EFFECTIVE LIBRARY AND INFORMATION CENTRE MANAGEMENT

Effective Library and Information Centre Management

by
Jo Bryson

Gower

Published by
Gower Publishing
Gower House
Croft Road
Aldershot
Hants GU11 3HR
England

Gower
Old Post Road
Brookfield
Vermont 05036
USA

Reprinted 1994, 1996

British Library Cataloguing in Publication Data
Bryson, Jo, *1950-*
    Effective library and information centre management.
    1. Libraries. Management
    I. Title
    025.1

ISBN HBK 0566 05637 2
       PBK 0566 05640 2

Printed and Bound in Great Britain by
Hartnolls Limited Bodmin Cornwall

Contents

EPILOGUE

List of figures

List of tables

Preface

Strategies for Effective Library and Information Centre Management
has been written with the view to being both a management handbook for librarians and information professionals working in or
managing public library systems, special libraries and information
centres, and a management textbook for students in librarianship
and information studies. This book is intended to communicate the
strategic management issues which face libraries and information
centres today, and provide ideas which may be used to stimulate
librarians and information centre managers to find entrepreneurial
and effective solutions to these issues.

It is also intended that the book acts as a reference tool on
management issues for those who are recently qualified and working
in libraries or information centres, those who by virtue of their
position have little or no access to others for support or advice on
management issues, or those who have received very little or no
formal management training. Each chapter has been written with
the intention of considering its topic in an manner which reflects
modern trends in management, and which are then applied to
libraries and information centres. It should be noted that the terms
libraries, information centres, library and information centre managers, and information professionals are interchanged throughout
the book.

The concepts and practices of library management have changed
considerably over the past 10 years. Librarians and information
centre managers can no longer afford to take a closed system
approach, nor portray their role solely as the 'keepers of the books'.
Information is not just a basic resource of the library, but also its
raison d'être, and is now regarded as a valuable commodity which
can be added to and manipulated to create value-added products

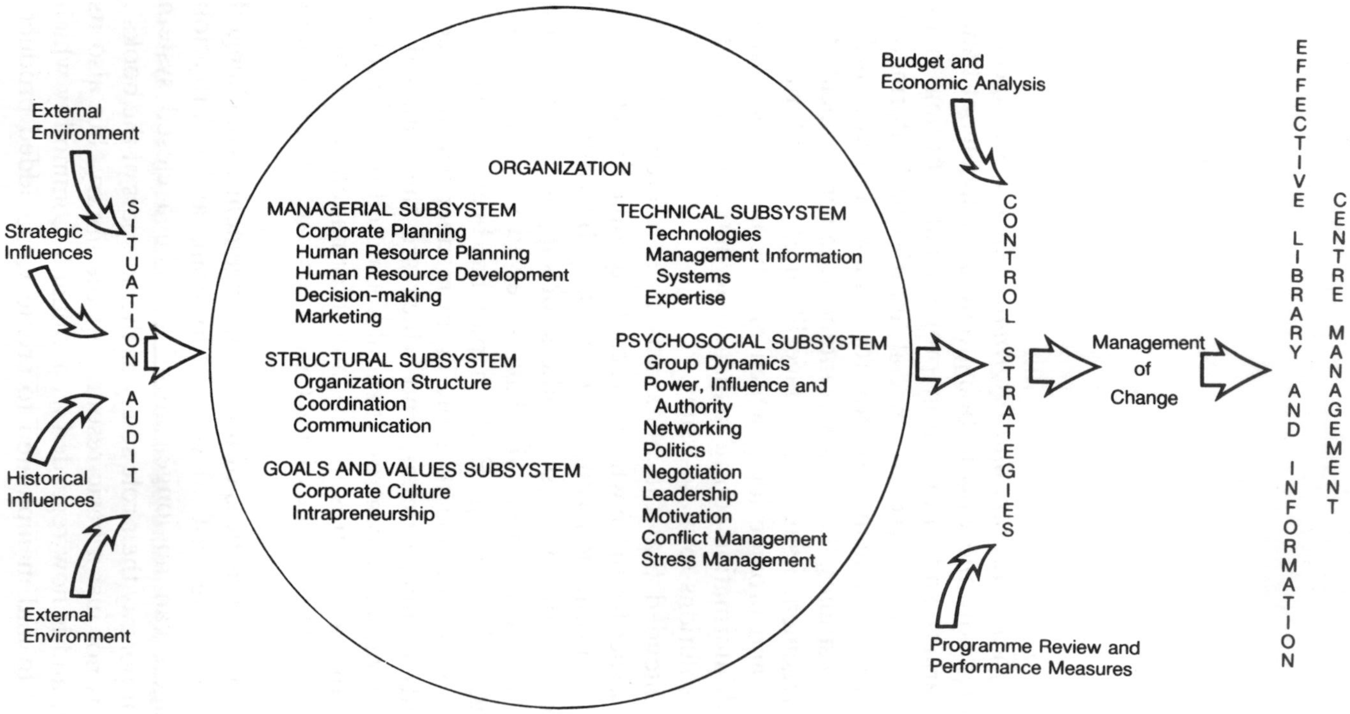

EFFECTIVE LIBRARY AND INFORMATION MANAGEMENT

Management of Change

STRATEGIES

CONTROL

Budget and Economic Analysis

Programme Review and Performance Measures

ORGANIZATION

MANAGERIAL SUBSYSTEM
Corporate Planning
Human Resource Planning
Human Resource Development
Decision-making
Marketing

STRUCTURAL SUBSYSTEM
Organization Structure
Coordination
Communication

GOALS AND VALUES SUBSYSTEM
Corporate Culture
Intrapreneurship

TECHNICAL SUBSYSTEM
Technologies
Management Information Systems
Expertise

PSYCHOSOCIAL SUBSYSTEM
Group Dynamics
Power, Influence and Authority
Networking
Politics
Negotiation
Leadership
Motivation
Conflict Management
Stress Management

SITUATION

External Environment

Strategic Influences

AUDIT

Historical Influences

External Environment

Figure P.1 Strategies for effective library and information centre management: a textbook approach

which can be traded. If libraries and information centres are to survive in an information economy, they must become more dynamic, competitive and business-oriented.

In keeping with the above, librarianship today is no longer solely dependent upon good stock management. There is a growing realization that other resources – human, technical, financial and information – have to be managed effectively and efficiently. Moreover, to be successful, the library or information centre's products and services have to be marketed effectively.

Many libraries today are multi-million dollar operations which require considerable management expertise to ensure that they achieve their goals and objectives whilst being cost-effective. To achieve this, library and information centre managers have to be, and be seen to be, innovative and intrapreneurial. This book has also been written to reflect the dynamic role of library and information centre managers today. Special attention has been paid to the concept of managing in times of economic restraint, changing work attitudes and environments, and the movement towards the commercialization of library services or privatization. The influences of technology, management style, corporate culture and the changing external environment upon the organizational environment, and the part which these play in enabling the library to be competitive and intrapreneurial are important issues which are addressed throughout the book.

A systems approach to strategic management has been selected as the basis for the design and layout of the book. Such an approach is based upon work carried out by Kast and Rosenzweig and is useful as it allows the library or information centre manager to consider all the management issues which influence the library or information centre. The library manager can systematically move from considering the library and its parent organization's external environment, and its influence upon the management of the library or information centre, to an examination of its internal environment.

A subsystems approach is taken when considering the internal environment. A library's or information centre's internal environment can easily be divided into Kast and Rosenzweig's five subsystems – that is, the managerial, structural, technical, psychosocial and goals and values subsystems. Using this approach, the library manager can again systematically move through the management issues affecting the internal environment. He or she can consider in turn each of the five subsystems, noting their influences upon each other and the areas which require their attention.

Such a comprehensive and detailed approach is necessary when considering the trends towards greater accountability for modern managers. In an era where there is an increasing emphasis upon 'user payment for service' in the public and academic library environments, and cost-cutting and resource-shedding in public and private sector organizations, consumers of library and information services are likely to appraise more critically the types and range of services being provided. Unless the library is meeting the needs of the market in an effective and efficient way, its funding and survival will be questioned.

In keeping with its role as a textbook, the introductory part of the book provides the reader with some basic concepts of the functions of management as they are today, together with the strategic influences which affect the management of libraries and information centres. This part will be of interest not just to students of librarianship and information studies, but also to those already holding positions in libraries and information centres who may not have had any formal management education.

Part II provides a strategic approach to understanding the library or information centre's external and internal environments and that of its parent organization. The concept of parent organization is used throughout the book. This refers to the organization to which the library or information centre is attached – that is, the local government authority, the government department, private sector organization or academic institution. It is an important concept, as the internal and external environments of the parent organization often dictate the environments of the library or information centre. The need to manage effectively the library's internal environment in a way which complements the external environment cannot be stressed too strongly.

If the influence of the external environment is ignored, the library or information centre may find that its goals and objectives are incompatible with the strategic needs and direction of the community which it serves. In addition, its sources of financial and human resources may be depleted, its organizational structure and technical resources rendered inappropriate, and its goals, values and psychosocial subsystems incongruous with the needs of the organization.

Part III introduces the reader to the managerial subsystems which operate in libraries and information centres. These encompass the key components of management over which the library or information centre manager has control: planning, decision-making, human resource planning and development and marketing. It should be noted that many of the other subsystems are influenced by factors over which the library manager has little control.

The library or information centre manager may often be judged by the way in which he or she manages these key components. For without proper planning, marketing, decision-making and human resource management, the library or information centre will not effectively achieve its strategic objectives. It should also be noted that these components play an important part for the organization's long-term survival and success.

Part IV considers the structural processes which support the library or information centre by providing the coordination required for it effectively and efficiently to achieve its goals and objectives. An inappropriate structure will hinder the library as the structure dictates the communication processes and lines of authority within organizations.

Also in this Part, the topic of communication is addressed. Good communication is a necessary ingredient for effective management as it affects the processes of planning, organizing, decision-making, controlling, motivating and leadership. Communication skills are exceptionally important for librarians and information centre managers as these skills are used in dealing with their consumers in satisfying their demands and requests for service.

Part V considers the technical resources which need to be managed. The use of technology creates a number of management issues which have to be attended to. The technology is an important part of the transformation process which converts inputs such as financial, human and information resources into outputs in the forms of goods and services. As such, it must be appropriate to the requirements of the library or information centre. The technology used will also affect the working environment of the library and information centre. Modern information technologies have had far-reaching effects upon working environments and work processes. Explanations of these effects are included to provide the library manager with a greater understanding of these important issues.

In Part VI, some background information is provided into the psychosocial environment which exists in organizations. This is often a very perplexing area for library and information centre managers as the dynamics involved are intangible. In the course of their day-to-day tasks, employees at all levels are subject to complex interpersonal dynamics, forces of power, and politics which can seem to be most complex without an understanding of the dynamics involved. The approach taken to these topics is to describe some of the issues at stake, so that library and information centre managers can at least recognize some of these dynamics and provide rational explanations as to their various occurrences.

This Part also covers the topics of leadership, networking, motivation, negotiation, conflict and stress management. These are all important areas which have to be understood by library managers as they will become directly involved with these in their daily routines. Various strategies for managing these areas are provided as a guide for those who lack long-term experience in dealing with such issues.

Part VII considers two very important emerging issues in management – corporate culture and intrapreneurship. Both of these issues are critical to the survival and success of present-day libraries and information centres. Successful libraries have a corporate culture which matches the characteristics of the library and which value innovation and intrapreneurship. Advice is offered as to how to develop a successful corporate culture and create an innovative environment.

Part VIII considers the topics of budgeting, performance reviews and managing change. Knowledge of effective financial management is necessary as this is an important library resource. The library or information centre manager will be personally accountable for all expenditure and income for the library.

Knowledge of performance measures is equally important as it is by these means that the values and benefits of the library or information centre can be demonstrated. In an age of accountability, performance measures are often a legislative requirement of public-sector organizations.

xvi

Finally, the aspect of change is considered. Change is a part of life, particularly in a dynamic environment. This topic is considered at the end of the book as it is the final, yet ongoing, outcome of all the previous strategies.

In closing, the contents of this book are dedicated to all librarians or information professionals who have the desire to practice innovative and effective management skills to ensure the survival and success of libraries and information centres in an information age.

Jo Bryson
October 1989

PART I
INTRODUCTION TO LIBRARY AND INFORMATION CENTRE MANAGEMENT

Introduction

This Part aims at introducing the reader to the concepts of management. The first chapter discusses the reasons why librarians and information specialists need to be aware of management practices and why management skills are needed in libraries today. It provides an introduction to the various functions, roles and skills which are needed to effectively manage libraries and information centres and discusses the various levels of management which are to be found there.

Chapter 2 considers the strategic influences which affect the operations of libraries and information centres. The introduction of new technologies, changing work attitudes, shifting sources of funding, and the need for greater accountability impact upon the way in which libraries and information centres are to be managed in the future.

1 An introduction to management

INTRODUCTION

Management has been described as either an art or a science, but it is really a combination of both. The managerial task includes the coordination of human, information, technical and financial resources toward accomplishing organizational goals and objectives. The scientific approach lies in decision-making, planning and in the appropriate use of the technology. The artistic approach to management can be found in the tasks of communicating, leadership and goal-setting.

The management of a library or information centre is accomplished by a combination of basic management functions, roles and skills. Whilst each will be described separately in this textbook, they are in fact highly interdependent. Such functions and roles will differ in various types of libraries and information centres as each library is influenced by its external environment, the type of organization to which it belongs, its age, technology and corporate culture, and the attributes of its employees. Management functions and roles also differ according to the level of management, as they reflect the managerial responsibilities which are appropriate to each level.

Management skills are needed when dealing with all types of organized activities and in all kinds of organizations. Indeed, managing a library requires similar management skills to managing a football team or a large local government authority. Even a librarian or information professional working in a 'one-man-band' situation uses management skills to procure funds for the library, to decide upon its future direction and to plan for new services, and to communicate with management and other individuals within the organization in order to achieve their library's goals.

4

FUNCTIONS OF MANAGEMENT

Traditionally it has been accepted that the managerial task comprises five basic functions: planning, organizing, controlling, coordinating and commanding. More recently, these have been extended to include more specific functions such as leading, staffing, budgeting and reporting. Whilst it is useful to be aware of these functions, they should not be considered as separate activities since managers rarely engage in one practice to the mutual exclusion of the others. They are all interrelated in the management process.

MANAGEMENT ROLES

The functions of management are enacted in the various management roles. Henry Mintzberg (1973: 92–3), has studied a variety of managerial roles and has identified 10 interactive roles which are

Table 1.1
Management roles in libraries and information centres

Role	Description	Identifiable activities in libraries and information centres
Interpersonal *Figurehead*	Symbolic head; obliged to perform a number of routine duties of a legal or social nature.	Attendance of the chief executive or chief librarian at a farewell function for an employee.
Leader	Responsible for the motivation and activation of subordinates; responsible for staffing, training, and associated duties.	Discussions with individuals or groups as to their career paths and training and professional development needs.
Liaison	Maintains self-developed network of outside contacts and informers who provide favours and information.	Serving as an office bearer in a professional association and attending meetings where professional issues are discussed.
Informational *Monitor*	Seeks and receives wide variety of special information (much of it current) to develop thorough understanding of organization and environment; emerges as	Telephone conversations with officers of government agencies or departments, lunchtime meetings with suppliers of resources e.g. book suppliers.

5

Table 1.1 *continued*

Role	Description	Identifiable activities in libraries and information centres
	nerve centre of internal and external information of the organization.	
Disseminator	Transmits information received from outsiders or from other subordinates to members of the organization; some information factual, some involving interpretation and integration of diverse value positions of organizational influencers.	Holding staff meetings, personal conversations with selected subordinates.
Spokesperson	Transmits information to outsiders on organization's plans, policies, actions, results, etc.; serves as expert on organization's industry.	Production of Annual Report, appointment to select committees in library and information centre areas.
Decisional Entrepreneur	Searches organization and its environment and initiates 'improvement projects' to bring about change; supervises design of certain projects as well.	Initiation of new services, implementing a user/non-user survey of library facilities and services, problem solving in an unorthodox or original manner.
Disturbance Handler	Responsible for corrective action when organization faces important, unexpected disturbances.	Responding to situations such as strikes, bankrupt suppliers etc. which cause resource schedules not to be met.
Resource Allocator	Responsible for the allocation of organizational resources of all kinds – in effect the making or approval of all significant organizational decisions.	Allocating funds, personnel, equipment and personal time to various departments. May or may not be involved in how resources are further split or earmarked.
Negotiator	Responsible for representing the organization at major negotiations.	Bargaining with others to obtain additional funds for a special library project. Negotiating new award conditions for library staff with trade union representatives.

Source: Adapted from *The Nature of Managerial Work*, Henry Mintzberg, pp.92–93. © 1973, Henry Mintzberg, reprinted by permission of Harper and Row, Publishers, Inc.

performed by managers. Mintzberg separated these into three groupings: interpersonal, informational and decisional. Each of these can be readily identified in libraries and information centres (see Table 1.1).

Whilst these roles are described separately, they are in practice highly integrated, each role being dependent upon others. The relative importance of each role is influenced by the manager's personal leadership style, the type of organization, its external environment, subordinate attributes, technologies used and the organization's corporate culture.

LEVELS OF MANAGEMENT

Managers operate at different levels of an organization, and their activities and skills differ according to their place in the hierarchy (Figure 1.1). Generally managers are described as being either top-level, mid-level or first-line managers. The number of people at each level of the hierarchy traditionally decreases as one moves towards the top. Non-managerial personnel form the bulk of any organization's employees, there are a smaller number of first-line managers, even fewer mid-level managers and there is only one chief executive at the top.

It is important to realize that there are often two hierarchies of management operating within libraries; that of the library, and that of the organization to which the library belongs. For example, within a university or local government authority, the chief librarian may be regarded as being top management within the library, but mid-level management within the infrastructure of the university or local authority.

Top management

Top management is responsible for planning for the future and for scanning the external environment in order to identify potential changes which may either threaten or provide opportunities for the organization. In libraries or information centres, top management performs a boundary spanning the role, interacting with external organizations in the tasks of lobbying or politics, and representing

7

8

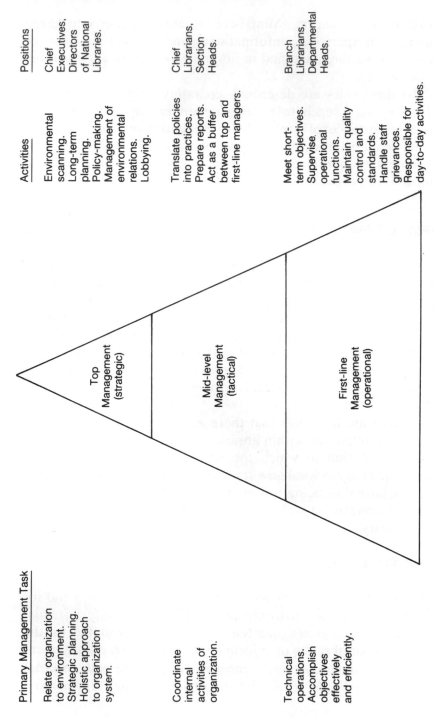

Figure 1.1 Levels of management and their associated tasks, activities and positions in libraries

Positions

Chief
Executives,
Directors
of National
Libraries.

Chief
Librarians,
Section
Heads.

Branch
Librarians,
Departmental
Heads.

Activities

Environmental
scanning.
Long-term
planning.
Policy-making.
Management of
environmental
relations.
Lobbying.

Translate policies
into practices.
Prepare reports.
Act as a buffer
between top and
first-line managers.

Meet short-
term objectives.
Supervise
operational
functions.
Maintain quality
control and
standards.
Handle staff
grievances.
Responsible for
day-to-day activities.

Top
Management
(strategic)

Mid-level
Management
(tactical)

First-line
Management
(operational)

Primary Management Task

Relate organization
to environment.
Strategic planning.
Holistic approach
to organization
system.

Coordinate
internal
activities of
organization.

Technical
operations.
Accomplish
objectives
effectively
and efficiently.

the library in community affairs, business deals and government negotiations. Managers at this level spend much of their time with their peers, counterparts from similar organizations, and to a lesser extent their subordinates.

In planning for the future, top managers take note of information received from their contacts in the external environment and from summarized information obtained in the form of reports from their subordinates (mid-level management) on the organization's internal environment. In establishing policies they take an holistic viewpoint, being responsible for overall control of the organization and, as part of this process, they identify the goals to be achieved by their subordinates.

Mid-level management

Mid-level managers receive broad overall strategies and policies from top management and translate these into specific action programmes which can be implemented by first-line managers. They also spend considerable time analysing data, such as statistics provided by first-line managers, and summarize these in reports to top management. In acting as a buffer between top and first-line management, mid-level managers spend much of their time using high-level communication skills in talking on the telephone, attending meetings and preparing reports. Mid-level managers in libraries or information centres must have an in-depth knowledge of their particular department or branch and its relationship with other departments or branches in order to perform the necessary coordination function which is part of their role.

First-line management

First-line managers are directly responsible for the day-to-day administration of resources in order to meet short-term objectives. Theirs is primarily a supervisory and grievance-handling task calling for strong technical and interpersonal skills. They spend little time with top management or managers from other organizations, dealing mainly with their subordinates and clientele. In libraries and information centres first-line managers lead hectic, interrupted work lives. They spend most of their time problem-solving and

9

communicating with those in their immediate supervisory area, much of which is on a one-to-one basis. They are also charged with maintaining quality control or standards and, in libraries or information centres, this can mean ensuring that requests for information are answered correctly and as quickly as possible, that proper overdue procedures are carried out, or ensuring that materials are shelved correctly.

An understanding of the levels of management is important in order to ensure each management level is performing its proper functions and tasks. It is false economy for top management to be involved in the day-to-day operations of the library at the expense of proper planning, whilst first-line management cannot be expected to have an holistic view of the total organization in order to make decisions affecting many areas.

MANAGERIAL SKILLS AND LEVELS OF MANAGEMENT

A skill can be described as the ability to translate knowledge into action that results in a desired performance. Traditionally it has been considered that managers use three skills in carrying out their tasks: technical, interpersonal and conceptual. To these may be added diagnostic and analytical skills. Not all of these skills are used in equal proportion. Managers at different levels in the organization need different kinds of skills, and libraries and information centres are no exception to this rule. As librarians or information personnel progress up the hierarchy of the organization, technical and interpersonal skills diminish in importance compared to the conceptual, diagnostic and analytical skills.

Technical skills

Technical skills comprise the skills needed to accomplish tasks. In libraries and information centres these include the knowledge and technical expertise required to use on-line information systems, trade and national bibliographies, computer terminals, video disk players or a knowledge of the various bibliographical organization schemes. Technical skills are most used by first-line managers in

10

libraries and information centres where training and supervision of staff in work activities is important. In order to answer questions and gain the respect of their subordinates they must be skilled and knowledgeable in the equipment, facilities, systems and techniques used in the library or information service.

Interpersonal skills

Interpersonal skills are used by managers as they interact with people within and outside the organization, and they featured prominently in Mintzberg's 10 managerial roles. They are used to maintain the network of contacts and human relationships which are necessary in order for the goals of the organization to be achieved. Interpersonal skills are also used to communicate with, understand and motivate both individuals and groups.

Top management in libraries use interpersonal skills to obtain knowledge about the external environment in which the library organization operates, and in lobbying and dealing with the decision-makers. Mid-level managers use interpersonal skills in liaising between top and first-line management, in discussing needs and translating policies into actions. First-line managers rely heavily on interpersonal skills to create a work environment in which tasks are happily and effectively accomplished. A manager who has good interpersonal skills is likely to be more successful than a manager who is poor in this area.

Conceptual skills

Conceptual skills can be defined as the ability to understand the relationships of individual parts to the whole, and the whole by breaking it into parts. It also requires an understanding of cause and effect relationships within and outside the organization. In libraries and information centres, conceptual skills require an holistic approach to understanding how the various departments' or services' goals and activities contribute to actual outcomes and the relationships and impact of external environmental forces upon these goals and activities. These skills allow top and mid-level management to take an overall view and determine whether individual department needs complement those of the organization, and react to potential problems appropriately.

Diagnostic skills

Diagnostic skills provide the ability to acquire, analyse and interpret information to determine the cause of changes in either the inputs, outputs or transformation processes of the organization. In libraries or information centres such changes may be either symptoms of problems or favourable situations. For example, a high staff turnover in a technical services department may be a symptom of a human relations problem where the librarian-in-charge is lacking in interpersonal skills, or, alternatively, a product of a monotonous work environment in which the solution may be found in job enrichment. A favourable situation can be detected when an increase in the issue rate of materials in the library is the favourable result of a change in the book selection policy.

Analytical skills

Analytical skills allow the librarian or information professional to determine the cause of change and to either provide corrective action or take advantage of the situation. They complement diagnostic skills in that they provide the means to identify the key variables in a situation, to determine how they are interrelated and to decide which ones need attention. Various strategies for dealing with the issues at stake can be considered and the most appropriate one decided upon. Diagnostic skills enable managers to understand a situation; analytical skills enable them to determine the appropriate course of action.

REFERENCE

1. Mintzberg, H. (1973), *The Nature of Managerial Work* (New York: Harper and Rowe).

2 Strategic influences on modern library and information centre management

INTRODUCTION

Library and information centre managers can no longer afford to ignore the psychological, technical, sociological and political changes taking place in both the external and internal environments of their organizations. Their impact is a two-way process. Changes in the external environment affect the organization's internal environment, whilst decisions made at managerial level will impact upon both the external and internal environment. As a result, a major and increasingly important task of management is to place the library or information centre strategically in its environment in order to assure its continued success and security.

MANAGING IN A TURBULENT ENVIRONMENT

Meeting increased demands with fewer resources

Changing environments require new skills for library and information centre managers. Two of the most prevalent impacts upon non-profit-making organizations, the sector to which most libraries and information centres belong, are increased demand coupled with reduced government support. These place increasing pressure upon managers to deliver more with less. The matter is further complicated as information is now regarded as a commodity or organizational resource. Managers in public libraries and libraries attached to tertiary institutions are faced with the ethical issues and problems of providing free information services with dwindling resources where greater emphasis is being placed by government upon self-supporting or 'user pays' principles. Added to this is government pressure for greater financial accountability and for stakeholders to become increasingly more active in the operations of libraries and information centres.

Demands for lower personal taxation and increased privatization of many services influence how libraries and information centres are funded, structured and managed. Some types of library services will certainly be charged for in the future and methods of evaluating these and their relationships to the remaining 'free' services will need to be determined.

In an effort to curtail expenditure it may not be easy to abandon services or levy charges. There may be enormous exit barriers to some services both on a social and economic scale. Library and information centre managers may find themselves locked into many more programmes than they can afford. They will therefore need skills in politics, lobbying and negotiating in order to secure the necessary resources in a competitive environment. Strategic planning and marketing skills will be needed to identify and focus upon key groups to which services should be aimed. A low coverage of too large a client market is inferior to a good quality service for a focused market; and no library should be in the business of duplicating the services of other agencies.

Meeting performance criteria for efficiency and effectiveness

Changes are occurring in the way in which libraries are evaluated. In the past, libraries have often been evaluated solely from a financial or economic perspective; that is, whether or not they have met their budgetary targets. Today there is increased emphasis on measuring performance; that usually means efficiency and effectiveness. Meeting efficiency criteria involves the manager in value analysis; that is, ensuring that the optimum level of service is provided for the lowest possible cost, something that all managers should be able to do. However, the ability to meet the effectiveness criteria is not always as easy to demonstrate, since invariably the interests of stakeholder groups are not stable. Indeed, many have individual needs which they wish to be met, and which often defeat the concepts of economies of scale and efficiency.

Meeting the needs of employees, stakeholders and users

Like most other organizations, libraries and information centres should have a corporate social responsibility, which involves satisfying the needs of the employees, public and community. This leads to the need for managers to integrate social objectives with the 'business' objectives in order to meet self-actualization and environmental demands. One of the methods by which this can be achieved is by worker participation in management. Employees are increasingly becoming involved in corporate governance, and this involvement places greater emphasis on communication within the organization and the information-disseminating role of the manager so that employees are fully informed of the issues at stake.

Increased importance is being placed upon the quality of life. For libraries and information centres this is manifested in the quality of working life for the organization's employees and a higher standard of living reflected in changed consumer demand patterns for library services. New values and structures are evident in society, which will not only be reflected in the demand for new resources but also in the work attitudes of staff and the corporate culture of the organization to which the library belongs.

Stakeholders are those persons who take an interest in the library, or who have the capacity to influence its ability to achieve its objectives. Examples of stakeholders for a special library operating in the private sector are unions, activists such as environmental, health and safety groups, shareholders or owners, political groups, suppliers, other libraries or information centres, employees and associations for librarians or information personnel. Any of these stakeholders can have an effect upon the organization's direction by impeding or facilitating the accomplishment of the library's goals. Some have more effect than others, but the library or information centre manager cannot afford to ignore any of them, and all need to be managed. This requires the library or information centre manager to identify who they are, their levels of influence and how each may politically, socially or economically affect the library's operations, functions and future plans. These actions form part of an environmental analysis or situation audit. It is also important that the library or information centre manager ensures that sufficient resources are allocated to deal with them. Good public relations with all stakeholders is a necessary part of marketing the library.

Meeting the challenges and opportunities of technology

Over the past 10 years, libraries and information centres have been greatly affected by changes in information technology, and the rate of change is still accelerating in this area. The introduction of the various information technologies have lead to reorganized structures, changes in work patterns, demands for new skills, job retraining schemes and, in some cases, a reclassification of positions. Networking facilities have already caused managers to make new policies on interlibrary lending and reciprocal borrowing arrangements, whilst it is anticipated that aspects of service delivery will change in the near future. Library and information centre managers need to be aware of the penetration levels and rates of the new technologies in order to measure their effect on the delivery of services and operations of the library or information centre.

Such environments require the library or information centre manager to have the ability to think quickly with an holistic orientation and perspective; to be politically sensitive yet entrepreneurial and risk-taking, and to focus upon the process of planning and decision-making.

THE STRATEGIC APPROACH TO MANAGING LIBRARIES AND INFORMATION CENTRES

Strategic management provides a comprehensive approach to managing the impact of a dynamic environment upon the psychological, sociological, political and other subsystems which can be found in a complex organization. In so doing, it considers the organization's functional and managerial ability to position itself to cope with a changing environment.

The strategic approach recognizes that an organization's long-term performance is affected by its strategic culture, managerial capability, logistic capability and capacity, its technological thrust and its financial resources. These five features are critical to the

16

organization's success. If it loses any of these or they fall below a certain level or capacity, the organization will cease to operate efficiently or effectively. As a result it may lose its strategic position in the external environment and eventually disappear.

Strategic management uses a planning approach, and as such requires the sanction and involvement of top management. Top management is also required to provide the knowledge and foresight to determine both the activities of the external environment, and the organization. However, the planning process should also be a democratic, people-interactive process. Whilst not everyone can be the planner, everyone should be involved to some extent in the top-down process.

In planning for survival and success in a dynamic environment, everything must be considered. The internal and external environment of the organization is studied, the results being used to provide input into the situation audit which evaluates the present situation. It may comprise of a strategic four-factor analysis, critical success factors, a SWOT (strengths, weaknesses, opportunities, threats) analysis or an organization capability profile. The internal nature of the organization (strategic culture, structure, leadership style, technological thrust, and so on) should be evaluated with the external environment in mind. Financial and market analysis provide additional valuable information. Once all of the required information has been obtained, strategies for survival can be planned.

Strategic management requires both strategic thinking and strategic planning and is a useful approach for managers as it enables the library or information centre to quantify and qualify its contribution to the community or organization on a long-term basis. It provides the opportunity for the library or information centre to justify its existence in other than financial terms. It also allows the library or information centre to maintain or enhance its position in the community by capitalizing on its strengths and opportunities whilst positively overcoming its threats and weaknesses. Using these strategies management can focus on long-term strategic goals and environmental changes, with the result that they are better able to manage and control change and make their services more appropriate to user needs.

Strategic management provides a comprehensive and effective management technique which can be used in dealing with complex

17

and changing environments. A full discussion on the techniques of strategic management and how they can be used in libraries and information centres can be found in Chapter 3.

PART II
STRATEGIES FOR UNDERSTANDING THE LIBRARY'S OR INFORMATION CENTRE'S ENVIRONMENT

Introduction

Libraries and information centres operate within the context of two environments – internal and external. Both of these environments affect the way in which the libraries are planned and managed and, unless the library or information centre manager has a clear understanding of them, they will be working in a vacuum.

Most libraries and information centres operate in complex and changing external environments which frequently produce new challenges which must be mastered to ensure the library's future survival and success.

A library or information centre also has an internal environment which has to be managed on an equally important basis, and which is affected by the external environment in terms of its complexity, its organization structure, and its management styles. The library or information centre manager cannot afford to ignore this.

Having determined what comprises the external and internal environments of the library or information centre, the manager must then decide upon how well the library is functioning within the context of these environments. This is achieved by a number of processes. Some of the processes which can be used are a SWOT analysis, the identification of critical success factors, a capability profile, and a strategic four-factor analysis.

Such an audit of the external and internal environment and the library's performance is sometimes omitted by managers as being too time-consuming. Unfortunately they fail to see the advantages to the library in terms of reducing the risk factor in decision-making and providing the opportunity of capitalizing on the library's strengths and opportunities whilst minimizing the threats and weaknesses. Planning is made far more effective by the use of such audit processes.

This section aims to take the reader through a step-by-step guide to assessing and understanding the operating environments of the library or information centre, and the library's or information centre's performance therein.

3 Situation audit

INTRODUCTION

The situation audit provides library and information centre managers with important background information which is used in strategic planning. After scanning the external and internal environments of the library or information centre and carrying out some analyses, the librarian or information centre manager should be able to determine the role of the library in its environment, its influence and image, and the services which it provides. The situation audit should also provide information on existing and potential users of the library, stakeholders and other influences found in the environment, and competitors of the library.

A knowledge of these factors should make the library or information centre manager more aware of the opportunities and threats facing the library and their ability to manage these. If such a knowledge is extensive, covering all of the relevant domains in both the external and internal environment, it reduces the element of surprise and, therefore, risk. The planning task can be made more effective, as many variables are known. Although accident and chance will still play their part in a dynamic environment leading to sudden, unexpected changes, it is the manager's task to lessen the element of surprise as much as possible in order to ensure that the library or information centre is secure in its position.

The situation audit is essential as, with any plan, there is a certain amount of optimism as to what can be achieved. Top management assumes that the future can, and should, be better than the past. The planning process allows for growth and typically produces goals which are not fully met in reality. As a result there is a gap between what it was thought the organization would achieve and what is actually achieved.

The first stage of the situation audit is an analysis of the external and internal environments of the library or information centre. This provides background information for the other analytical processes mentioned later in this chapter and for marketing and other management strategies used in libraries.

STRATEGIES FOR ASSESSING THE EXTERNAL ENVIRONMENT OF LIBRARIES AND INFORMATION SERVICES

The need to assess the library or information centre's external environment cannot be stressed enough, for it is with a clear understanding of the external forces which impact upon the internal environment that planning must take place. In a dynamic external environment management faces new realities, new challenges and new uncertainties on a daily basis. A detailed knowledge of the changing external environment and its subsequent effect upon the organization's internal environment is therefore necessary to avoid unrealistic decisions being made.

The assessment of the external environment is therefore one of the first roles in the situation audit stage of the strategic planning process. It allows managers to identify trends, issues, opportunities, threats and provides information for other assessments such as the four-factor analysis.

Complexity of the environment

In scanning the domains of the external environment, library and information centre managers will be able to determine whether their particular organization is operating in a simple or complex, stable or unstable environment. This is useful information as the complexity and stability of the external environment affects the structure, management style and corporate culture of the internal environment. If only four or five domains really have an impact upon the organization, the external environment may be considered to be simple. A complex environment exists when over 10 domains readily impact the organization. If domains continually change in the intensity of their impact and, as a result, services change moderately or continually, the environment may be considered to

23

be unstable. An unchanging environment is a stable one. Turbulence does not strike all libraries and information centres in the same way or at the same time. Libraries and information centres can operate in different environments; one fundamental difference being that of the private and public sectors.

Environmental domains

All libraries and information centres have the potential to be affected by the domains in the environment. These consist of economic conditions, availability of financial resources, geographical situation, technological innovation, their historical development, clientele and markets, demographic patterns, supply and demand of human resources, availability of materials and other library resources, the industry in which they operate, political climate, cultural–social conditions, future trends, law and government (see Figures 3.1 and 3.2).

Economic conditions

Economic conditions reflect the general economic health of the country and area in which the organization operates. Unemployment rates affect public library services as these libraries are traditionally used more in times of unemployment. High unemployment may also lead to a much larger labour market from which library managers may select their staff. Purchasing power is affected by the economic conditions at home – that is, how much the library can spend on books and related materials. Overseas libraries' purchasing powers are also affected by the economic conditions in the two main publishing countries, Britain and the United States; their exchange rates, inflation rates, and production capacities will affect the supply and purchasing prices of material being ordered. Economic conditions therefore affect the availabilities of supplies, labour and demand for output. During periods of economic recession the incomes of libraries operating in government and non-profit-making organizations are greatly affected as incomes fall, yet demand for their services rises. Historically, major growth periods in libraries have coincided with periods of economic prosperity as

24

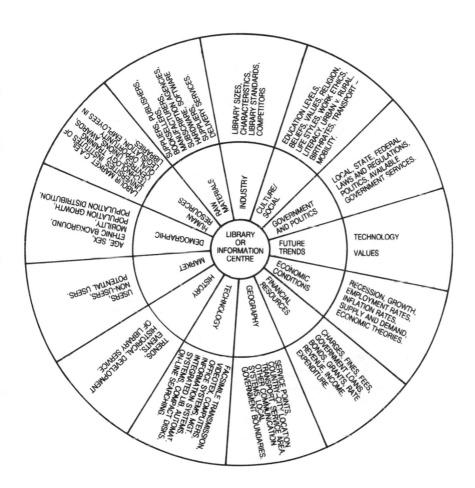

Figure 3.1   The external environment model

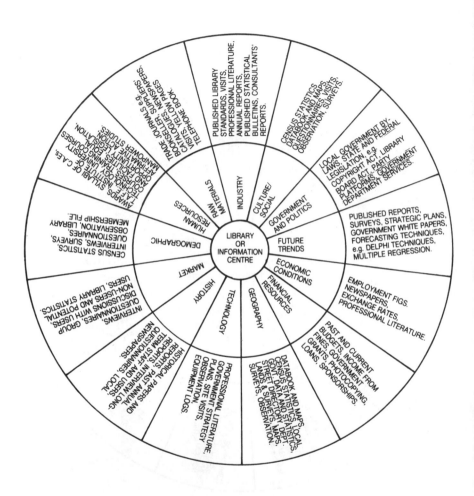

**Figure 3.2   Sources of information for the external environment
model**

it is during these times that tax revenues have risen, providing more monies for the public purse.

Library and information centre managers should therefore be involved in projecting the general course of the future economy of the nation. Such projections should include the changing characteristics and trends of the economy in terms of inflation, employment, money market and exchange rates. As many library and information centres purchase materials published in overseas countries or use overseas databases, the economics of these countries should also be considered in order to predict trends in future price structures.

Information relating to economic conditions can often be obtained by reading the business supplements to newspapers, monitoring exchange rates and scanning professional literature for articles on overseas economic conditions and their effects on libraries in other countries.

Financial resources

In the past, financial resources for libraries and information centres operating in the public sector have been virtually guaranteed. As a result, the library or its funding bodies seldom questioned the responsiveness of the library to the needs of the marketplace. The growth of government expenditure is now at a level where inefficiency and ineffectiveness can no longer be tolerated. There is a trend towards smaller government involvement and costs incurred being directly placed with the consumer. As a result, the library and information centre manager needs to be more accountable, market-oriented and entrepreneurial. Entrepreneurial and marketing activities require certain information. The library or information centre manager needs to be aware of alternative sources for funding such as employment generating schemes, grants or sponsorships from the private sector and other income-producing activities or value-added services which may operate out of the library without destroying its fundamental purpose.

Modern budgeting techniques assign 'total costs' to operating facilities. Hence the library may find that interest and loan repayments for capital items are allocated to their budgets rather than that of the overall organization. Knowledge of economic policies affecting interest rates is therefore needed.

27

Geographical environment

The geographical environment impacts upon the provision of a library or information service in that it either facilitates or hinders its usage. All libraries should be strategically sited to provide a high profile. The geographical environment may consist of a single building or it may be an area of many square kilometres.

Special libraries or information centres serving the employees of a particular organization should be strategically located near a busy thoroughfare, near the main entrance to the building or near to the canteen. They should not be hidden away where they can be easily overlooked.

Public libraries should be located in or near shopping centres, within easy reach of car parks and public transport stops. Natural features such as rivers, hills or lakes may physically separate communities necessitating the duplication of library services to serve small isolated pockets with bookmobiles. Man-made features such as busy highways or freeways, may deter some potential library users from using the library. These should be taken into account when planning new library services. Territorial boundaries, such as state borders, local government boundaries or campus sites may determine the extent of service provision to users.

Technology

Technology may be defined as the use of available knowledge and techniques to produce goods and services. The complexity of the technology influences the skill level and organization size required to use it. In libraries, knowledge of classification and cataloguing schemes, use of integrated on-line library automation systems, access to local, national and international databases can all be considered technology. New information technology developments also have an impact on libraries.

Satellites and ISDN networks provide new dimensions for information transmission and video conferencing. Videotex, EDI facilities and electronic mail offer opportunities for interlibrary loans and access to library collections. It may be that, in the future, remote access may become the preferred form of library usage. This has implications for library staff and buildings.

The information technology industry – particularly in the fields of communications – has experienced rapid technological changes in recent years, and further breakthroughs with far-reaching effects are envisaged. If libraries fail to keep up with technological change, they may find that they miss opportunities. Because technological change affects the human resources within an organization, new skills may need to be taught and some people may need to be totally retrained.

Information regarding the technological conditions, advances or changes which are relevant to the library or information centre may be obtained from reading professional and information technology literature, using forecasting methods such as the Delphi survey technique, consulting government information technology plans and attending suitable conferences.

Past trends

The present and the future is always shaped by the past. In order to try to predict the future, it is necessary to consider trends of the past. Whilst the future is never certain, the likelihood of recurrent trends of the past being repeated when the same conditions apply again tends to make the exercise of predicting the future more successful. Policies determined or changed in the past will determine the guidelines under which the library operates. Historical decisions will have impacts on sources of funding, provision of services and levels of staffing.

Market analysis

In order to develop effective services, the library or information service manager must be aware of their market – that is, their present or potential clients, and their status. The market influences the library through demands for various services. Library managers should continuously analyse these demands in order to provide the most appropriate levels of services. The needs of potential users must also be considered as the library may not be reaching its full market potential. In this case, the library may have to reduce or delete some little-used services in order to diversify into an area of increasing demand. Library and information centre managers should try to understand and anticipate potential market changes resulting from either a changed market base or changing needs.

Market research may be carried out by using surveys and questionnaires, group interviews and discussions with users and non-users, and by analysing information about the make-up of existing membership files.

Demographic profile

The make-up of the population served by the library or information centre should be demographically analysed. For public libraries, the age of the population, income distribution, levels of education, population distribution and mobility, ethnic origins and areas of employment are useful in determining the types of services and opening hours of the library. Special libraries and information centres will find employee profiles detailing subject areas of interest, position held, qualifications, useful in planning and delivering information services.

Human resources

Libraries and information centres, like all organizations, must have a supply of trained and/or qualified personnel. Without an adequate supply of human resources, libraries would not be able to provide their services. The supply of professional labour relies upon throughput from the tertiary institutions such as universities, institutes of technology or polytechnics. Changes in the environment must also be reflected in the changes to courses taught within these institutions if graduates are to have the required skills with which to perform their tasks. Input from the profession is needed to ensure that courses are updated professionally.

Demands from unions alter employment awards and conditions. These may affect budgets, rosters, makc-up and classifications of staff. Government legislation, such as equal opportunity or affirmative action, may affect human resource selection procedures. Manpower studies provide some input in regards to the future supply and demand of qualified or experienced library personnel.

Raw materials

Libraries and information centres acquire raw materials from the external environment. These raw materials include books, serials, audio-visual materials, furniture, communication, hardware and software systems. Libraries rely upon library suppliers, publishers, booksellers, manufacturers, telecommunication and hardware/ software suppliers; shipping agencies and port authorities where goods are imported, and delivery services for the supply of raw materials. Any changes affecting any of these agents will affect the supply of materials which will consequently affect the level of service. Examples of such changes are industrial disputes, cutbacks in production levels, increased labour costs or discontinuities in services.

Industry trends

Industry includes competitors or potential competitors in the same type of business. The size of a particular type of library may determine whether it acts as a leader or a follower of innovation of its type. Libraries are grouped according to the characteristic of ownership, services and markets. To ensure a common bond with various types of libraries, library standards exist. These are industry-wide standards which are provided to portray minimum standards or guidelines for different types of libraries.

An accurate forecasting of the development of the library or information sector is necessary for future planning. Such forecasts should be made relating to future trends of size and services, structural changes within the library environment and its competitors. Private information consultants and the mass media are two examples of competitors within the information industry.

Social and cultural environments

The social climate and culture of the environment in which the library or information service operates will affect its services. Social values will be reflected in stock selection policies and services and employee attitudes to work.

31

Government and politics

The political environment has a major influence upon the management of a library or information centre in respect of how managers act towards users or employees. Librarians may also try to influence the political environment by lobbying key people to preserve or introduce policies which they believe are in keeping with their own or public interest.

Stakeholders may exercise a major influence on the strategic decisions made by libraries and information centres operating in the private sector. Stakeholders do not normally become politically active in 'day-to-day' routines, but may have considerable say about new initiatives in services.

Future political actions may lead to the privatization of some libraries and mergers of others. Political actions may also determine the future provision of public sector libraries and the extent of their services.

The impact of the external environment upon the library and information centre

Size

The complexity of the external environment is related to the size of the organization. As an organization grows in size the complexity of its external environment increases, which in turn increases the complexity in the organization. The larger the library or information centre, the more specialized are the functions and this leads to departmentalization. The more complex the environment in which the library is operating, the greater number of departments and tasks will be needed. When the external environment becomes more complex and unstable, organizational departments must become highly specialized to handle the uncertainty in their external environment.

Internal management structure

The external environment is related to internal management structures. Burns and Stalker (1961) found that when the external environment was stable, the internal environment of the organization was generally characterized by rules, procedures and a clear hierarchy of authority – a typical bureaucratic structure. In this case, the organization could concentrate on current operational problems and day-to-day efficiency, and long-range planning and forecasting was easy because future environmental demands would be similar to the present. The organization was therefore mechanistic in nature.

In a complex, unstable environment, managers had continually to analyse the relevant environmental elements. Plans were constantly updated as a result of the rapid changes, and decisions were pushed down the hierarchy to where information relevant to the decision was held. Communication systems needed to be open and so an organic structure was used. Burn's and Stalker's classification of organizations (mechanistic and organic) can be further developed by providing a framework for the assessment of the characteristics of the internal subsystems (see Table 3.1).

Lawrence and Lorsch (1969), have also concentrated upon analysing the relationships between the organization's environment and its internal structure. They considered the effect of the external environment at a departmental level. Their first hypothesis was that the greater the degree of certainty in a sub-environment (department), the more formalized the structure of the subsystem.

The authors also considered the attributes of different departments in a study of 'differentiation and integration'. They believed that differences in a department's sub-environment would force the department to develop particular attributes as a coping mechanism, resulting in corresponding differences in the structures and orientations of departments. The organization would be differentiated; each department maintaining its own technology, holding different time horizons and goals, and having a different structure and interpersonal orientation. In fact, each department would create its own subculture.

This hypothesis may be demonstrated in some libraries or information services where departments responsible for bibliographic control, and which have little interaction with the external environment or operate in a more stable environment, may have a more mechanistic approach. Work practices are often characterized by

33

Table 3.1

A framework for assessing the organizational structure according to its managerial, technical, goals and values, and psychosocial subsystems

	Mechanistic Organizations	Organic Organizations
Managerial Subsystem	Controlling, high task, low relationship Assumes that people need to be governed by strict rules. Leader keep tight hold of reins, makes all decisions and avoids risks Formal hierarchy for coordination, control and authority. Authority at top, little delegation. Authority significant – top down Position power Little acceptance of expertise power Structure dictates distribution of power, control, reward, information and communication systems. Coercive and reward power Seniority outweighs competence and experience – length of service important in determining leader	Innovative, creative, high task, high relationship Interdependent, mature relationship Authority dispersed, much delegation Use of mentors and role modelling Network structure of control, authority and communication Authority insignificant Emphasis on personal expertise power Power – expert Reward power – pay for performance Risk taking, experiential
Technical Subsystem	Closely defined job description, division of labour Abstract nature of task is distinct from those of concern as a whole Operations governed by instructions Specialized differentiation of functions	Tasks continually adjusted and redefined Total situation of concern determines task Duties defined by purpose and staff interrelationships Sophisticated, often automated Project work

	Emphasis on routine Highly formalized Precise definition of rights, obligations and technical methods attached to each functional role	Lateral rather than vertical communication, providing information and advice rather than instructions and decisions
Goals and Values Subsystem	Feelings repressed Hidden agendas Emphasis on written communication Interaction is vertical (superior–subordinate) Formal, aloof, distrustful Value system – win–lose, strive to preserve status quo, reactive not proactive to change Rules and procedures ferment distrust and encourage mediocrity Little to promote learning and growth Loyalty to concern, leader and/or part of the organization, stresses obedience to superiors Precise definitions of rights, obligations and methods into functional positions Power struggles and abuses of power Highly political	Multi-channelled communication, innovative, risk-taking Two-way communication – mutual respect Relaxed, trusting, mutual respect, informal Win–win, collaborative, supportive Provides for quality learning environment both physically and psychologically Importance attached to expertise and affiliations outside organization in industry, technology and commercial environments Commitment to organization as a whole or to profesional goals Much professionalism High regard for mentors and role modelling Individuals seen as agents for organizational learning Opportunity for self development and socially useful work
Psychosocial Subsystem	Less motivation for self-improvement, learning blocks Hygiene factors important sources of motivation Assumes subordinates are immature and dependent Little professionalism	Self-directed motivation Herzberg's motivators important Assumes subordinates are interdependent and mature Much professionalism

Table 3.2

The effect of the environment upon the managerial, technical and structural goals and values, and psychosocial subsystems

	Stable Environments	Unstable Environments
Managerial Subsystem	Authoritarian, close supervision Task-oriented Individuals have less control over jobs as decisions are highly centralized Use of staff and advisory personnel Minimum delegation of authority	Participative, appropriate to solving complex problems in groups or committees Decisions made at lower levels of hierarchy Relationship-oriented Less emphasis on use of staff functions Much delegation and decentralization Leader must provide initiating structure if task is too ambiguous.
Technical Subsystem	Many rules and procedures, highly specialized jobs, downward communication Structure and management must be appropriate to task The right person must fit the right job Many control points, frequent checks by management Detailed planning based on standard rules and procedures	Flexible rules, broad jobs with diverse tasks Individuals perform diverse tasks Diverse products, demands are complex, diverse, rapidly changing. Emphasis on research and development, jobs less well defined.

Structural Subsystem	Organized by function Bureaucratic and mechanistic Structure and management of group must be appropriate to task Well-defined hierarchical group structures more appropriate for routine problems	Organized by product, service or subject. Subject specialists responsible for selection, cataloguing, classifying material and reference service. Open and structured Departments and individuals are integrated
Goals and Values Subsystem	Stresses advantages of hard work and Protestant work ethic Downward communication Type of organization is appropriate to goals and values of organization and to environmental culture Emphasis on efficiency	Lateral, upward and downward communication Decreased emphasis on individualism and increased emphasis on group/social ethic 'Higher-level' incentives, interesting jobs and achievement are held as important Increased sensitivity, openness, supportiveness. Emphasis on intuition and creativity, achievement of milestones rather than control points
Psychosocial Subsystem	Employees motivated to accomplish tasks for which there is a reasonable probability of success Have to perform to standards Individual has less control over his job Appraised according to clear performance standards	Higher level incentives such as interesting jobs and achievements are important Needs increased sensitivity, openness and supportiveness Performance criteria less clear, based upon critical incidents

rules and procedures, by close supervision, very little personal decision-making, and the existence of uniform standards to which subordinates must conform. This may be contrasted by situations which occur in reader services departments. Here staff have to be more creative in their search for information, making decisions regularly, and are subject to much less direct supervision.

Library and information centre managers should understand the complexity and uncertainty of their library's external environment, and design their organizational structure accordingly (Table 3.2).

STRATEGIES FOR ASSESSING THE INTERNAL ENVIRONMENT OF LIBRARY AND INFORMATION CENTRES

The task of assessing the internal environment of an organization makes it possible to identify organizational strengths and weaknesses and to develop programmes which both build on the strengths and overcome the weaknesses. The task is made more meaningful if models are used. Such models make the task of identifying the various systems and subsystems which operate in the internal environments of libraries and information centres much easier. Some systems are so interrelated that it is difficult to distinguish one element from another. At other times, several systems interact with each other to provide other outcomes. This can lead to confusion about which system is actually being studied. By analysing the organization in terms of models a clearer assessment can often be achieved.

Kast and Rosenzweig's organizational system

The first model is one based upon Kast and Rosenzweig's (1984: 8) organizational system. The organization is seen as being an open, sociotechnical system comprising five integrated subsystems, namely: goals and values; technical; psychosocial; structural; and managerial (see Figures 3.3 and 3.4).

Managerial subsystem

The managerial subsystem spans the entire organization through top

38

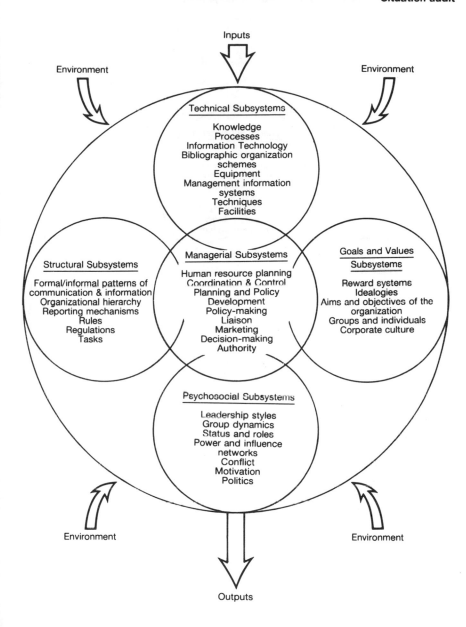

Figure 3.3 The internal environment model
Source: Adapted from Kast, Fremont and Rosenzweig (1984)

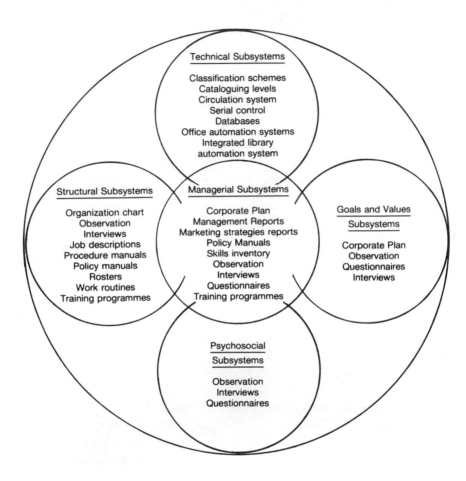

Figure 3.4   Sources of information for the internal environment model

management's task of relating the organization to its external environment. This is achieved through the planning and programme development function, staffing, coordination and control, policy-making, liaison, marketing, organization development, decision-making, and authority; these being the basic functions of top management.

In assessing the managerial subsystem, the organizational values, objectives and policies should be considered to identify whether these are strategically relevant, and whether they are being met. The allocation of resources, responsibility and authority should be effective in order that goals are achieved within the policy constraints. The structure should adequately reflect the complexity and stability of the external environment. Control processes should be in place to provide feedback mechanisms and keep the organization strategically on course for survival and success.

Information for assessing the managerial subsystem can be obtained from the organization's corporate plan, from marketing strategy reports, policy manuals, management reports, interviews and questionnaires and general observation.

Technical subsystem

The technical subsystem is concerned with transforming inputs to outputs. It includes the techniques or skills employed and the methods, information, technology and equipment used. Knowledge and management information systems are also part of the technical subsystem which will vary between different types of libraries and different departments. The employees and managers in each of these will have different informational and technology needs dependent upon their skills and responsibilities. The technology may also determine the organization structure and the psychosocial system.

The technical subsystem may be assessed by considering whether the technology used is the most appropriate and effective, whether it fits the organization structure and corporate culture, and whether it is responsive to the environment. It should also be efficient. In libraries and information centres, efficiency and effectiveness should be considered when designing or choosing classification schemes, when selecting the level of cataloguing to be used, or in

41

preparing a systems analysis for a library or office automated system.

Structural subsystem

The structural subsystem provides for formalization of relationships between the technical and psychosocial system. It involves reporting mechanisms and organizational structure, formal and informal patterns of communication and information flow, organization hierarchy and the system of rules and regulations. The structural subsystem determines the ways in which the tasks of the organization are divided and integrated.

This structural subsystem should allow for effective communication throughout the organization, with clear lines of authority and communication channels reflected in the hierarchical structure. The type of structure should reflect the complexity and stability of the external environment and the type of technology used. Information regarding the structural subsystem may be obtained through organization charts, job descriptions, procedure manuals, policy manuals, observation of work routines and communication patterns, interviews and questionnaires.

Psychosocial subsystem

The psychosocial subsystem consists of the interaction of individuals and groups through group dynamics, leadership styles, politics, conflict, friendship, motivation, power and influence networks. It is influenced by the attitudes, expectations, feelings and personal goals of individuals and groups. The technology, corporate culture and external environment will also affect the psychosocial subsystem. This subsystem can be analysed through the use of interviews, questionnaires and general observation.

Goals and values subsystem

The goals and values subsystem is important in determining the organization's corporate culture and general climate. The aims and objectives of the organization will only be accomplished in an

42

environment where there is congruence between what the organization is trying to achieve and what it is. The goals and values subsystem may be assessed through interviews, questionnaires and general observation, and by relating these to the strategic plan section of the organization's corporate plan.

Beer's social systems model

A second model which is useful in understanding the relationships between the various systems in the internal environment of an organization is Beer's (1980) social systems model of organizations. Beer identifies eight major organizational components: the environment, people, organizational structures, organizational behaviour and processes, human outputs, organizational outputs, corporate culture and dominant coalition.

Within these components, the people, organizational structure, behavioural and process, and human outputs systems interact with and are influenced by the external environmental domains of the market, social factors and technology, the organizational culture and the dominant coalition.

In explanation, people have needs and expectations which are either enhanced or frustrated by aspects of the organizational structure. These can include the organizational structure itself, policies, job structures, meeting structures, control and accounting systems or simply the geographic layout of the building.

Together, the interaction of people and organizational-based structures influence the behavioural processes found within organizations. These include leadership patterns, types of supervision, communication, conflict management, decision-making processes, problem-solving processes, planning and goal setting and other interpersonal behaviours.

The influence of these systems interacting with each other lead to some human outputs based upon perceptions and feelings of well being. Attitudes about organizational effectiveness, commitment, feelings of competence, intrinsic and extrinsic satisfaction, trust and supportiveness, elements of collaboration and reality orientation will all be governed by people, structures and behaviour.

All four of these systems interact upon and are influenced by the

43

corporate cultural system and the dominant coalition which refers to the skills and attributes of top management. Finally, the external environment affects the operations of these internal systems.

The result of all these systems working together provides for economic outcomes and quality of life within the organization. Economic outcomes can be demonstrated by profit, growth and return on investment. In libraries and information centres, levels of service and other performance factors could be substituted for profit and return on investment. Quality of life can be measured by employee turnover, absenteeism and the competitiveness of the library or information in labour markets.

STRATEGIC AUDIT FOR A LIBRARY OR INFORMATION CENTRE

A strategic audit for a library or information centre can be undertaken by using Wheelen and Hunger's strategic audit (1986: 38–45). (See Table 3.3.)

Table 3.3
A strategic audit for a library or information centre.

I.	*Current Situation*:	
A.	1.	Where are libraries and information centres going in the next ten to fifteen years?
	2.	How are they performing in comparison to their competitors in the private sector, eg: information brokers?
B.	1.	What are the library or information centre's current mission, objectives, strategies and policies?
	2.	Are they clearly stated or are they merely implied from performance?
	3.	At what point is the library or information centre now? Where does it aim to be in the future?
	4.	Mission: What business is the library or information centre in? Why?
	5.	Objectives: What are the corporate, departmental and functional objectives? Are they consistent with each other, with the mission and objectives, and with the internal and external environments?
	6.	Policies: What are they? Are they consistent with each other, with the mission, objectives, and strategies, and with the internal and external environments?

44

II.   *Strategic Managers*

A.   Ownership level (Board of Directors, Council, Ministers):
1. Who are they?
2. As stakeholders do they have much influence on policy decisions of the library or information centre?
3. What do they contribute to the library or information centre in terms of knowledge, skills, background and connections?
4. What is their level in strategic management? Do they merely rubber-stamp top management's proposals or do they actively participate and suggest future directions?
5. How sympathetic are they to the library's purpose?

B.   Top Management:
1. What person or group constitutes top management?
2. What are top management's chief characteristics in terms of knowledge, skills, background and style?
3. Has it established a systematic approach to the formulation, implementation, evaluation and control of strategic management?
4. What is its level of involvement in the strategic management process?
5. How well does top management interact with lower-level management?
6. How sympathetic is top management to the library's purpose?

III.   *External Environment : Opportunities and Threats*

1. What general environmental factors are affecting the library or information centre?
2. Which of these are the most important at the present time? In the next few years?
3. What percentage of environmental factors are deemed to be important now? In the next few years?

IV.   *Internal Environment : Strengths and Weaknesses*

A.   Organizational structure:
1. How is the library or information centre presently structured?
2. Is decision-making authority centralized or decentralized?
3. Is the structure clearly understood by everyone in the library or information centre?
4. Is the present structure consistent with current corporate objectives, strategies, policies and programmes?

B.   Corporate Culture:
1. Is there a well-defined or emerging culture composed of shared beliefs, expectations, and values?
2. Is the culture consistent with the current objectives, strategies, policies and programmes?
3. Does the corporate culture value initiative, or does it stifle it?
4. Are there department subcultures? Are these consistent with the corporate culture?

45

   5. What is the culture's position on important issues facing the library or information centre?

C. Corporate Resources:
   1. What are the library or information centre's current marketing objectives, strategies, policies, and programmes?
   2. Are they clearly stated or merely implied from performance and/or budgets?
   3. How well is the library or information centre performing in contrast to other similar libraries?
   4. What are the library or information centre's current financial objectives, strategies and policies?
   5. Are they clearly stated or merely implied from performance and/or budgets?
   6. Are they consistent with the organization's mission, objectives, strategies, policies, and with internal and external environments?
   7. How well does the library or information centre perform compared with other departments on a financial basis?
   8. What is the library or information centre's approach to quality control in the services which it provides?
   9. Are these clearly stated or merely implied?
   10. Are they consistent with the organization's mission, objectives, strategies, policies, and with the internal and external environment?
   11. What is the vulnerability of the library or information centre to local or national strikes, reduction or limitation of resources from suppliers and substantial cost increases of resource materials (books, journals, etc.).
   12. What are the library or information centre's current human resource management objectives, strategies, policies, and programmes?
   13. Are they clearly stated or merely implied from performance?
   14. Are they consistent with the organization's mission, objectives, strategies, policies, and with the internal and external environments?
   15. Is there a high turnover of staff? If so, why?
   16. How well is the library or information centre performing in terms of improving the fit between the individual employee and the job?
   17. Are appropriate techniques being used to evaluate and improve corporate performance? Consider job analysis programmes, performance appraisal systems, training and development programmes, up-to-date job descriptions, skills inventories.

V. *Strategic Factors*

   1. Are the current mission and objectives appropriate in the light of the key strategic factors and problems?
   2. Should they be changed? If so, what will the effect be on the library or information centre?
   3. What are the long- and short-term problems facing the library or information centre?
   4. Can the current or revised strategies be met?

46

VI.   *Strategic Alternatives*

    1. Are alternative strategies needed?
    2. If so, which alternative strategies are feasible?
    3. What are the pros and cons of each?

VII. *Implementation*

    1. What kinds of programmes should be developed to implement the recommended strategy?
    2. Who should develop and/or be in charge of the programmes?
    3. Are the programmes feasible? Are there sufficient financial, technical, human and information resource allocations?
    4. Will new standard operating procedures need to be developed?

VIII. *Evaluation and Control*

    1. Is the current information system capable of providing sufficient feedback on implementation activities and performance?
    2. Is the information timely?
    3. Are appropriate standards and performance measures being used?
    4. Are reward systems capable of recognizing and rewarding good performance?

Source: Wheelen, Thomas and Hunger (1986) adapted from pp.38–45. Reprinted with permission.

CRITICAL SUCCESS FACTORS

Critical success factors can be used to identify the most important ingredients for a library's or information centre's success. They focus upon the key determinants of success in the operating environment. Examples of critical success factors are a motivated, knowledgeable staff, quality assurance, key political factors or legislative requirements.

Critical success factors should be viewed as a tool for identifying certain key components in the library's goals. As a result, the library or information centre is able to clarify certain goals and formulate objectives which will allow it to be successful by drawing attention to key issues. Such issues may be reflected in written policies or activity statements, examples of which are statements that indicate the need for staff to provide a rapid response to customer enquiries, or policies which direct the library to be unbiased in its treatment of all information.

47

SWOT ANALYSIS

The SWOT (strengths, weaknesses, opportunities and threats) analysis provides an objective assessment as to whether the library or information centre is able to deal with its environment. The more competent an organization is, the more successful it is likely to be. Strengths and weaknesses deal with factors internal to the organization, whilst opportunities and threats are concerned with its external environment.

A strength is a resource or capability an organization has to effectively achieve its objectives. In a library or information centre, a strength may be its outstanding collection of stock or a particularly helpful and creative member of staff whose knowledge of the stock enables the library's information service to function very effectively.

A weakness is a limitation, fault or defect in the organization that will keep it from achieving its objectives. Limited opening hours or a cramped floorspace may prevent a library from extending its services further to cater for an expressed need.

It is often difficult for the library or information centre manager to carry out an objective assessment of their library's strengths and weaknesses. Usually, only outsiders can remove themselves from the emotional and personal issues involved. Information for the assessment can be gathered through interviews with staff, evaluation of internal reports and other documentation, questionnaires, surveys and interviews with users and non-users.

An opportunity is any favourable situation in the organization's external environment. It may be a trend or change which supports the demand for a service which has not previously been identified or filled. An opportunity usually allows the library or information centre to enhance its position, and may be brought about by a technological change which allows the organization to offer a new service or fill an existing need. The combination of OPAC facilities in an automated library system and existing communications technology has allowed readers to access the library's catalogue from a remote point and so provides the facility for a new service. The production of talking-books or spoken-word cassettes on a commercial basis, at a reasonable cost and free of some copyright legislation, has allowed the public library the opportunity to meet an already existing need for the elderly or infirmed.

A threat is an unfavourable situation in the library's or information centre's external environment that is potentially damaging to it or its strategy.

It may be a barrier, a constraint, or anything that might inflict problems on the library or information centre. Privatization is a threat to many services offered by library and information centres in the public sector.

The SWOT analysis allows strategies to be planned which can materialize the strengths and opportunities and overcome the threats and weaknesses facing the library or information centre. It is used extensively in marketing processes.

CAPABILITY PROFILE

The capability profile is a means of assessing the library's or information service's strengths and weaknesses in dealing with the opportunities and threats in the external environment. The organization's capability in the fields of management, marketing, technology and finance helps to identify the strengths and weaknesses in dealing with variables in the internal and external environment.

Managerial capability can be gauged by considering the extent and use of strategic plans, the image of the library or information centre, its speed of response to changing conditions, management communication and control, the organization's ability to attract and retain highly creative people and its ability to respond to the external environment.

Marketing capability can be demonstrated by user loyalty and satisfaction, percentage of users versus non-users, quality of service, and ability to grow.

The presence of technical skills, level of technology used, resource and personnel utilization, economies of scale, newness of equipment, application of computer technology, level of coordination, and integration and effectiveness of service may determine the library's or information service's technical capability. Financial capability is determined by access to capital and stability of costs.

A bar chart is prepared detailing the degree of strength or weakness of each category. After completing the chart the relative strengths and weaknesses can be determined. Whilst the capability profile is highly subjective, it is still useful. It provides the means for examining the current strategic position of the library or information centre and highlights areas needing attention.

STRATEGIC FOUR-FACTOR ANALYSIS

This analysis identifies the key factors which are critical to strategic planning, management and control (see Figure 3.5).

The four factors include strategic planning, organizational considerations, strategic control factors in the internal environment and resource requirements. Factors in the external environment influence the strategic plan as alternative approaches to dealing with the external environment are considered. The capability of the organization to meet demands imposed by the external and internal environment will also affect the choice of strategic approach. The strategic control focuses upon the internal requirements involved in implementing the chosen strategies (operational plan). The fourth

External environment/Strategic plan

Goals, objectives, missions, stakeholders, social responsibility, opportunities, risks, threats, legislation, regulations.

Resource requirements

Financial resources, productive capacity, human resources, expertise, research and development.

Strategic Management

Organizational considerations

Organizational structure, power, politics, leadership, groups, peers, organizational climate.

Internal environment/Strategic control

Implementation, control, technology, lifecycle, performance, rewards.

Figure 3.5 Strategic four-factor analysis
Source: Rowe, Masan and Dickel (1986): Reprinted with permission.

50

axis shows how funding sources and other factors are assessed in order to acquire resources.

The strategic four-factor analysis allows for the information needed for effective strategic management to be simply organized so that the relationships between the four strategic areas can be displayed.

REFERENCES

Beer, M. (1980), *Organisation Change and Development : a systems view* (Glenview: Scott, Foresman).

Burns, T. and Stalker, G.M. (1961), *Management of Innovation* (London: Tavistock Press).

Kast, F.E., Fremont, E., and Rosenzweig, J.E. (1984), *The Nature of Management (Modules in Management)* (Chicago, Ill.: Science Research Associates).

Lawrence, P. and Lorsch, J. (1969), *Organisation and Environment* (Homewood, Ill.: Irwin).

Rowe, A.J. *et al.* (1986), *Strategic Management and Business Policy: A Methodological Approach* (2nd edn.) (Reading, Mass.: Addison-Wesley).

Wheelen, T.L. and Hunger, J.D. (1986), *Strategic Management and Business Policy* (2nd edn.) (Reading, Mass.: Addison-Wesley).

PART III
STRATEGIES FOR MANAGERIAL PROCESSES

Introduction

This section aims to introduce the reader to the managerial subsystems which operate in libraries and information centres. It provides an insight into five key managerial processes: planning, human resource planning, human resource development, decision-making and marketing.

Corporate planning is a very important management task as it is essential to the long-term survival and success of the library or information centre. It requires an insight into the library's external and internal environments, its overall performance, and the future. It relies upon objective judgement and creative ability to determine the library's strengths and weaknesses and to take advantage of opportunities, whilst minimizing threats. Corporate planning is an important management process from which decisions about the library's or information centre's future flow. The corporate planning process is discussed in Chapter 4.

Human resource planning is important as libraries and information centres are very labour-intensive. People are a very valuable organization resource both in monetary terms and in behavioural outcomes. If people are managed correctly, their value is increased considerably, yet if they are managed inefficiently, the cost to the organization is extremely high. A properly balanced, highly motivated and well trained workforce will enhance the library's output and performance.

A systematic approach to human resource planning can be used to ensure that the tasks of the library are performed by those who have the appropriate skills, knowledge and attributes. This includes the process of job analysis, the writing of job descriptions and job specifications, the conducting of interviews and proper induction procedures; all of which are described in Chapter 5.

The induction process is the first stage of what should be continuous human resource development. Training and development needs can be identified through performance appraisals, career counselling can be used to map a course for personal achievement, and, finally, separation interviews can give feedback relating to working conditions. An introduction to these topics can be found in Chapter 6.

Chapter 7 deals with the topic of decision-making. Decision-making is needed to determine courses of action. An organization cannot function without decisions being made. Some decisions are simple to the extent that librarians and information professionals make decisions in their work activities without realizing the fact. Other decisions are more complex requiring judgement and extensive knowledge. The complexity of decisions generally reflects the management level of those involved.

Managers have different decision-making styles. This is reflected in the extent to which they include others in their decision-making processes. Participative decision-making is also linked to organization style.

The last chapter in this section deals with marketing strategies. These are closely linked to the corporate planning process in that they ensure that the library's or information centre's services are appropriate to, and satisfy the consumers' needs. Strategic marketing identifies viable market positions and programmes for the survival and success of the library or information centre.

4   The corporate planning process

INTRODUCTION

Corporate planning is a continuous and complex process. It allows libraries and information centres to adjust to dynamic environments and to respond effectively to new situations so as to ensure their survival and success.

To be effective, corporate planning requires the commitment and involvement of top management. There has to be a clear understanding throughout the organization of the need for corporate planning and of its value. The process will fail if inadequate time or resources are spent on it, or if there is a lack of commitment to the process.

The corporate planning process recognizes that organizations cannot achieve everything they would like to do. Instead, it allows for the allocation of resources and the planning of strategies on a priority basis to best achieve those activities which lead to the effective accomplishment of the organization's mission. A by-product of its success can be found in increased communication and coordination amongst various parts of the organization, resulting from the process of determining the organization's goals. (See Figure 4.1).

In the light of changing environments and uncertainty, one important strategy is that which facilitates the organization's growth and survival in an environment where competition for resources is upmost.

ROLES AND RESPONSIBILITIES

Prior to embarking on the corporate planning process the roles and responsibilities of all the stakeholders must be clearly defined.

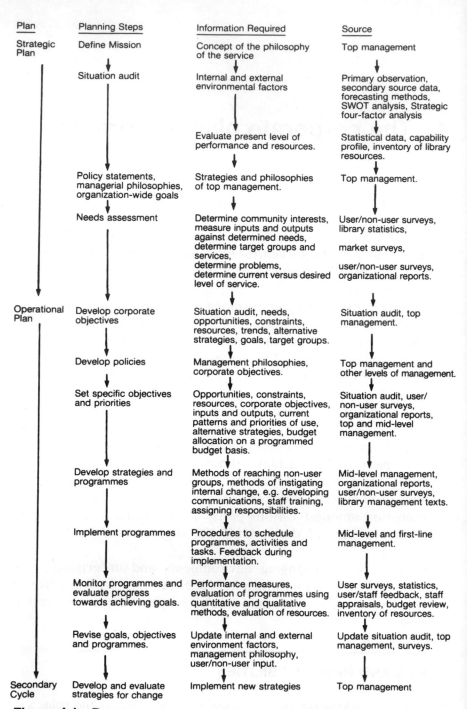

Plan	Planning Steps	Information Required	Source
Strategic Plan	Define Mission	Concept of the philosophy of the service	Top management
	Situation audit	Internal and external environmental factors	Primary observation, secondary source data, forecasting methods, SWOT analysis, Strategic four-factor analysis
		Evaluate present level of performance and resources.	Statistical data, capability profile, inventory of library resources.
	Policy statements, managerial philosophies, organization-wide goals	Strategies and philosophies of top management.	Top management.
	Needs assessment	Determine community interests, measure inputs and outputs against determined needs, determine target groups and services, determine problems, determine current versus desired level of service.	User/non-user surveys, library statistics, market surveys, user/non-user surveys, organizational reports.
Operational Plan	Develop corporate objectives	Situation audit, needs, opportunities, constraints, resources, trends, alternative strategies, goals, target groups.	Situation audit, top management.
	Develop policies	Management philosophies, corporate objectives.	Top management and other levels of management.
	Set specific objectives and priorities	Opportunities, constraints, resources, corporate objectives, inputs and outputs, current patterns and priorities of use, alternative strategies, budget allocation on a programmed budget basis.	Situation audit, user/non-user surveys, organizational reports, top and mid-level management.
	Develop strategies and programmes	Methods of reaching non-user groups, methods of instigating internal change, e.g. developing communications, staff training, assigning responsibilities.	Mid-level management, organizational reports, user/non-user surveys, library management texts.
	Implement programmes	Procedures to schedule programmes, activities and tasks. Feedback during implementation.	Mid-level and first-line management.
	Monitor programmes and evaluate progress towards achieving goals.	Performance measures, evaluation of programmes using quantitative and qualitative methods, evaluation of resources.	User surveys, statistics, user/staff feedback, staff appraisals, budget review, inventory of resources.
	Revise goals, objectives and programmes.	Update internal and external environment factors, management philosophy, user/non-user input.	Update situation audit, top management, surveys.
Secondary Cycle	Develop and evaluate strategies for change	Implement new strategies	Top management

Figure 4.1 Requirements for the corporate planning process

Source: Adapted from Figure 1, 'Cycles of the Planning Process', taken from *A planning process for public libraries* by V. Palmour, M. Bellassai and N. De Wath: © 1980 by ALA.

Planning is a human-oriented process. All stakeholders who have the potential to be affected should be involved. This includes library staff, readers, the funding allocators and others who are in a legitimate position to influence the library or information centre.

By its nature, corporate planning requires top management to be highly involved in the process. Whilst it is acknowledged that top management will not produce the plan alone, their personal commitment and involvement is crucial to its long-term effectiveness. They should be the initiators of the process and oversee its progress.

An important responsibility of top management is to create an environment for corporate planning which dispels fears and encourages enthusiasm. Planning must not only be wanted, but it must be seen to be wanted. The enthusiasm for corporate planning can be enhanced by discussing the successes of other organizations who have used it, by explaining how library and information centre functions might be bettered through planning, and revealing how corporate planning would improve the decision-making process.

Most of the goals, objectives and strategies will be realized through the activities of the various departments of the library. The initial handling of the planning process will therefore greatly influence the employees' perceptions of it and their long-term enthusiasm for its implementation. The process may require attitude changes amongst the staff and careful handling of the situation may pay dividends at the time when the planning process is implemented. If all staff are involved in the planning process of their own particular areas and are allowed to participate in some decision-making, they will identify more readily with the corporate plan and show enthusiasm for its implementation.

Managers must be motivated to spend time on corporate planning. There should be a formalized system which allocates time and resources to the task, and an organizational approach which allows the manager's contribution to the planning process to be assessed as part of their individual performance appraisal.

It is the responsibility of top management to determine whether consultants are to be used as facilitators. Consultants should not be used to actually produce the corporate plan, since this is an internal task. However, they can be used to determine user/non-user needs by conducting interviews or surveys to ascertain viewpoints, or to act as the advocate or facilitator to overcome personality or territorial influences when setting goals and objectives.

THE CORPORATE PLAN

An outcome of the corporate planning process is a document called 'a corporate plan'. This is a written record of an organization's objectives and how it proposes to achieve them. The corporate plan has two main components: a strategic plan and an operational plan. The strategic plan expresses the organization's aims and, in broad terms, how it intends to achieve them. It should be geared to increase the organization's flexibility, ability to adjust to change, and capacity for creativity. It does not focus on daily operational or budgetary issues, but provides the mission statement and long-term strategic goals which lead to the definition of corporate or organizational objectives, policies and standards.

Operational plans should list the services to be delivered and an estimation of the resources required for their operation. A set of results or outcomes, qualified by a timetable for their achievement, is provided for each service or project. Measures of performance to assess the level of achievement of the objectives and detailed plans for the acquisition, development and use of human, technical, informational and financial resources are also included in the operational plan.

The corporate plan should therefore be objectives-driven as it is primarily concerned with outcomes. It should also present a clear rationale for specific objectives; give a clear impression of the relative priorities being given to individual outcomes; provide a choice of strategies; and provide a justification for all programmes, activities and resources.

THE STRATEGIC PLAN

Define the mission

The first task of the planning process is to define the library's or information centre's mission. This identifies the purpose of the library or information centre and should clearly articulate its purpose. It is often useful to view this as a means to solving a problem. For instance, a special library may view its mission as responding to the problem of ensuring that the information needs of its parent organization are met. This is preferable to saying 'to provide books and related materials which meet the information needs of the parent organization', since the latter statement could inhibit the library's role in the following manner:

1. It may narrow the perception of the library by the stakeholders.
2. It assumes that the library itself will provide all the information, when it could legitimately act as a facilitator of an information exchange.
3. It locks the library into dealing solely with books and related materials which are mainly sources of external information.
4. It does not provide the library with the opportunity to take advantage of any emerging information technologies or partake in any other course of action.
5. It does not allow the library to consider the option of being responsible for the organization and management of the parent organization's internal information – for example, the records management system.

Situation audit

The mission statement is set in the context of the organization. A detailed scenario of the organization can be gained through the situation audit as discussed in Chapter 3. The situation audit includes:

- the identification of the internal and external environmental factors which impact upon the organization;
- critical success factors, SWOT analysis, capability profile, strategic four factor analysis and other audit functions;
- a summary of the key issues facing the organization;
- an outline of the present level of resources and organization performance;
- statements of policy and managerial philosophies;
- the formal and informal mandates imposed on the organization;

61

- the desired future in terms of major results or outcomes;
- a statement of organization-wide goals which represent the philosophical basis for its operations and articulate the desired future conditions to be achieved.

Needs assessment

The needs assessment provides additional environmental information for the development of the operational plan. It enables the library or information centre to:

- identify the difference between current provision and desired level of service;
- forecast future needs;
- plan provision to meet such needs in good time;
- ensure that the operational policies are effective in reaching real needs.

The needs assessment should not relate solely to users of the library. Individual staff, group, departmental or divisional needs should also be considered.

Many sources of information can be used for a needs assessment: previous user/non-user surveys, census information, organizational reports, other written documents, community analysis and other empirical data. A needs analysis should not rely solely upon the librarian's professional judgement or on indicators such as the volume of complaints, comments or suggestions made by users, since these methods do not always provide an accurate assessment of needs. Underestimation can arise, or alternatively, librarians may not be aware of needs of certain non-vocal sectors of the community. Often the needs of non-users are overlooked. Overestimation of needs can also arise by overlooking the fact that a vast majority of library users may be satisfied with the existing provision of service.

The preliminary stage of clarifying what is meant by need in a particular programme area can be useful, forcing library members to examine what their real objectives and definition of need are. The concept of need implies a normative judgement: a particular level of need is arbitrary and depends upon one's attitude. Ideas of what constitutes need change over time as affluence increases, in a similar way to which motivational needs change according to Maslow's theory of motivation. 'Wants' and 'needs' should be distinguished: to get to work you may *want* to drive a Mercedes or Porsche, yet you may really only *need* a push-bike.

In attempting to assess needs, it is important to try to survey the needs of both users and non-users of the library service. Surveys of this kind can provide valuable data, although they are comparatively expensive and need careful planning to provide valid and useful results. If surveys are not planned properly, incorrect information may be obtained which could result in the implementation of a programme totally unsuited to the real needs of the community. This could be more costly to the organization in both financial and social terms than the original costs involved in the correct planning function.

Implemented correctly, surveys can provide the library or information centre with details for forward planning not obtainable elsewhere. There is a danger, however, of a tendency to rely upon a survey as a 'proven management technique' instead of trusting an officer's gut feeling which arises out of his/her close involvement and working knowledge of the situation. Various data collection and analysis techniques are available.

Having determined future needs, and using information obtained from the situation audit relating to present level of performance and levels of existing resources, the library or information centre manager can begin developing corporate objectives.

THE OPERATIONAL PLAN

Develop objectives

Objectives are statements of why certain things are done. They are an expression of a purpose for solving a problem. When an objective is stated as a problem it is apparent that there are several solutions. For example, lending books is only one method of overcoming a problem in the provision of information to the library's or information centre's community.

Objectives have different time horizons. Corporate objectives are of a long-term nature and should allow for the improvement and coordination of corporate operations. Specific objectives comprise mid-term and short-term objectives which are in turn translated into programmes and activities. These determine the services to be delivered and are output- and/or outcome-oriented. Specific objectives are framed with the inputs, outputs and constraints in mind and their resources are allocated through established functions such as the budgeting process. More specific information about objectives is included later in this chapter.

Develop programmes

The development of programmes takes place after considering all of the alternative strategies whereby each specific objective can be achieved. It should be a creative and innovative exercise, allowing for the best possible alternative to be selected. An improper choice of programmes will waste planning time and money, will result in frustration for staff and the misuse of funds, ultimately rendering the process futile.

The programmes selected should represent the best possible use of funds when considered against all other possible uses. Each programme should lead to improved organizational performance and derive the greatest possible benefit for the least cost.

In libraries and information centres, the evaluation of programme alternatives should assess not only the financial and economic aspects, but also the social and political benefits. Quality and quantity of output (services) should be measured against inputs (resources).

Implement programmes

Programmes are implemented by organizing activities and allocating tasks. Implementation of the plan at this level is possibly the most difficult task as it invariably means change. Strategies for dealing with change should be devised prior to the introduction of new programmes. Responsibilities are assigned, and monitoring and control processes devised, to measure progress towards the attainment of goals.

Successful planning processes tie implementation strategies into action plans. They also build management structures and recruit or train people with skills and outlooks which reinforce the strategies. Such an integration of strategy and structure provides for a synergistic whole.

In implementing programmes, emphasis should be placed upon the outcomes of decisions rather than the techniques by which the decisions are made. The secret in implementing the corporate planning process in a library or information centre is to establish a medium by which the quality of service is increased by motivation and increased commitment to the organization's goals. Positive results should be highlighted and reinforced. Short-term improvements can be made permanent through positive reinforcement, monitoring and review.

Information-sharing is paramount. Library and information service staff are entitled to be fully informed. The need for staff to have the opportunity to contribute and be involved in day-to-day decision-making is important, for this collective approach anticipates that all employees will have a commitment to the achievement of organizational goals and shares the onus of high performance amongst all members of the organization. Mutual discussion regarding the implementation of programmes includes agreement upon resources and assistance necessary to achieve stated objectives. This may lead to more effective and cooperative coordination throughout the organization. Improvements in superior–subordinate relationships may be expected due to the increased communication and participation in the objective-setting process and feedback in the periodic performance appraisals.

Critical to the success of implementing the planning process is the need to determine the proper sequencing and relationships of activities. Appropriate beginning and completion dates must be set in order to avoid plans being implemented before the strategies for dealing with the resultant changes are considered. Appropriate financial, human, technical and informational resources must be made available at the right time and in the right place.

Programme review

The success of corporate planning can be recognized in the achievement of the organization's goals. Very often the planning process is considered complete upon implementation of the programme. This is not so. The last and most significant part of corporate planning is the evaluation of the planning process and measuring the successes of the selected programmes. Evaluation through monitoring and review processes is the accountability aspect of planning: it determines whether the library's or information centre's goals are being achieved. It also provides the organization's members with important feedback which can be used to improve the total effectiveness of the library as a service agency responding to the needs and wants of its patrons. More detailed information on this topic can be found in Chapter 27.

POLICY-MAKING

Policies are guides to decision-making processes. They are usually created either to solve a problem or as a declaration of intention for a specific course of action. Policies, like objectives, can be either general or specific. General policies are used on an organization-wide basis and are broad and comprehensive. These affect all departments and all levels of staff. Specific policies usually occur at operational level, having significance for a particular department or being relevant to day-to-day issues or activities. Only those staff who are directly concerned with that department or who deal with the specific issues, such as resource selection policies, will be affected.

Policies ensure that decisions are made in keeping with managements' philosophies. They are usually carried out by others than those who design them. Good policies are developed with this in mind, for if they cannot be implemented effectively they will fail.

The policy-making process should be well planned and well thought-out in terms of strategic timing, costs, issues at stake, and the values and attitudes of the stakeholders to these issues. All policies imply some form of change, be it at strategic or operational level. As a result, conflict can arise which may in turn jeopardize the policy.

Effective policies solve problems or channel decisions towards achieving the goals of the library or information centre and its organization. Once overall policies have been established, they can become effective tools for moving decision-making to lower levels of the organization, by providing answers to routine questions. This ensures that individuals, groups or departments can take initiative in making decisions but that the outcomes will still be in line with the ultimate achievement of the organization's goals.

Policies are usually found in a policy manual, although many organizations also have a set of unwritten policies. The policy manual is a way of communicating within an organization and serves as an induction tool for new members of staff.

Policies are ratified at the ownership level. In the case of a special library within a private company, the ownership level will comprise the chairman and board of directors who are elected by the company's shareholders, whilst in the case of a public library the ownership level is the mayor and councillors or aldermen who are elected by the ratepayers.

OBJECTIVES

Hierarchy of objectives

Objectives may also be distinguished according to their level in the hierarchy (Figure 4.2). At each higher level in the hierarchy the objectives are more general and relevant to a greater proportion of the organization's activities so that the corporate objectives at the top of the hierarchy are relevant to 100 per cent of the organization. Corporate objectives concern all activities of the organization and are usually long-term.

Specific activities are either departmental objectives or short-term ones for the whole organization, and are always measurable and achievable. These are then translated into programmes, activities and tasks. Activities and tasks are directly related to the subsets of the specific objectives and are usually short-term or repetitive, are measurable and relate to groups or individuals.

A hierarchy of objectives also exists based upon an element of time. It is pyramid-shaped, with the broadest and most future-oriented objectives at the pinnacle of the pyramid and the immediate or short-term objectives at the base.

The long-range objectives (2–5 years) are of importance because

67

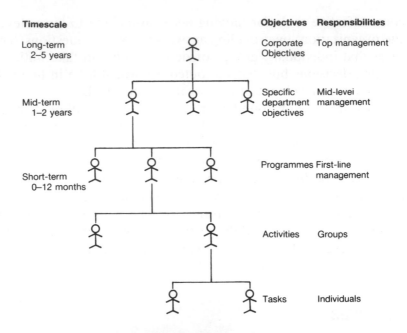

| Timescale | | Objectives | Responsibilities |

Figure 4.2 The hierarchy of objectives

they provide direction for the organization over the next several years and consequently affect the nature of the medium-range and short-term objectives. Medium-range objectives (1–2 years) should be fairly precise in definition and quantification as it is possible to forecast the environmental climate to some degree of accuracy for this time span. Immediate or short-term objectives represent the bulk of the objectives in the corporate plan and should be very specific and concrete.

Writing objectives

Effectively formulated objectives should result in concrete outcomes desired by the organization. However, formulating meaningful statements of objectives takes careful thought and analysis. The intention of the objective must be clear and its focus well understood: it should not merely specify the action but also stimulate it. Objectives should be clearly stated and understandable to all responsible for their achievement. They must be challenging but still capable of achievement. They must be written so that they can be analysed and occasionally reviewed.

Objectives should be defined in terms of results or conditions to be achieved rather than in terms of the activities to be performed, as it is against objectives, that performance will be measured. They should be stated in positive terms – that is, in terms of what is to be done rather than in terms of what is to be avoided. Above all, objectives should be quantified, since the more concrete the infor-information the more likely will be the achievement of the 'real' meaning. The quantity of results ('how much') is just as important as the type or kind of results. Time limits, percentages, volume amounts and frequency rates are measurable points which can be incorporated into library or information centre objectives. Quantified objectives define and clarify the expected results better than a verbal description. They provide a built-in measure of effectiveness.

Successful planning

Success in corporate planning depends upon an understanding of the process by those involved. It requires a commitment by top management and good communication channels throughout the organization. Because the planning process should be tailored to meet the needs of each organization, it may not be necessary for every step outlined above to be followed since these will vary according to each library's needs and resources. However, it is necessary that adequate resources be available as inputs, and that outputs are designed so as to be practical.

The plans themselves should be flexible, enabling smooth and quick adjustments when necessary. However, they should not need extensive modification and should be abandoned if this is the case. When the plans have outlived their usefulness they should be replaced by another as part of the continuing cycle. Corporate plans should be simple and provide for the accomplishment of goals with the fewest possible variables. Complex plans are difficult to implement and monitor.

The corporate planning process will be less than successful if management assumes that the planning function can be delegated to a planner. Planning should not be rejected as a management technique on the basis that previous attempts to plan have failed;

that there is insufficient knowledge of the planning process; or that effective long-term goals cannot be developed in the light of a dynamic environment. Planning is, and should be, a learning process. It should not be separated from the entire management process and, like other management processes, it is just as political as it is rational.

Corporate planning is a continuous process which requires a periodic reassessment of the total operating environment. It is not a practice of taking last year's plan and adding to it by extrapolating trends. It requires completely rethinking the future in the light of the current environment and prospective future changes.

Corporate planning is ongoing. It should not be forgotten between cycles because the cycle is continuous, the environment forever changing, and it is impossible to eliminate uncertainty about the future.

5 Human resource planning

INTRODUCTION

Personnel are an organization's most expensive, yet most valuable, resource. In any organization's budget – and this is particularly true of labour-intensive organizations such as libraries or information centres – the wages and salaries component is usually the highest of all expenditures. Managed appropriately, an organization's workforce is its lifebreath. Managed inappropriately, the workforce becomes an expensive commitment that leads to few rewards but many problems.

Successful planning and management of human resources is critical for overall organizational effectiveness. Future manpower needs are related to corporate goals and objectives. Human resource management involves more than developing procedures for annual review, and equal opportunity. It is a complex process that ensures that staff are given the opportunity to develop both their personal and professional competencies and so maximize their output.

Every librarian has to be concerned with human resource management. For many years, effective human resource management has been ignored by some, due to the belief that worker productivity was not as important for libraries as, for example, the new cataloguing regulations and their effect on in-house systems. The recent development of the human relations approach to management, and an emphasis on tighter budgetary control, has now led librarians to plan for the more effective and efficient use of their staff. Motivation, training and personal development have become recognized techniques for improving worker performance and efficiency. There are now attempts to 'marry' the job, the person and the situation – in other words, a contingent approach.

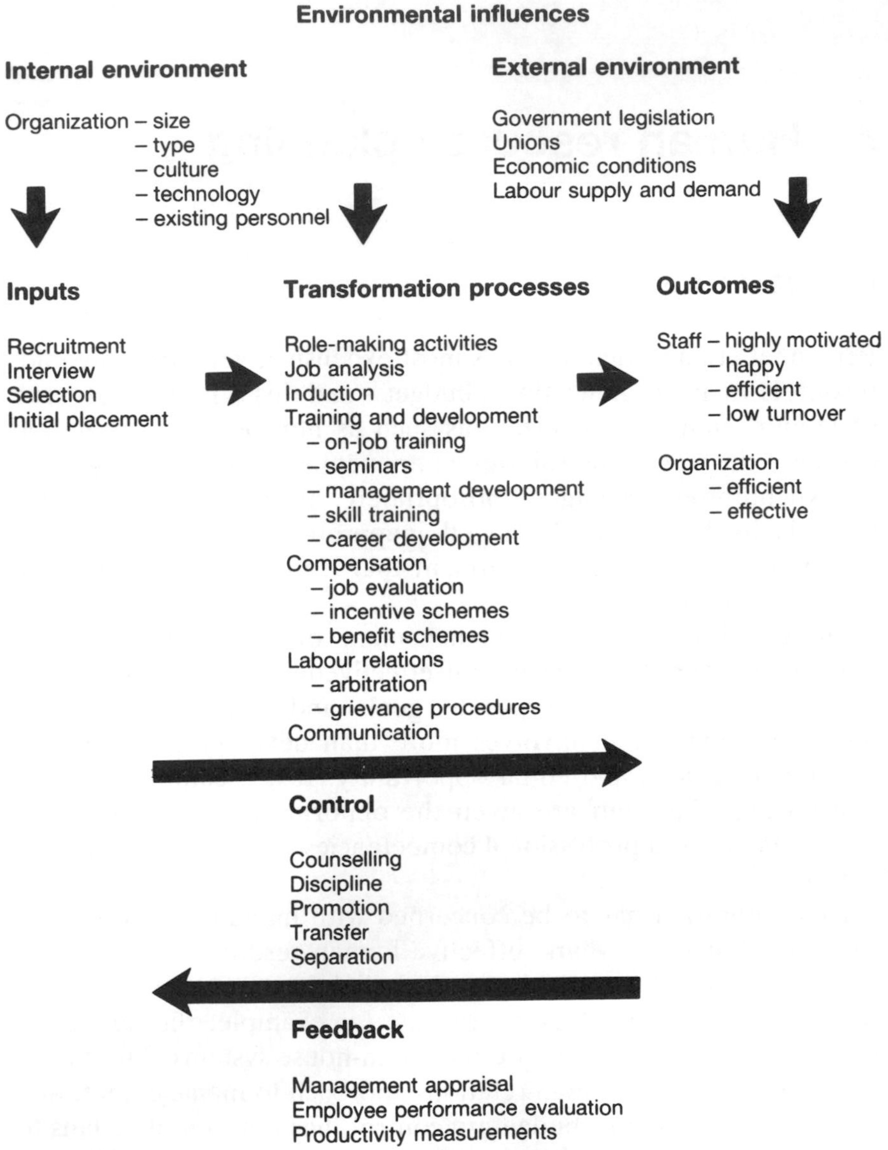

Environmental influences

Internal environment

Organization – size
         – type
         – culture
         – technology
         – existing personnel

External environment

Government legislation
Unions
Economic conditions
Labour supply and demand

Inputs

Recruitment
Interview
Selection
Initial placement

Transformation processes

Role-making activities
Job analysis
Induction
Training and development
    – on-job training
    – seminars
    – management development
    – skill training
    – career development
Compensation
    – job evaluation
    – incentive schemes
    – benefit schemes
Labour relations
    – arbitration
    – grievance procedures
Communication

Outcomes

Staff – highly motivated
       – happy
       – efficient
       – low turnover

Organization
    – efficient
    – effective

Control

Counselling
Discipline
Promotion
Transfer
Separation

Feedback

Management appraisal
Employee performance evaluation
Productivity measurements

Figure 5.1   The systems approach to human resource planning

The systems approach can be applied to human resource planning (see figure 5.1). The job analysis determines the kind of person necessary properly to fulfil the responsibilities of the job as described by the job description and job specification. Skilful recruiting procedures provide for the successful selection and placement of the right person to fit the job. Proper orientation and induction allows the new employee to become conversant with the organizational goals and also forms the basis for future development of both the person and the job.

Efficient and effective outcomes result from the transformation processes of good job analysis and design, training and development, appropriate compensation and labour relations, good communication systems and role-making activities. Control is in the form of counselling, discipline, promotion, transfer or separation. Feedback mechanisms comprise management appraisal, employee performance evaluation and productivity measures. The result is a highly motivated staff leading to increased organization efficiency and effectiveness.

The external and internal environment also affects human resource planning. External factors, such as government legislation and policies together with other legal requirements, may determine some employment practices. Unions may be influential in classifying positions or work practices. Awards govern conditions of employment. The supply of labour is affected by economic conditions, changes in academic requirements and the organization's ability to attract and keep appropriately skilled people.

Internally, the size, structure and type of organization affects human resource planning. Its degree of specialization, personnel configurations, professionalism, formalization, and its technology and corporate culture has the potential to attract different types of people.

Effective human resource management is planned and executed at a macro (strategic) and micro (operational) level. Macro human resource management refers to human resource planning and forecasting. Overall organizational objectives are converted into specific personnel actions, as the procurement, development and utilization of human resources depends upon the organization's strategic plans for its future (growth, diversification, contraction, and so on). Micro human resource management refers to the production of job analyses, job descriptions; and other personnel processes which affect individuals.

MACRO APPROACH

The macro approach to human resource planning can be broken down into various stages. Stage one consists of the determination of manpower objectives based upon the environmental analysis and the corporate goals relating to productivity, growth, development of the organization, together with budgeting constraints. This is followed by projections for the planning period (manpower needs), based upon size of labour force, skill inventory, employee earnings, and productivity levels, as compared with the inventory of current manpower status (manpower availability).

The third stage requires the identification of gaps between projected manpower status and desired manpower objectives, expressed either as a match, excess or deficit of personnel. This may relate to specific skills, occupations or levels of staff and may not be organization-wide.

Alternative actions are generated to overcome anticipated manpower gaps. Such alternatives may include recruitment and/or lay-off of personnel, redesign of jobs, reorganization of work processes, changes in the requirements for the abilities sought by recruits, skill-training programmes, revision of wage structure and/or system of compensation, and changes in work rules.

The final stage involves the monitoring and evaluation of feedback regarding the performance of the library's programmes, and revision and alteration of the programme and/or objectives as necessary. This stage of monitoring, feedback and revision ensures that the human resource planning process is continual and dynamic rather than periodic and formal.

The macro approach to human resource planning encourages organizations to plan for their future staffing structures and to take into account changes in services and technology. Exercised properly, and on a continuing basis, it should eliminate problems of oversupply or undersupply of particular skills within an organization. It also aids in the determining of training needs in relation to required skills (see Figure 5.2).

74

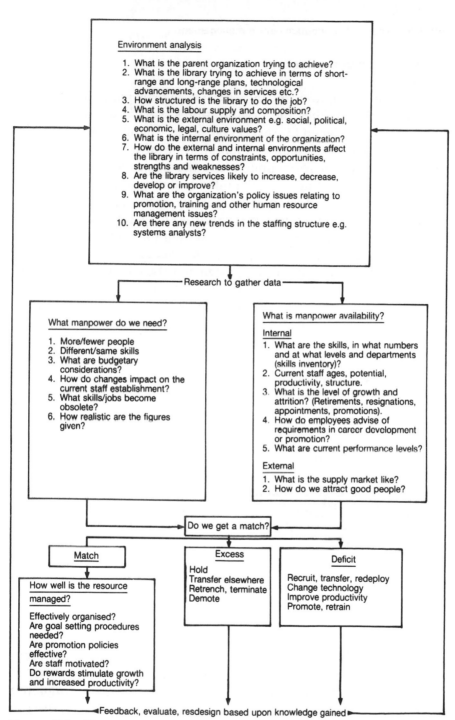

Environment analysis

1. What is the parent organization trying to achieve?
2. What is the library trying to achieve in terms of short-range and long-range plans, technological advancements, changes in services etc.?
3. How structured is the library to do the job?
4. What is the labour supply and composition?
5. What is the external environment e.g. social, political, economic, legal, culture values?
6. What is the internal environment of the organization?
7. How do the external and internal environments affect the library in terms of constraints, opportunities, strengths and weaknesses?
8. Are the library services likely to increase, decrease, develop or improve?
9. What are the organization's policy issues relating to promotion, training and other human resource management issues?
10. Are there any new trends in the staffing structure e.g. systems analysts?

Research to gather data

What manpower do we need?

1. More/fewer people
2. Different/same skills
3. What are budgetary considerations?
4. How do changes impact on the current staff establishment?
5. What skills/jobs become obsolete?
6. How realistic are the figures given?

What is manpower availability?

Internal
1. What are the skills, in what numbers and at what levels and departments (skills inventory)?
2. Current staff ages, potential, productivity, structure.
3. What is the level of growth and attrition? (Retirements, resignations, appointments, promotions).
4. How do employees advise of requirements in career development or promotion?
5. What are current performance levels?

External
1. What is the supply market like?
2. How do we attract good people?

Do we get a match?

Match

How well is the resource managed?

Effectively organised?
Are goal setting procedures needed?
Are promotion policies effective?
Are staff motivated?
Do rewards stimulate growth and increased productivity?

Excess

Hold
Transfer elsewhere
Retrench, terminate
Demote

Deficit

Recruit, transfer, redeploy
Change technology
Improve productivity
Promote, retrain

Feedback, evaluate, resdesign based upon knowledge gained

Figure 5.2 The macro approach to human resource planning

75

Skills/manpower inventory

A skills or manpower inventory is a management information system which describes the organization's workforce. Such inventories may be designed for several purposes – monitoring workforce capabilities and performance, identification of employees for promotion, transfer and/or training, and the projection of workforce capabilities. Depending upon the intended purpose, these inventories range from distributions of employees by salary, age, sex, and so on to individualized employee files indicating qualifications for job openings. The usefulness of any data system for employee inventories depends upon the appropriateness, accessibility and current validity of the data. A simple file system may be adequate for a small, relatively stable organization, whilst a computerized data system, updated daily, may be required for a large, more dynamic organization.

Many systems used for manpower or skills inventories are designed to identify qualified candidates for staff openings. Most inventories call for information on age, sex, tenure, skills, rated potential, salary, job and organizational assignment and any other information found useful in predicting turnover, performance and job movements within the organization.

MICRO APPROACH

The micro approach to human resource planning reflects the interface of individuals with their jobs. As part of operational planning, it covers personnel selection and placement, training, appraisal and staff development. The micro approach is systematic, beginning with a job analysis and ending with the exit interview at the time of separation between the employee and the organization (Figure 5.3).

Job analysis

Job analysis is the process of studying and collecting information relating to the operations and responsibilities of a specific job. It is fundamental to the preparation of the job specification and job description.

The process of collecting data usually consists of interviews

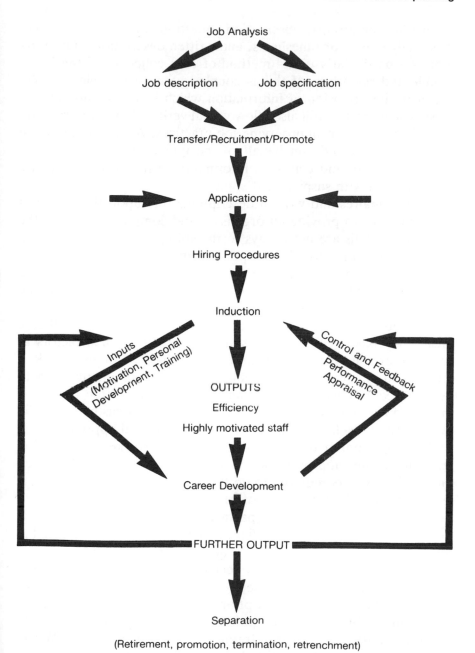

Figure 5.3 The micro approach to human resource planning

(individual or group), observation, questionnaires, filming activities, daily diaries or timesheets, and written descriptions. Observation is a particularly useful method of data collection if the job is simple and repetitive. If this is coupled with an interview, it will result in the provision of information which is not readily observable. The interview will also allow verbal verification of information already obtained from observing job practices. A sincere, attentive and assuring attitude on behalf of the interviewer is required to ensure accurate and complete information, since job analysts are often viewed with suspicion.

Questionnaires and written descriptions rely upon the ability of the jobholder to provide an organized and complete report of the job. These skills are not always forthcoming at lower levels in the organization hierarchy where report writing and analytical skills are not required. In such cases, daily diaries or timesheets provide a more structured approach to analysing tasks. They can therefore be used more widely throughout the organization.

The job analysis provides details on a quantitative as well as a qualitative basis. Quantitative statements refer to such factors as the size of the work group, and the number of times a task is performed per hour, day or week. Qualitative statements refer to working conditions, and personnel requirements. Often the job is broken down into elementary units or tasks; the focus being on the work activity itself. This is called the task-oriented approach.

A second approach to analysing jobs is the worker-oriented job element. In this approach the units of analysis are the generalized human behaviours required to do the work. Similarities and differences are described in terms of processes that are common to all jobs, not idiosyncratic to one particular job. The third approach is to analyse the underlying abilities and aptitudes; jobs are studied in terms of the profiles of abilities required to perform the work.

A variety of information is collected. This includes a description of the work activities performed – for example, report writing, or applying a bibliographic description to an item or recording details of accounts which have been paid – and the purpose of the work, the procedures used and the frequency of the procedures. Work-orientated behaviours are listed. These include details of machinery, technology or equipment used – for example, a personal computer, fax machine or word processing facilities – as well as proportions of time spent sitting, standing, moving about and the amount of time devoted to, or the importance of, communication or decision-making skills. Individual demands such as aptitude, personality or physical characteristics are also included in work-orientated behaviours.

The job analysis should also collect information on accountability – the superiors and subordinates and levels of responsibility. The nature of the supervision – that is, clerical, administrative, technical or professional – and its extent, as in continuous or close super-vision, should also be noted.

Job description

The first and immediate product of the job analysis is the job description. This is a descriptive, factual statement of the duties and responsibilities of a specific job. The following information is usually provided:

1. *Job identification*: Includes such information as job title, alter-native title, department, division and code number for the job.
2. *Job summary*: Provides a short definition of the job itself, which is useful as additional identification when the job title is not sufficient. It also serves as a summary to orient the reader towards an understanding of the detailed information that follows.
3. *Duties performed*: This is the heart of the job description. It tells what is to be done, how it is to be done and the purpose behind each duty. If possible, duties should be arranged in chronological or some other systematic order. An estimation of the approximate percentage of time devoted to each major duty is helpful as is the degree of supervision received.
4. *Achievable results*: Provides some measure of performance or standards which describe the minimal acceptable employee performance of each job's duties.
5. *Reporting–supervising functions*: Identifies the immediate superior and subordinate positions and the degree of super-vision received and given.
6. *Combination tasks/relationship to other jobs*: Identifies the vertical and horizontal relationships of workflow and proce-

79

dures, and the positions within the organization with which coordination is required.

7. *Machines, tools and materials*: Lists and defines each major type of technology, knowledge and equipment used; where possible trade names should be identified.

8. *Working conditions*: Checklists are often used to indicate working conditions, using such alternatives as hot, cold, dry, dusty, noisy, etc. Hazardous conditions should be noted.

Definitions of technical terms and other comments which clarify the above can be included.

Job descriptions form the basis for human resource planning, recruitment and position management. They can be used to provide intending applicants and new appointees with details of the idiosyncrasies of the position. Job descriptions are also useful in settling industrial disputes. Results-oriented job descriptions provide for some measure of performance and the beginning of a description of inputs and outputs for the position. They also serve as a useful basis for staff appraisal.

Job descriptions need to be updated continuously if they are to be effective; otherwise they become irrelevant and ignored. Unfortunately it is often the case that job descriptions are only updated when positions become vacant and new staff are to be appointed. An ideal opportunity to update the job description is at the time of the annual performance appraisal interview. Because library and information centre positions usually centre around technology, environmental changes in such technologies make the updating of job descriptions an important task in libraries. For this reason it is also helpful to write job descriptions in dynamic terms (see Figure 5.4).

Job descriptions need to leave some scope for initiative and innovation on the part of the jobholder. If they are too specific and detailed, they can allow the jobholder merely to continue the practices of their predecessor, thereby stifling initiative and creativity and failing to lead to an improvement in efficiency.

The value of job descriptions depends very much on how they are used and updated in the library or information centre. At best their value extends beyond the recruitment stage. They should be referred to at times of staff appraisal and when considering staff

```
┌─────────────────────────────────────────────────────────────────────┐
│                        CITY OF NOAH VALE                              │
│                        Job Description                                │
├─────────────────────────────────────────────────────────────────────┤
│ DIVISION                DEPARTMENT              POSITION NUMBER        │
│ COMMUNITY SERVICES      LIBRARIES                    :40              │
├─────────────────────────────────────────────────────────────────────┤
│ Title                   Special Allowances      Classification        │
│ ASSISTANT LIBRARIAN     Nil                         C4               │
└─────────────────────────────────────────────────────────────────────┘
```

	CITY OF NOAH VALE Job Description	
DIVISION COMMUNITY SERVICES	DEPARTMENT LIBRARIES	POSITION NUMBER :40
Title ASSISTANT LIBRARIAN	Special Allowances Nil	Classification C4

1. *Job Summary*
   The Assistant Librarian assists at a semi-professional level with the day-to-day operations of the library service.
2. *Organizational Relationship*:
   Reports to: Branch Librarian
   Supervisers: Library Assistants
   Coordinates with: Childrens Librarian

3. *Duties performed*:

	Frequency %	Supervision received
Principal Duties:		
Rostered enquiry desk duty.	30	Min
Supervise issue, discharge and shelving of books and other materials	20	Min
Accession, catalogue and classify books, pamphlets and cassettes	10	Min
Bibliographic checking/verification of requests	10	Min
Subsidiary Activities:		
Attend to telephone enquiries	5	Min
Supervises shelf tidying and general library tidying	5	Nil
Any other duties as directed by Branch Librarian	5	
Combination Tasks:		
Assist Children's Librarian in organizing and conducting children's activities	15	Min

4. *Achievable Results*:
   All tasks will have been completed when library users' enquiries are efficiently and effectively answered, when all materials have been correctly issued, discharged or shelved; when an accurate bibliographic description has been assigned to all newly accessioned material; when all outstanding requests have been correctly verified; and when all material is placed in its proper location and the library is neat and tidy.
5. *Equipment Used*:
   VT100 Visual display terminal
   Calculator
   Xerox photocopying machine
6. *Working conditions*:
   Air-conditioned, clean building.

Figure 5.4   An example of a job description for an assistant librarian

81

development and manpower planning. To be of true value, they should be results-orientated and written in dynamic terms to allow for changing work environments.

Job specification

Whereas the job description describes the job, the job specification describes the desired attributes of the person doing the job. It is a statement of the minimum acceptable human qualities required to perform a job properly. Such requirements are usually established for individual jobs on the basis of judgements (such as those of the job analyst), but in some instances they are based upon statistical validation procedures.

The job specification can include the following aspects:

1. *Information inputs to the position*: Interpretations of perceptions, verbal or auditory interpretation, environmental awareness, visual input from materials – for example, visual appraisal of condition of stock.
2. *Mental processes*: Decision-making, information processing, use of job-related knowledge.
3. *Work output*: Manual or control activities, physical coordination required, skills and technical abilities, use of equipment, technology.
4. *Relationships with other persons*: Supervising of staff activities, public contact, communication of instructions, directions or other related job information, interpersonal communication skills.
5. *Job context*: Potentially stressful/unpleasant environment, potentially hazardous job situations, personally demanding situations.
6. *Other job characteristics*: Attention-demanding activities, vigilant/discriminating activities, structured/unstructured activities, continuity of workload.

Minimum educational requirements and work experience are also included.

The job specification should be used as a guideline to the knowledge, skills and aptitudes required to perform a specific job

---

CITY OF NOAH VALE
Job Specification

DIVISION	DEPARTMENT	POSITION NUMBER
COMMUNITY SERVICES	LIBRARIES	:40

Title
ASSISTANT LIBRARIAN

---

1. *Job Summary*
   The Assistant Librarian assists at a professional level with the day-to-day operations of the library service.

2. *Educational Requirements*
   Completion of an accredited course leading to a degree in library and information studies.

3. *Experience*
   Previous work experience in a public library-related environment would be an advantage.

4. *Abilities Required to Perform Work*

   4.1 Good general knowledge and ability to interpret written and verbal requests for information.

   4.2 Possession of effective written and verbal communication skills.

   4.3 Ability to translate theoretical knowledge of librarianship gained in learning environment into the work situation, eg: demonstrated knowledge of bibliographic organization.

   4.4 Basic working knowledge of an online, integrated library automated system.

   4.5 Ability to efficiently and effectively organize own work after initial instruction.

   4.6 Ability to relate effectively with people of all ages, and to recognize and provide for their information needs.

   4.7 Ability to display empathy with children is important.

   4.8 Enthusiastic and energetic personality.

   4.9 Reliable and cooperative.

Figure 5.5 An example of a job specification for an assistant librarian.

83

(Figure 5.5). It should not be allowed to dictate the recruitment process to the extent that, all other things being equal, an applicant who is qualified and capable but deficient in some aspect fails to be appointed.

The main qualifications or qualities required for a job are easy to analyse, as there are fairly acceptable standards of education recognized by all; however, the degree to which each is required to fill the job is harder to ascertain. The degree of training is usually defined in specific terms – the completion of a specific programme, for example – or it may be defined quantitatively such as the typing or data input at so many words per minute. The ability to read, write or count and, in the case of non-English-speaking migrants, the ability to understand a minimum of English may be a job qualification. The degree of experience required is best defined in actual job experience, either in the job itself or in a related job. A time measure of experience is sometimes specified, for instance, 'a minimum of three years experience in managing a public library'.

The degrees of requirements about aptitudes, intelligence and personality required to perform the job are usually expressed in such terms as possession of an outgoing personality, clerical aptitude, above-average intelligence.

As it is used in the recruitment of personnel, the job specification can be condensed and form part of the original advertisement. It should be given to prospective candidates along with the job description so that they are fully informed of the position for which they are applying.

The job specification should form the base upon which applications are initially screened. It should be used as a comparison between the qualifications of the candidates and the basic qualifications of the job. At the time of the interview, the interviewer should gear questions to evaluate the interviewee in terms of the qualities and qualifications outlined in the job specification.

THE RECRUITMENT PROCESS

Recruitment sources

In general, there are two potential sources for prospective candidates for a position – internal and external. Filling a position internally has the advantage of increasing the general level of morale by providing an example of career path development within the library or information centre. It is a reward mechanism for good work, and may stimulate others to greater achievement. The process of recruiting internally may be more predictable in its outcome as human resource or management personnel should have access to information relating to the candidate's history of work performance within the organization. This may be more reliable than the curriculum vitae or external references furnished by external candidates.

Internal promotion is not always in the organization's best interest. External sources may provide more highly skilled candidates than those on the existing staff, or the organization may need some 'new blood' injected into it.

A number of external sources for recruiting library personnel are available. These include recruitment advertising, employment agencies, recommendations by present employees, educational institutions, unsolicited or casual applicants or networking.

Advertisements

Advertisements may be placed in the local or national press, trade journals or professional media. The choice of media will depend upon the level of the position to be advertised. Information relating to the organization, job specifications and the job itself should be included in the advertisement to assist in self-screening. The advertisement should include details of the name of the library or information centre, the name of a contact person and telephone number for further details, closing date, person or place to whom applications should be sent and application details required.

The advertisement layout, design and copy should reflect an accurate image of the library or information centre. It should reflect the organization's size, whether the organization is conservative or progressive, centralized or decentralized, dynamic or static. High-quality design can boost the immediate response as well as the organization's image. Advertisements are governed by media deadlines. In general, the more frequent the publication, the shorter will be the deadline. Thus, a local newspaper will have a shorter deadline than a professional or trade journal.

Employment agencies

Employment agencies can be used to screen potential applicants. Employment agencies want to keep their clients happy by effectively working toward the client's goal, and they do this by effective advertisement design and placement of staff. Both public and private employment agencies can be used. Often government employment agencies have a professional division for the recruitment of qualified library or information centre personnel. One concern of using employment agencies, particularly private ones, is the commission which they charge and the cost of their artwork and typesetting. However, some of these costs would also be incurred by the library in its own placement of advertisements and in time spent sifting through letters of application and the advising and conducting of interviews.

Recommendations

Current employees may suggest prospective candidates for job vacancies. It can be presumed that the employee knows both the organization and the acquaintance, and would therefore want to please both. The hiring of relatives is an inevitable component of recruitment programmes, and some organizations have policies which allow or disallow this practice. Such a policy does not necessarily coincide with hiring on the basis of merit, but interest and loyalty to the enterprise can be offsetting advantages.

Library schools

Many libraries make special efforts to establish and maintain constructive relationships with school faculties and administrations. Staff of departments of librarianship or information science within tertiary institutions are often in positions to advise on outstanding candidates or suitable newly qualified professionals. Departments such as these often maintain a job register or have bulletin boards where advertisements can be displayed.

Unsolicited applications

Unsolicited applications, both in person or by mail, provide a source of recruitment. Policies differ between libraries or information centres as to how such applications are handled. Some keep all applications for future reference, whilst others note only outstanding ones. Some libraries refuse to take such applications, advising applicants to apply again when formal advertisements appear in the media.

Interviewing

The most widely used method of selecting individuals for jobs is the interview. The aim of the interview is threefold; to collect information about the candidate; to give information to the candidate; and to begin the induction process for the successful candidate.

Interviewers are essentially fortune-tellers for they are in the business of predicting the successful candidate's likely future behaviour in the organization. To do this the interviewer has various roles: as an initiator or leader in conducting the interview as they think fit; as a participant in communicating with the others present; to act as an observer noting behaviour, speech and other non-verbal communications; to be an analyst, listening, watching and analysing actions; to evaluate by interpreting correctly and drawing conclusions to what has been seen and heard; as a mind-reader in putting aside what has been said in exchange for what has not been said but is in the mind; to make objective judgements at the *end* of the interview; to listen for meaning in order to determine the context correctly; to counsel and to identify emotions, relating these to their cause.

Interviewers must be able to perform two basic functions: to acquire only relevant information and to interpret data correctly, once acquired. To carry out these functions the interviewer needs to have the following qualities: a warm and engaging manner and an ability to quickly establish rapport; a sensitivity to social situations; a quickness in perceiving implications in the remarks of others; a sensitivity to vocal intonation and hesitation; a mental level as high as or higher than that of applicants, enabling him to take control of the situation; and an analytical mind with the ability

87

to make critical judgements, enabling correct evaluation of all factors. Interviewers should also have an open mind and be adaptable, and should also possess a mature personality, showing evidence of sound practical judgement.

If it is used as the sole selection process for a position, it is most important that the interview is not only based upon the need to appoint the most appropriate person to the position, but that there is also an awareness of the ethical and legal reasons for the interview to be completely objective. Library and information centre managers should be aware that a substantial degree of subjectivity can creep into the interview if it is not structured correctly. This can arise by a lack of knowledge in the person(s) conducting the interview; a concern that the library is viewed in too favourable a light; a lack of interpretation or communication by those taking part in the interview; and the 'halo effect' which causes the interviewer(s) to read into discussions an intent which was not intended.

A considerable amount of planning is required for employment interviews. To overcome the likelihood of any subjectivity a structured interview is required. This necessitates basing the interview exclusively upon those job duties and requirements which are critical to job performance. There should be an interview committee so that answers are rated by more than one person. It is preferable that both males and females are employed on the interviewing committee, and that there is a balance of management and personnel skills between them.

All procedures should be consistently followed to ensure that each applicant has exactly the same chance. The committee should determine in advance a set of questions which can be consistently applied to each applicant, and the same questions should be asked in the same order by the same member of the committee. Incomplete answers or problem areas should be probed whilst maintaining an atmosphere of trust. It is useful for the interviewing committee to have determined sample answers to questions in advance so that interviewee responses can then be rated on an explicitly defined scale. Answers to questions should be documented for future reference and in case of legal challenge. Basic information questions given on the application forms should not be repeated. In general, employment interview objectives are usually intangible, dealing with such traits as character, social adjustment, attitude, and expression and capacity for growth and advancement.

Interviews are a two-way process. The interviewer should deliver appropriate and accurate information about the organization to the interviewee. The prospective candidate also evaluates the organization and makes decisions as to its suitability as an employing body. The interview is often the first contact with the organization and provides the first impression of its dynamics.

The interviewers should show concern for the applicant's feelings while maintaining control over the interview. They should convey a feeling of interest in the applicant by reacting appropriately to the applicant's comments, questions and non-verbal behaviours. An atmosphere of warmth and trust should be created. Interviewers should make use of encouragement and praise in order to put the applicant at ease.

Other selection tests should preferably be administered in conjunction with the interview, since such tests provide a more objective approach to personnel selection. Reference checks, psychological testing and job simulations offer additional dimensions to the selection process, either serving to support the interviewer's decision or, alternatively, justify a possible reappraisal of the decision-making process and the final decision.

If an incorrect decision is taken on the strength of one interview the results can be expensive, not only in financial terms for the organization, but also in mental anguish and the lowering of morale for both the employee and his or her co-workers who will be unsettled by the inevitable resignation or dismissal.

Correct interviewing procedures set realistic job expectations. As a result, the position may fail to meet the needs of some successful applicants, who will therefore reject the job offer. For those who accept, their work experience will confirm their expectations. Their needs will match the job, there will be high job survival, job satisfaction and less likelihood of resignation. The outcomes result in a motivated, satisfied staff.

If initial job expectations are set too high or too low it may attract a high rate of job offer acceptance. However, work experience will subsequently fail to match the new employee's expectations, resulting in dissatisfaction and a realization that the job does not suit. Frequent thoughts of resignation affect other members of staff leading to low morale and an unsettled staff.

Induction

One very important facet of personnel management which is often overlooked is the induction process. All too often it is felt that the appointment of an individual to a position ends the selection process, but the induction process is, in fact, one of the most vital processes of library or information centre management. It is the process which establishes what is required of the new appointee, and which produces a well-informed staff.

Induction orientates and introduces the new employee to the organization and may be done on either a formal or informal basis. The first phase is often conducted by the staff personnel unit (if one exists) and is one of information provision: it should cover background information to the organization; employee benefits; salary schedules; safety; probationary period; time recording and absences; holidays; grievance procedures; hours of work; lunch and coffee breaks; use of telephone facilities, and so on.

The second phase is performed by the immediate supervisor. It provides information relating to the library environment and includes visits to branch libraries or orientation of other departments within the organization, introductions to all senior staff and a complete overview of special programmes or facilities within the organization. It is at this stage that the new employee will begin to be aware of the norms and values of the parent organization's and library's corporate culture and subcultures. They may need some explanation as to why certain things occur and what values are most prevalent within the organization. A typical induction programme follows the format listed below.

First day

Review employee's work experience, education and training.

Greet personally. When the new employee arrives don't keep them standing or waiting unattended. Make them feel welcome. Greet them by names, and address them by it often. Show friendliness.

Put them at ease. They are likely to feel nervous or uneasy at first. Avoid any impression that they arrived at an awkward time. If you can't see to them immediately, apologize and arrange for someone else to look after them. Discuss their background and interests.

Show interest. Make them feel that the job genuinely needs them. Ask questions in a friendly tone – don't interrogate. Invite questions from them and act in accordance with the genuineness of the invitation. Enquire if they have any problems.

Explain the work to be done. Do not make it sound too difficult. Tell them their wages again, and when, where and how they will be paid. Have their job description available for discussion.

Introduce the new employee to their co-workers and their immediate subordinates (if any). Tell them who they report to, and who reports to him or her.

Point out amenities. Prevent them from feeling awkward; show them the work layout, particularly things which immediately concern them – for example, restroom facilities, canteen, locker room, car park. Have their desk or office and supplies ready.

Show them the work. Show them where they will be working. Introduce them to nearby workers. Avoid nicknames that could offend. Stay with them for a short time. Explain the work of the department, its relationship to the total organization and other departments. Clarify their position in the department, and its relationship to others in the department.

Instruct. Before instructing them in their jobs, find out what they already know. Explain the task carefully step-by-step and be patient if they are slow to grasp what you tell them – repeat key points till you are sure they understand. Indicate safety hazards. Alert them to job standards. Don't give detailed instructions till they are at ease and have lost their nervousness. Even though you have assigned instruction of the new employee to an assistant, take time yourself to make the new person feel that you are concerned about their training.

Arrange guidance. Tell them whom to approach with work problems. Provide them with a policy and procedures manual. Make sure they are not left alone to fend for themselves – this includes lunch time and coffee breaks. Ensure that someone explains lunch arrangements and invites them to eat in company.

Maintain contact. Make sure you see them again on the job later in the day. Make sure they know where they are to report the following morning.

Second day

Make early contact. Contact them within the first few hours of work. Check over things of the first day. Answer their questions readily. Look interested in their welfare.

Inform. At this point you could let them know in more detail how their work fits into overall activities. Don't overburden them with information or rules. Give information on things that affect them personally.

Maintain contact. Make a point of seeing them, even if briefly, once more through the day. Encourage them to talk about problems they have met.

Within the first week

Give further information. Contact them at least daily for the rest of the week. Help them to develop a sense of belonging. Ask them if they are interested in such things as social club activities, and tell them how they can take part.

Review. Show interest in their progress. Help them with problems they have met, but avoid criticism. Be alert for personal problems that arise which could affect the newcomer's work performance. Clear up any misunderstanding.

Second week

Explain rules, norms and values. Explain why rules are necessary and point out their application to other employees. Discuss the norms and values of the library and of the parent organization and how these affect library staff.

Discuss informally. Informal contact should be made about every second day. Listen for dissatisfaction. Counsel them or tell them what you propose to do.

End of first month

Maintain regular contact. Regular contact during the first month should help prevent grievances setting in. Make a point of talking with them briefly at least three times a week.

Check progress. By this time, if they have stayed, they should have settled down. Check their work. Correct errors by arranging further instruction, not by pointing up the failures. Don't reprimand in public – relieve their embarrassment by correcting them in private.

Praise them. If they have done a job well, tell them so. Let them know that their efforts are appreciated.

Within first three months

Review progress regularly. If they have trouble settling down, a transfer to other work might be discussed.

Comment. If their performance improves, let them know. Be generous and sincere in your comments.

6 Strategies for human resource development

INTRODUCTION

Human resource development is an ongoing management function. It begins with the induction process and is followed by staff training and development and career counselling along clearly identified lines of need. The feedback for these functions is obtained through the performance appraisal system and through separation interviews with staff who are about to leave.

The primary purpose of human resource development is to increase personal satisfaction through the extension of individuals to take advantage of their maximum capabilities; to improve human performance on the job; to overcome deficiencies; and to improve the quality of working life. Collectively, these outcomes should lead to increased organizational efficiency as a result of a knowledgeable and highly motivated staff.

TRAINING AND DEVELOPMENT

Library and information centre managers must recognize that the primary responsibility for training is theirs. The task may be delegated to a qualified and experienced training officer if such a position is available, although management still needs to be involved. Management must recognize that training cannot be substituted for selection. Training cannot create ability in the absence of capability, or transform ordinary mentality into brilliance, or create skill where aptitude does not exist – it can only develop the potential that is already latently there.

The work environment provides the greatest continuing opportunity for personal development and job-related learning on an individual basis. Courses, seminars, conferences and other training activities cannot be substituted for on-the-job opportunities for personal growth. Such opportunities are found in planned job rotation, job exchange systems or secondments and acting in relief positions.

Since stop–go training has an inhibiting effect upon learning, it requires the same kind of thoughtful, detailed, judicious planning as any other function of management. Training will only be taken seriously by employees if management views it seriously. Managers must persevere in maintaining training programmes during times of economic pressure as their curtailment represents a false economy.

Training does not consist of just one activity – the training session. Provision must also be made for support systems, policies and/or follow-up programmes to ensure the learners' effective use of their newly acquired knowledge, skills and attitudes on the job.

Identifying training needs

It is essential that training programmes are based upon identified needs. Organizations are extremely complex and the assumption that training, or rather the lack of it, may be the particular cause of the problem is a management decision which must not be made without investigation into the other systems which operate within the organization, in order to eliminate them as problem sources.

If it is established that the problem lies in the human system, there is a need for a further investigation to see if the area overlaps with some other system – such as, for example, the technical system. Low productivity may mean that the supervisor is not supervising subordinates correctly, or that the equipment being used is inadequate or unsuitable. Low output may also be caused by low morale, for which the reason needs to be found; by the supervisor's lack of skill in training people how to use the equipment; or by the supervisor's lack of skill in recognizing machine inadequacy. Only some of these problems will be corrected by training. Of those problems to be corrected by training, each will need a specific training session tailored to address its own unique problem.

Individual training needs can be identified during the performance appraisal interview, which may also be used to identify areas where specific training is required by one department or the whole organization. Changes in policy or the introduction of new technologies will also present the need for training or re-training of those affected.

Potential areas for training can also be determined by identifying the organization's weaknesses; by determining what skills, knowledge or attitudes are or are not carried out, and hence determining occupational training needs; and by discovering individuals' deficiencies in particular skills, knowledge or attitudes in order to determine who needs training in what.

Individual training is usually carried out on the job, with the immediate supervisor politely and considerately pointing out weaknesses and making suggestions as to how to overcome them. Particular groups have their own training needs. It is useful for groups such as subject specialists or library assistants to collectively determine their own training needs. As a result of their involvement in the planning process, the participants should readily partake in the training session and perceive it as being connected, and of value, to their work activities.

Designing the training programme

A good training programme should be based upon the needs of the learner – that is, on what the learner needs to know or should be able to do. It should be shaped to provide balance and flow, as well as to provide many good ideas which could easily be put into practice. Learning materials should be varied in order to avoid boredom. A combination of didactic and experiential methods is necessary.

When designing a training programme it must be remembered that it generally involves adults. Research has shown that adults learn in significantly different ways to children. The mature adult will make an arbitrary decision as to whether any new behaviours will be acquired, based on previous experiences and issues. Adults see themselves as self-directing in their learning needs, expecting to be able to answer some of the questions from their own experience and not just to be told. They need to test new concepts and behaviours against what they have previously learnt. This has a number of ramifications for the design of the training programme.

First, the training programme should be designed so as to be problem-centred rather than content-centred. It should permit and encourage the active participation of the learner, who should be encouraged to introduce past experiences into the process in order to re-examine those experiences in the light of the new data. Second, the climate of the learning should not be authority-orientated. The evaluation process should be a mutual activity between the learners and the instructor, leading to a reappraisal of needs and interests.

To some extent, the potential use of the new skill, knowledge or behaviour influences the type of training programme to be provided. If the planned outcome is that of increased knowledge, there is generally less need for discovery learning. If the learning is to be applied in an innovative way, then more experience-based learning is needed. If the desired outcomes are to have frequent learning-on-the-job applications or to be used in an operating mode – such as the operation of a word processing system – there is a need for more experiential learning. Retention is another aspect to consider. The longer the learner needs to retain what is learnt in the training programme, the more experiential the training programme needs to be.

If the training programme is to result in attitude or behavioural changes as an outcome of the learning process, attempts to change the participants' behaviour should be incorporated into the training programme. By design, the training programme should contain a great deal of simulation, group and individual participation, role play and case discussion in order to create participant behaviour in the training room and provide for immediate feedback on the success or failure of that behaviour.

The training programme should be designed so as to provide the optimum blend of didactic and experimental learning depending upon the type of learning required. Whatever the course content, it must be relevant, understandable, able to be absorbed, and associated with the work environment. Didactic training methods include lectures, reading, demonstration and panel discussion. Experiential methods of training can be provided through field trips, structural discussion, brainstorming, case studies, in-baskets, role-playing, sensitivity training and encounter training.

Establishing a climate for the training programme

In order to facilitate effective training, it is important to establish a discerning climate for the programme. This can be achieved with an acceptance that, whilst all human beings can learn, individuals must be motivated to learn. The individual(s) must be aware of the inadequacy in their present behaviour, skills or knowledge and have a clear picture of the behaviour to be adopted. The learner must have guidance in order to correct improper performance before a pattern emerges. This is particularly true for on-the-job applications. Appropriate materials for sequential learning must be provided, and these should be varied to avoid boredom. The learner must be provided with time in which to practise the learning and must derive satisfaction from it. Repetition reinforces the learning process, so the learner should receive opportunities for the reinforcement of the correct behaviour. The learning activity will be accomplished more readily when it is appropriately geared to the learner's physical and intellectual level of development.

Maintaining behaviour acquired through training

Maintenance of behaviour is anything which keeps an acquired skill or knowledge up to a performance standard – for example, getting feedback on the quality of one's work, and having the opportunity to use the skills.

A good training programme will impart knowledge, skills or behaviours, develop reasons why the learners should want to master these and provide the opportunity for practice. Learners should return to the workplace able to use the new 'tools' correctly. For the knowledge, skills or behaviour to be locked in, they must be applied back on the job. For this to happen there must be active support and involvement by the immediate supervisor. Supervisors should be involved in the pre-training and post-training meetings with management to determine the purpose of the training programme for the.individuals involved, to set the goals and objectives of the training session(s) and to evaluate the outcomes of the training programme.

To maintain behaviours, library or information centre managers and supervisors should use the terminology and concepts learned at the training programme. They should phrase questions in terms recognized by the participants as coming from the session and refuse to accept answers which are not similarly phrased. Participants should perform real work, not made-up practice sets, during training. They should also be encouraged to maintain a notebook of key ideas learned and possible on-the-job applications throughout the workshop. This should be followed up after the training session as part of the evaluation process, and should be used to demonstrate positive outcomes of the training session.

Evaluating the training programme

The evaluation process is both an information-gathering and decision-making process. At the end of the day, a 30-minute review should be held between the trainer and participants to gather information and evaluate the training session. Items for review should include the pace of the training session, problems with materials, groups, the trainer and general housekeeping problems. These reviews can yield valuable information, as they bring problems to light whilst they are still fresh in everyone's mind, provide immediate feedback, and allow problems to be recognized and solved before they affect the future training programme.

Any evaluation that takes place should evaluate the training process and not any other outside factors which could influence a change in behaviour. Pre- and post-tests on trained and untrained groups can be used to evaluate what has been learnt as a result of the training programme.

CAREER DEVELOPMENT AND COUNSELLING

The largest increase in jobs in the 1990s is forecast to be in the service and information-handling sector leading to an increase of new and varied positions in this field. As a result, career planning in libraries or information centres will take on renewed importance as opportunities develop for alternative career paths.

Career planning is a joint effort involving the organization, the manager and the employee. It must form part of the overall organizational planning. The organization must provide a structure and climate that encourages career planning and development; it should formulate and make known its own goals and priorities. Unless staff can see where the organization is heading, it is difficult for them to determine whether their future lies in the same direction.

The organization should also make known its human resource development policies and practices, such as equal opportunity programmes, funding or time granted for further study or attendances at conferences. Career planning and development relies upon the existence of such policies and a commitment to their development by management through the provision of budget allocations to meet financial needs.

To encourage the development of professional knowledge and expertise, and to allow employees the opportunity to put into practice their newly acquired skills, the organization must provide career paths and salary gradings related to experience.

The library or information centre manager has a responsibility to provide appropriate resources, assignments, coaching and counselling to assist employees in the realistic planning and attainment of career objectives. They should develop the talents of their subordinates, providing encouragement and support. As part of the appraisal system they should help employees choose their goals and identify the means to attain them. From a professional point of view the manager can act as a role model, providing professional qualities which subordinates may strive to achieve.

The individual has to accept primary responsibility for his or her own growth and development. He or she should identify his/her long-term career plans and seek access to organizational resources for growth. He or she is also responsible for providing feedback on the organization's performance in career management policies.

Individuals should develop action plans to assist in career planning. This is a process of identifying critical achievements in their working post; producing an inventory of their current skills and knowledge together with their anticipated future needs (a 'where am I now?' analysis); identifying the ideal job ('where do I want to get to?'); and defining the opportunities, constraints and critical success factors in achieving the ideal position ('how can I get there?'). The action plan determines the strategies, qualifications, skills necessary to achieve the ideal position ('what will I do?').

100

Problems can arise in career development when there is a feeling of lack of progress or where there is a lack of challenge in the current position with no foreseeable prospect of change. Career development is also affected when there is a conflict of interest between personal loyalty, professional loyalty or organizational loyalty, since failure to reconcile loyalty dilemmas can cause stress and a feeling of futility or confusion. Problems with immediate supervisors can also lead to a sense of frustration in career progression. At times like these a mentor can be useful. Mentors provide encouragement and support, help to develop people's talents and often open doors to the future.

PERFORMANCE REVIEWS OR APPRAISALS

Performance reviews have several important uses. They are a means of improving staff motivation and expertise; they provide feedback to employees on their level of performance, allowing them to capitalize on their strengths and overcome their weaknesses; and they can be used to develop an inventory of human resources which forms the basis for career planning from an organizational point of view.

All the organization's employees should be subject to an annual performance appraisal. This includes those who are employed at top management level as well as those at mid-level and first-line management. Performance appraisals should be conducted by the immediate supervisor.

Performance reviews provide a method of career counselling and encouragement for staff members to plan for their future. They allow the manager and subordinate mutually to set goals for the future and for each to determine their individual strategies to achieve these goals. The opportunity to sit down and plan in a mutual way is often lost in the day-to-day crisis management of many organizations. A formal appraisal system ensures that this is not the case, resulting in more rational and consistent goal-setting down the line.

Appraisals should be viewed in association with the training and development of staff because it helps to identify training needs which have to be met if staff are to improve their performances. If

101

the appraisal is to be successful, the organization must be able to offer the training opportunities identified to staff. If it cannot do this, the appraisal will cause frustration or resentment and will be viewed in a negative light.

Whilst feedback on performance is formalized in the annual appraisal interview, monitoring of performance and coaching should be on a continuous basis. Staff have to be informed about their existing performances in order to be stimulated to improve them. Praise or criticism relating to individual events is best given at the time of the event, not held back until the annual appraisal interview.

If performance is valued by the organization, the performance review system forms part of its culture: management and staff hold the belief that the appraisal system is worthwhile and necessary, appraisals are given priority by management and care is taken to ensure that they are properly conducted. There is an emphasis upon personal development within the organization, with good personal performance being valued by a reward system based upon results. Promotion is based on capability, not necessarily seniority. Regularly scheduled appraisals allow managers to confer with their subordinates and translate individual and organizational goals into a joint commitment, leading to a mutual agreement about what needs to be achieved and a culture where cooperation is a norm and feedback a value.

Performance appraisal systems

There are a number of different methods for measuring employee performance. Three of the most simplest methods are ranking, graphic rating scales, and checklists.

Ranking

Ranking is the most simplest form of systematic rating. Employees are compared with others in order to create a simple rank order of worth. In so doing, the appraiser does not distinguish between the person or their performance which could lead to subjective assessments. No attempt is made to itemize what is being appraised so as

CONFIDENTIAL

DIVISION COMMUNITY SERVICES		DEPARTMENT LIBRARIES		POSITION NUMBER		
SURNAME		FIRST NAMES				

Employees should be rated according to an objective assessment of the person's actual performance. Consider only one factor at a time. Carefully read each description and mark the one most closely associated with actual performance.

These headings are not necessarily in order of importance nor do they carry equal weight.	A	B	C	D	E	COMMENTS
ATTENDANCE AND PUNCTUALITY. Is the officer regular or irregular in attendance?	Frequently away/and or late	Very seldom away or late	Rarely away but sometimes late	Regular and punctual	Rarely late but sometimes away	
APPEARANCE AND DRESS. What is the officer's personal appearance?	Excellent	Neat and tidy	Passable	Untidy	Unsuitable and extreme tastes	
INTEREST. What degree of interest does the officer display?	Lacks interest generally	Shows lack of interest to a marked degree	Exceptionally keen and enthusiastic	Displays above-average interest	Displays a reasonable amount of interest	
ALERTNESS AND COMPREHENSION. How readily does the officer grasp what is required?	Readily comprehends	Slow to comprehend and adapt	Exceptionally quick even in a new area	Very slow and dull	Very quickly understands	
APPLICATION. What is the officer's application to the task in hand?	Keen and industrious	Steady worker	Usually industrious with occasional lapses	Poor worker and can distract others	Exceptionally energetic and enthusiastic	
KNOWLEDGE OF THE JOB. To what extent does the officer possess the knowledge and ability necessary for the job?	Has barely sufficient to cope with general requirements	Needs to refer too frequently even on routine matters	Very well informed with unusually sound knowledge	Well informed with good knowledge of work area	Fairly well able to cope with most aspects	
NEATNESS AND PRESENTATION. Is the officer's work tidy or untidy?	Very neat and tidy	Neat	Adequate	Somewhat untidy	Careless and untidy	
WORK OUTPUT. What is the officer's effective output?	Consistently slow, tending to hold up the office	Very fast worker, consistently producing considerable volume of work	Quick worker with greater output than normal	Normal output and keeps up with work flow	Rather a slow worker	
ACCURACY AND RELIABILITY. How accurate and reliable is the officer's work?	Exceedingly accurate and reliable	Rarely makes errors	Normally accurate and reliable	More errors and omissions than normal	Many errors and omissions	
LEADERSHIP. To what extent can the officer organize and inspire others	Leads and organizes efficiently	Shows indications of leadership	Job does not normally require leadership	A bad influence on others	Outstanding organizer and leader	
TEMPERAMENT. How well does the officer stand up to varying situations and pressures?	Steady and balanced	Normally steady but unusual situations can upset officer	Becomes ruffled and acts impetuously under pressure	Unusually well balanced and reliable under pressure	Very effective and reliable	
Signature *Assessor*	Position			Date		
Signature *Interviewee*	Position			Date		

Figure 6.1 An example of a performance assessment form using the graphic rating scale

103

to identify strengths and weaknesses. The appraiser is merely asked to rate a number of people simultaneously and produce an accurate rank order.

Graphic rating scales

Graphic rating scales identify certain factors to be rated, such as neatness, personality, leadership, initiative, loyalty, dependability, appearance and quantity and quality of work output. Employees are assessed as to their performance in each factor with either four or five degrees of rating. The graphic rating scale is one of the most popular in use, but it is, however, time-consuming to fill when a large number of people have to be assessed (see Figure 6.1).

Checklists

Checklists are used to help identify employee performance. They are quick to administer, but should not be used as the sole evaluation process. A series of questions is presented concerning the employee to which the rater answers 'yes' or 'no'. Questions may be weighted by the personnel departments; there is, however, no indication of this on the form.
Sample questions on a checklist may be:

Is the employee always neat and tidy?	Yes/No
Are orders always followed?	Yes/No
Does the employee display a good working knowledge of the job?	Yes/No
Is he or she ever late in meeting deadlines?	Yes/No

One disadvantage of the checklist is that it is open to bias. To overcome this some questions may be stated twice in a slightly different manner. Checklists rarely relate to specific positions and are often difficult to use in other than very general situations as they do not provide the degree of scrutiny generally required when appraising performance.

STAFF TURNOVER AND SEPARATION

Staff turnover can be both beneficial and detrimental to the organization, depending upon the net consequences. On the positive side there is some financial gain as a controlled turnover of staff will reduce the organization's average labour costs as new staff are usually appointed at the first level of the appropriate salary structure. This is particularly true in organizations where there are annual salary increments for as the tenure of staff increases, so does the salary expenditure. Controlled staff turnover can facilitate the injection of new blood into an organization and can increase its flexibility when introducing new technologies.

From a negative point of view, staff turnover is expensive in terms of finance, time and staff morale. The economic costs can be found in severance pay, advertising and recruiting new personnel, in their orientation and training, in downtime of equipment, lost output and low productivity until the new person gains the knowledge and skills of the previous incumbent.

There is an optimum turnover rate which is the point between having insufficient employee turnover and having too much. Too slow a turnover rate will result in a staid organization; too high a turnover rate is usually an indication that there is a problem in the organization and is unsettling for those who remain.

In libraries and information centres, different jobs will usually have different turnover rates. The economic climate will also influence the turnover rate. The library or information centre manager must try to lower the turnover rate of the high performers and increase the turnover rate of the low performers in order to obtain a greater return on investment. Positions in which the tasks are simple to learn, such as library shelvers, can attract a higher turnover rate than those where a knowledge of the organization or stock is needed, such as subject specialists or reference librarians.

Redundancy

This occurs when employees are released from employment because the organization no longer has need for their services. Redundancies may be temporary or permanent. They are likely to arise through the introduction of new technologies, where opportunities for retraining or reskilling are few, or where employees for reason of ability or age are incapable of being retrained or reskilled.

Redundancy is a difficult problem, as the wishes and needs of the organization and its employees or representatives (unions) invariably differ, the organization usually wishing to take advantage of the opportunity to rid itself of less productive staff, employees usually trying to regulate redundancies through seniority.

Dismissal

This is probably the most stressful and distasteful method of separation, the employee being unsatisfactory in terms of behaviour, performance and/or attitude. Dismissal should only occur after attempts to improve or correct the offending aspect(s) of the employee have failed. Remember, at some stage of the recruitment process their skills and attributes were acknowledged as necessary for the organization. Having employed the particular staff member, the employer has some responsibility for developing the staff member according to the organization's own goals and values, and for ensuring that each employee is given every opportunity to succeed. This includes the provision of adequate communication, consultation, training and supervision. Employers must be careful to ensure that, before any staff member is dismissed, his or her case has been considered fairly and objectively.

Organizations should have a formal, written, grievance procedure which is known and accessible to both management and staff. No employee should be dismissed for a first breach of discipline, and no disciplinary action should be taken unless the case has been carefully investigated.

Retirement

Retirement may be mandatory or voluntary – that is, the organization may have a compulsory retirement age (usually 65), or provisions may be made for early retirement by those employees wishing to retire earlier. A fixed retirement age may lead to antagonism and resentment by those wishing and able to 'work on', yet allow less able staff to 'wait out' their final years with declining productivity. Voluntary retirement acknowledges that people age at different rates in terms of productivity, energy and creativity and provides a graceful exit for those who are no longer stimulated by the working environment.

The exit interview

Many managers overlook the opportunity to gain valuable information about themselves and their organization from the employee's point of view by failing to conduct an exit interview. Interested organizations take advantage of this often effective information-gathering exercise by ensuring that, upon separation, an exit interview is held with the employee. At this point, when the bond between the employee and the organization is to be broken, the employee may at last feel free to discuss matters which may have either been of concern or sources of grievances to themselves or others. The highlighting of the negative aspects of the organization, together with positive feedback, should, if taken notice of and acted upon, serve to make the organization a more effective, better place in which to work.

The value of interviewing employees as they are about to leave is that they may well feel more at liberty to make comments in the knowledge that their job is no longer threatened or that retaliative measures cannot be made against them. In this way, effective and ineffective communication channels or organizational design, recurring staff grievances, or inappropriate policies or procedures previously undetected by management may well be highlighted.

7 Strategies for decision-making

INTRODUCTION

Decision-making is an important management process, particularly when related to the planning function for, without decisions, nothing would ever be planned or accomplished. Some managers seem to make decisions quickly, whilst others always appear more hesitant. Much of this has to do with their personal decision-making style which is linked to their systems of thought.

Decisions can be simple and well-defined, or complex and ill-defined. The latter type are the hardest to make as little structure is provided for the decision-making process. Complex or non-programmable decisions rely to a great extent upon people's perceptions of situations, upon the information which is available to them at the time and upon past experience.

Modern management techniques encourage the use of participative decision-making, stressing that higher-quality decisions can often result from these practices. This has some limitations. It is most successful in an open organization or where subordinates possess the knowledge and abilities which enable them to make informed decisions. Vroom and Yetton's decision tree approach can be used to determine the extent of worker participation in decision-making.

In order to make an effective decision, information is required. The level and capability of the information will depend upon the management level at which it is used.

THE DECISION-MAKING PROCESS

Decision-making is a process of determining a particular course of action after having considered the environment and a range of

108

alternative solutions to a given problem. There are eight basic steps to rational decision-making:

1. The internal and external environment in which the decision is to take place is monitored.
2. The problem, the essential details and who is involved are investigated and defined. The exact nature of the problem is explored and diagnosed with the solution to the problem being seen as the goal.
3. Additional data is gathered.
4. Alternative solutions to the problem are generated. This involves consideration of the means by which the problem may be reduced or solved.
5. These alternatives are evaluated according to anticipated outcomes. The merits of each are assessed according to their probability of success and the relative advantages and disadvantages of each alternative solution are weighed against each other.
6. One solution is chosen.
7. Having chosen the solution it may need to be authorized before it is implemented.
8. The results are then evaluated through monitoring and reviewing the outcomes. If the results are ineffective, the decision-making process may need to begin again as part of the control process.

The first three steps are problem identification and the remaining ones are problem-solving steps.

PROGRAMMED AND NON-PROGRAMMED DECISIONS

The complexity of the decision process depends upon whether the decision is programmed or non-programmed. According to Simon (1960: 1–8) programmed decisions are repetitive and well defined, with operating procedures existing for resolving problems. New methods do not have to be worked out for solving these problems each time they arise as there is a certainty that the chosen alternative will be successful. A rational approach to decision-making is used. Such an example may be a decision to order a new set of library shelving from a well known library equipment supplier.

Non-programmed decisions are novel, unstructured and no procedures exist for solving them (ibid). They occur either because the organization (or manager) has not had to face the situation before, or where the number of considerations to be taken into account are large and undefined. Information about the situation is usually hard to obtain and there is little structure. Managers need to use more intuition and the benefit of past experience when making non-programmed decisions. An example of a non-programmed decision is the goal-setting exercise within an organization.

DECISION-MAKING AND PLANNING

Decision-making is an integral part of the planning exercise. Non-programmed decisions are made by top management when determining the organization's missions, aims and goals. The decision made at this level is concerned with what the organization is trying to do. In determining strategies or primary objectives the decisions are related to where the organization is wanting to go. Operational objectives require decisions as to how the primary objectives can be achieved. The budget-setting process determines how much money can be spent. The allocation of tasks requires decisions as to who is to be involved. Finally, performance monitoring requires decisions as to how well the organization is achieving its primary goals. As the decisions move to lower levels in the planning exercise, they become more programmable.

Some decision-making processes are now being carried out by computer application in order to make the processes more effective, and provide for faster and better decision-making in the future. This aspect of decision support systems is covered in Chapter 14.

PERCEPTIONS, EMOTIONS AND DECISION-MAKING

Decision-makers in libraries or information centres operate in a complex world of uncertainty. In making decisions they deal with what they perceive to be the facts. Their perception of the external environment is based upon discussions with their colleagues in external organizations, from reading selected reports and from personal observation. No matter how detailed their conversations or report reading, their information is still limited. As it is impossible to obtain every single piece of information relevant to the decision-making process, perception may therefore be limited.

A manager's interpretation of environmental stimuli is also influenced by learning from past experiences. This is also true of subordinates. As a result, everyone attempts to analyse the behaviour of others, but may not be aware of variables which affect such evaluations and so perceptions arise when making decisions.

A person's position in an organization may influence what is seen and the importance attached to perceived behaviour. As a result, the value of the decision and its outcome may differ at different levels within an organization. A decision which is regarded as solving a troublesome issue at one level may appear to be insignificant at another. Alternatively, what may appear to be a small decision taken at one level, may be felt to have great consequences at another.

It is important for library and information centre managers to be aware that decision-making is an emotional process. Feelings of self-worth biases and experiences affect the emotional processing of decision-making. Emotions are involved in diagnosing and defining the problem, in selecting acceptable solutions and in the implementation of the solution.

DECISION-MAKING STYLES

Right and left brain hemispheres

Various decision-making styles can be found amongst managers. One explanation for the different personal attributes and decision styles of managers can be found in the way in which they make use of the human brain.

The human brain can be divided into two halves. Looking down on the top of the exposed brain two hemispheres are present, the left and the right. The left brain controls the right-hand side of the body and the right brain the left side.

The right and left hemispheres have different thinking styles. The left brain in most people is particularly involved in thinking activi-

111

ties which use language, logic, analysis, reason and mathematical ability. It is also associated with awareness of detail, recognition and classification of problems and optimizing results over time. The right hemisphere is more associated with pictorial, image thinking, spatial awareness, creative ability and intuitive thinking. The right, it is argued, is much better at seeing wholes. Problem-solving, writing and planning requires high-level left side use, whilst the right brain is particularly associated with the ability to make non-logical connections and to see overall patterns or trends. It uses intuition as the basis for decision-making.

When to use different decision-making styles

There are four main decision-making styles; directive, analytical, conceptual and behavioural. Often more than one decision-making style is appropriate, and managers can select the style most appropriate for the situation.

Directive style

According to Rowe (1984: 18) managers with a directive style are efficient and logical yet generally have a low tolerance for ambiguity and low cognitive complexity. They are autocratic, have a high need for power and maintain tight control. They focus upon technical decisions, preferring a systematic structure. Decisions are made rapidly, with little information, usually obtained verbally, and few alternatives are considered. Only short-range, internal factors are usually considered.

Analytical style

Analytical managers have a greater tolerance for ambiguity than do directive managers, but require control over decision-making. As their decisions are based on careful analysis, they require more information and consider more alternatives. They are careful but enjoy variety. They are able to adapt to or cope with new situations. Analytical managers are problem-solving-oriented and strive for maximum output.

Conceptual style

Conceptual managers are broad in their outlook, achievement-oriented and consider many alternatives. They value commitments and integrity and are creative in finding solutions. They focus on long-range issues, are future-oriented and are able to negotiate effectively. They will frequently use participative decision-making techniques.

Behavioural style

The behavioural-style manager is concerned for the organization and development of people. They communicate easily, show empathy and tend to be persuasive. Their focus is short-/or medium-range. They use limited data as their emphasis is on decision-making through people.

PARTICIPATIVE MANAGEMENT AND GROUP DECISION-MAKING

Advantages

Proponents of the human relations school of management place emphasis on participative management techniques in decision-making, which involves the inclusion of individuals or groups in the decision-making process. The anticipated outcomes are higher-quality decisions, greater acceptance of the resultant decisions and a greater identification with the organization.

Subordinates often possess relevant, practical information relating to library operations which is unavailable to managers because they do not perform the same tasks. Subordinates are also likely to use this information if allowed to share in the decision-making process. At an operational level, it is probable that this will result in a more practical solution. Individual efforts of group members will provide a wider range of viewpoints in the decision-making process. This leads to greater creativity in the finding of a solution.

Subordinates who have been involved in the decision-making process are more likely to be motivated to ensure that the proposals are carried out as there is a feeling of commitment to the decision. This sense of involvement also leads to greater identification with the organization and its goals. Subordinates will probably have an increased awareness of the organization's purpose after participating in the decision-making process.

Participative management in organizations

Participative decision-making is linked to leadership and organizational style. A subordinate-centred (behavioural) leader is more likely to promote participative decision-making than a task-centred (directive) leader. The type of organization in which the library or information centre manager is operating may also determine whether a participative or authoritative approach is to be used. An open organization is more likely to encourage participative management than a mechanistic one.

The degree of subordinate or group participation in decision-making is limited by such variables as ability, interest, skill of the leader, and the area of freedom involved. Knowledge, ability and interest vary among individuals and groups. Organizational restraints may exist in terms of time taken to reach a decision, particularly when the external environment is changing rapidly. There may not be the time to explain the circumstances involved, the background to the decision and other variables necessary for knowledgeable decision-making, or for procedures to take place which allow the group to meet and make the decision. The subject of the decision may also prevent group decision-making. Strategic decisions requiring a detailed knowledge of the external environment will not be able to be made by those at the operational level.

Participative decision-making is useful for resolving differences among group members which, if left unattended, may prevent eventual agreement. The communication processes involved and the sharing of norms and values will positively influence the motivation of employees and result in less resistance. Groups are also likely to accept more risk than individual decision-makers, feeling that there is safety in numbers.

Disadvantages

There are also disadvantages to participative decision-making. It is

114

sometimes used as a substitute by management for making tough decisions. There is also a tendency to stall a decision by taking the problem from one committee to another. Both the failure to make a decision and indecision are ineffective management techniques. The need for the decision still remains and staff will recognize the failure or stalling of the decisions for what it is. Management also remains responsible for the implementation of the decision; it is in everyone's interest that the most sensible decision is made.

Group decision-making can be expensive in terms of staff time. A group decision invariably takes more time than an executive action. In order to estimate the full cost of participative decision-making the decision-making time should be multiplied by the number of people attending the group meeting.

Participative decision-making may sometimes produce lower-quality decisions or a compromise which is not truly effective. It can produce indecision and will occasionally backfire and actually produce a worse decision than might have been made by an individual.

If superiors are present, or if one member has a dominant personality, the decision of the group may in reality not be a group decision. This can have a lowering effect on group morale and act as a negative factor for motivation, providing for feelings of frustration and uselessness.

VROOM AND YETTON'S DECISION TREE APPROACH

Victor Vroom and Philip Yetton (1973) have developed a 'decision tree approach' for identifying a particular 'optimum' decision style that a manager would find appropriate in a given situation. Five alternative decision styles and procedures involving some or all of the leader's immediate subordinates are provided. Two varieties are autocratic, two are consultative and one is joint decision-making by the leader and subordinates. All five styles are feasible given certain situational conditions. The two key elements in selecting a style for decision-making are (a) ensuring that a quality decision is made; and (b) ensuring that the decision receives the acceptance necessary for effective implementation.

A decision process flow chart incorporates seven questions. Users

115

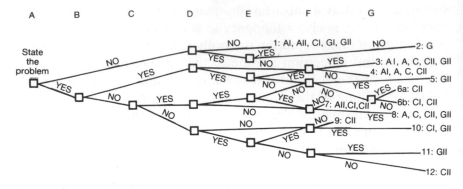

A. Does the problem possess a quality requirement?
B. Do I have sufficient information to make a high-quality decision?
C. Is the problem structured?
D. Is acceptance of the decision by subordinates important for effective implementation?
E. If I were to make the decision by myself, am I reasonably certain that it would be accepted by my subordinates?
F. Do subordinates share the organization goals to be attained in solving this problem?
G. Is conflict among subordinates likely in preferred solutions?

Figure 7.1   Decision process flow chart

Source: Vroom (1976: 19). © AMACOM, a division of American Management Associations, New York. Reprinted by permission of publisher. All rights reserved.

proceed through the decision process (tree) in accordance with their answers (Figure 7.2). A terminal point is reached which indicates the decision styles which are feasible for the decision structure.

Vroom and Yetton's five styles are:

AI   The manager makes the decision alone, using information available at the time and personally possessed.

AII   The manager obtains the necessary information from subordinates then determines the appropriate decision. The role played by others is that of providing the manager with the necessary information rather than of generating or evaluating alternatives. Subordinates may or may not be told of the nature of the problem.

CI   The manager shares the problem with subordinates individually and obtains individual ideas and suggestions, without bringing subordinates together as a group. The manager then makes the decision that may or may not reflect the subordinates' input or feelings.

116

CII   The manager shares the decision situation with subordinates as a group and solicits their ideas and suggestions in a group meeting. The resulting decision may or may not reflect the subordinates' input or feelings.

GII   The manager shares the decision situation with subordinates as a group, and the group generates and evaluates alternatives. The manager does not attempt to influence subordinates and is willing to accept and implement any solution on which there is consensus. The manager acts more as a chairperson for the group.

INFORMATION AND LEVELS AND NATURE OF DECISION-MAKING

The availability of information is vital to the decision-making process. Decisions are made at strategic, tactical and operational level and information is essential to evaluate the alternative courses of action at these three levels. The information required to make decisions about an activity within a library system differs from that required to make decisions about a total system, both in degree of detail and comprehensiveness. Depending upon their level within the hierarchy, managers will either need strategic (top), tactical (mid) or operational (line) information (Figure 7.2).

As top management deals mainly with the external environment, most of their information comes from external sources – for example, from meetings or during conversations with their peers. This information could relate to government funding allocations, strategic information about their suppliers, details of new technologies or of impending legislation. Due to constraints on their time, top management is only interested in a highly summarized view of the organization's internal information. They often employ research assistants to provide these summaries for them.

Mid-level management deals with information from both external and internal sources. Theirs are more tactical decisions and so require information relating to the allocation of human, financial and technological resources, budgeting and reporting upon resultant performance. Mid-level managers are usually interested in the gross performance of component operating units. Data is gathered from

117

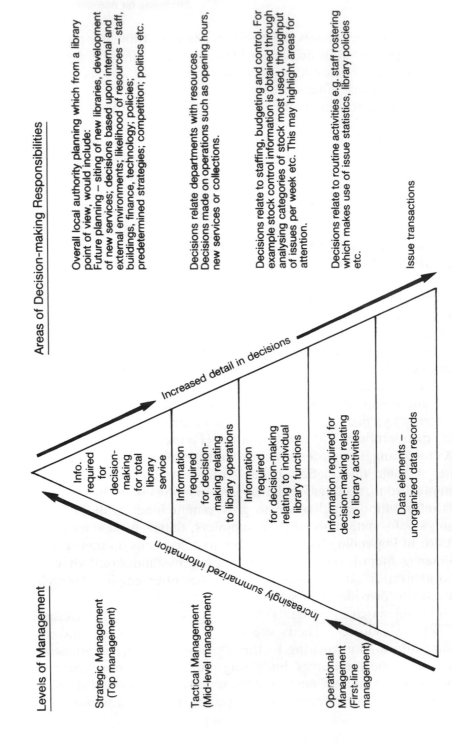

Figure 7.2 Information needs and decision-making activities within a public library system

Areas of Decision-making Responsibilities

Overall local authority planning which from a library point of view, would include:
Future planning – siting of new libraries, development of new services; decisions based upon internal and external environments; likelihood of resources – staff, buildings, finance, technology; policies; predetermined strategies; competition; politics etc.

Decisions relate departments with resources.
Decisions made on operations such as opening hours, new services or collections.

Decisions relate to staffing, budgeting and control. For example stock control information is obtained through analysing categories of stock most used, throughput of issues per week etc. This may highlight areas for attention.

Decisions relate to routine activities e.g. staff rostering which makes use of issue statistics, library policies etc.

Issue transactions

Increased detail in decisions

Increasingly summarized information

Levels of Management

Strategic Management
(Top management)

Tactical Management
(Mid-level management)

Operational Management
(First-line management)

Info. required for decision-making for total library service

Information required for decision-making relating to library operations

Information required for decision-making relating to individual library functions

Information required for decision-making relating to library activities

Data elements – unorganized data records

in-house sources and combined with other information from external sources, such as other libraries' annual reports. This is used for comparative purposes to measure performance, to help make decisions, and to prepare reports which are presented to top management. This information is also used to influence planning and policy-setting processes executed at higher levels.

At this level of management, external information is significantly different in source and character from internal information or that received by top management. It often comprises telephone conversations, hearsay and overheard snatches of conversations. If such information is intended to be used effectively in any decision-making processes at mid-management level, its reliability and relevance must be determined beforehand.

First-line managers obtain nearly all of their decision-making information in-house, using a very restricted subset of the organization's internal information. They receive instructions from mid-level management and gather data relating to individual library activities at a transaction level. They have to make operational decisions related to day-to-day matters or specific activities such as rostering of staff based upon policies and operational requirements.

SUMMARY

Emphasis is now placed upon participative management and group decision-making in order to achieve the best possible solution. Depending upon the situation, participative decision-making can result in a more creative or practical solution. Vroom and Yetton's decision tree approach can be used to determine the extent of worker participation in decision-making.

In order make an effective decision, information is required. The level and extent of the information will depend upon the management level at which it is used.

REFERENCES

Rowe, A.J. (1984), *Managerial Decision-making (Modules in Management)* (Chicago: Science Research Associates).

119

Simon, H.A. (1960), *The New Science of Management Decision* (Englewood Cliffs, NJ: Prentice-Hall).

Vroom, V.H. (1976), 'Can leaders learn to lead?', *Organizational Dynamics*, **4**, Winter, © AMACOM, a division of American Management Association.

Vroom, V.H. and Yetton, P.W. (1973), *Leadership and Decision-making* (Pittsburgh: University of Pittsburg Press).

8 Competitive strategies: strategic marketing for libraries and information centres

INTRODUCTION

Marketing is part of the total planning process. Strategic marketing makes use of many of the concepts and functions of strategic planning. Strategic marketing strategies ensure viable market positions and programmes for the survival and success of the library or information centre.

Any proposals for new services to new markets must be in line with the library's or information centre's mission and sufficient human, technical and financial resources should be available to support such services.

Market segments comprise individuals or groups who are actual or potential customers for a library or information service. Markets can be divided according to need, product, demography and geography, each market having its own particular characteristics.

Market targeting involves the evaluation, selection and concentration of those market segments which the library or information centre has determined it should serve. There are three strategies for market targeting: undifferentiated marketing, differentiated marketing and concentrated marketing.

There are various analyses which aid marketing strategies. These are exchange system analysis, image analysis, consumer satisfaction studies, competitive portfolio analysis and product life cycles.

The exchange system analysis is useful as it enables the library or information centre manager to identify what the patrons of the library or information centre are prepared to exchange for the services which the library offers. Its importance lies in the fact that both tangible and intangible items can be identified; thus allowing the more esoteric values which the library community holds to be identified. This may be useful information when either planning new services, or in justifying existing services.

Image analysis is exceptionally important in determining the library's or information centre's image to both the funding and governing bodies and its users. As a result of the image analysis certain market strategies may need to be undertaken.

Consumer satisfaction studies determine whether consumer expectations for services are higher or lower than those being provided. Product life cycles and product portfolio matrices help the library to determine which areas have the potential for growth.

Finally, diversification and service rejuvenation can help to instil new growth into ailing library or information centres.

STRATEGIC MARKETING

Strategic marketing takes place within the strategic management process of organizations and it develops strategies to ensure viable market positions and programmes for the survival and success of the library or information centre. Strategic marketing has been defined by Kotler *et al.* (1980: 56) as:

A managerial process of analysing market opportunities and choosing market positions, programmes and controls that create and support viable businesses that serve the organisation's purposes and objectives.

The strategic marketing process commences with an environmental and resource analysis and situation audit, which allows the library or information centre to identify opportunities which are in line with the basic mission of the service. A SWOT analysis and an organizational marketing system analysis can also be used at this stage. A SWOT analysis will not only identify the library's opportunities, but also the threats facing it in the external environment and the organization's internal capacity (resources, and so on) to deal with these in terms of its strengths and weaknesses (for further information please refer to Chapter 3). Any proposals must not only be in line with the library's or information centre's mission, but they must be able to draw upon the organization's existing skills. It may also be possible to share opportunities with other programmes, thus spreading the overhead costs.

Marketing opportunities for libraries and information centres are analysed by considering market segmentations, the size and growth rate of the client base, consumer behaviours, possible exit barriers and some forms of measuring and forecasting the attractiveness and effectiveness of such services in the future.

A market is attractive if:

1. it is of a good size – that is, if many people will use the service;
2. it has the potential for growth;
3. it is cost-beneficial on both a short-term and long-term basis;
4. there are adequate financial and technical resources and a competent and trained staff;
5. there are low exit barriers; and
6. the service is in line with the library's mission.

It may be the case that an opportunity satisfies most of these criteria, but that it has to remain dormant until, for example, financial or technical resources can be found or staff trained to provide the service.

First, a target market, which identifies a particular group(s) to which the service will be aimed, needs to be identified. This is followed by a process of competitive positioning, which involves researching competitors' services and the needs of the target market in order to find a market or market niche. This will determine whether the library or information centre is in a strong or weak competitive position, whether the programme is attractive and whether there is high or low alternative coverage.

Once a target market has been defined and the service's competitive position determined, a market strategy is devised. This includes the development of the marketing goals and objectives. Goals may include such aspects as increasing the quality of the library service, or its participation level, or its satisfaction level. Funds need to be allocated to the marketing budget. New services which are designed to meet new markets should have the important values explained to staff before commencing the service.

A marketing mix is a key part of the marketing strategy. A

four-factor classification called 'the four Ps' has been defined by McCarthy (1971: 44). These are product, price, place and promotion.

From a library's or information centre's point of view, product refers to services and involves the special features offered, the way they are offered and level of service. Price relates to whether a direct fee is attached to the service such as payment for an online

Table 8.1
Issues in strategic marketing analysis for
libraries and information centres

A. Market Analysis
1. What important trends are affecting the library and information industry? (environmental analysis)
2. What is the library's or information centre's primary market? (market definition)
3. What are the major market segments in this market? (market segmentation)
4. What are the needs of each market segment? (need assessment)
5. How much awareness, knowledge, interest and desire is there in each market segment concerning the library or information centre? (market awareness and attitude)
6. How do key publics see us and our competitors? (image analysis)
7. How do potential users learn about the library or information centre and make decisions to join? (consumer behaviour)
8. How satisfied are current users? (consumer satisfaction assessment)

B. Resource Analysis
1. What are our major strengths and weaknesses in staff, programmes, facilities, etc.? (strengths/weaknesses analysis)
2. What opportunities are there to expand our financial resources? (funding analysis)

C. Mission Analysis
1. What business is the library or information centre in? (business mission)
2. Who are the library's or information centre's customers? (customer definition)
3. Which needs are we trying to satisfy? (needs targetting)
4. On which market segments do we want to focus? (market targetting)
5. Who are our major competitors? (competitor identification)
6. What competitive benefits do we want to offer to our target market? (market positioning)

Source: Adapted from Kotler *et al.* (1980).

search or a photocopy and whether there are any price modifiers such as discounts or allowances. Place concerns the logistical provision of service and locations of service points. Promotion involves the advertising and publicity campaigns, the message communicated, the media used and the timing of such. Promotional campaigns should be realistic and affordable.

Finally the market strategy is implemented and controls put into place to ensure that the library's resources, services and objectives are correctly matched to the right markets.

Kotler (1980: 576) proposes 16 key questions which can be used during the strategic marketing analysis to determine the library or information centre's marketing strategy. (Table 8.1)

MARKETS AND MARKET SEGMENTATION

A market is a set of individuals, groups or institutions that are actual or potential customers for a product or service. Markets can be divided into groups with specific requirements; this is called market segmentation. In libraries and information centres there are need markets, geographic markets, product markets and demographic markets.

Need markets

Need markets consist of individuals or groups who have a common need. Libraries and information centres cannot satisfy all their users' demands just by lending books. Their consumers have diverse needs for facsimile services, information in varying formats (such as videotex, encyclopaedias or serials), for housebound services, story-telling sessions or on-line information services to name but a few. Yet there are certain groups within the library's or information centre's community who have similar needs. The need market for a homebound service would be the frail, the physically impaired, those people who are convalescing at home from surgery or hospitalization, young and old patients with terminal illnesses who are living at home, elderly people who can no longer drive and for whom public transport to the library is inaccessible, and others who for some reason cannot regularly visit the library.

Geographic markets

Geographic markets consist of those consumers who live in a region or a particular geographic locality. Geographic markets determine the type, size and siting of library and information centres together with their opening hours and services offered. Public library managers will actively seek out geographic locations in need of library services and serve them accordingly. For example, residents living in outer metropolitan areas may need later opening hours than those living in the inner city as their travelling time home will be longer. Later opening hours will allow families to visit the library as a unit. However, the dense population of inner cities will demand that library opening hours are longer than those of outer metropolitan areas or semi-rural localities. Rural areas having isolated pockets of population may be best served by a mobile library service. Special libraries serving organizations which have branch offices situated in regions or states will need to consider the specific requirements of each location and develop their services accordingly.

Each market has its own particular characteristics. The need market for a housebound service will differ from that of a geographical market requiring a mobile library service. Whilst each is served by 'a library on wheels' the library services offered to the housebound will most probably differ from those offered to people using the mobile library.

Product markets

Product markets are determined by a demand for a particular product or service. In public libraries a product market may be those people who have a demand for information. This can be further broken down into a market segmentation to those who have a demand for, say, technical or community information.

Demographic markets

Demographic market segmentation is one of the most popular methods of distinguishing market segments in libraries. They are often associated with clear market needs, and information relating to these markets is readily available. Demographic markets may be

126

identified by age, nationality, social needs such as those pursuing particular hobbies, sports or other forms of entertainment, or physical needs such as the physically impaired who may need ramp access to the library.

Markets which can be subdivided into identifiable segments or subsets require individual marketing strategies. The library or information centre manager should be aware of their market segments' current and potential future size; their major consumers (users) and potential customers (non-users) and their locations; their consumers' current levels of awareness of the range and levels of existing services; their needs and motives for using the services; and their concepts of what they may regard as being competitive alternatives to library services.

The strength in the market segmentation approach lies in the fact that it is based upon the end-user rather than the product or service. The end-user is assured of a service which satisfies as far as possible his or her individual needs rather than a mass-market offering. This is in line with the societal marketing concept.

Individual needs cannot be taken to the stage of a one-off situation, since this would not be cost-effective. Instead, the library or information centre manager must search for broad classes of users who have similar requirements. This is called a customer's product (service) requirement. Such an example can be seen in the case of a weekly storytelling session for preschool children. Such a session may satisfy numerous needs, some of which may not have been foremost in the library staffs' minds when they proposed the service, but which exist all the same. Examples of such needs may be a need for an only child to socialize with others of its age group; a need to provide the beginnings of a lifelong association with the library; a need to begin the learning process through books and stories; a need for a babysitting service; a need for the parent to get out of the house and talk to other parents; a need to promote the library to children of all ages; or a need for recreational activities. Thus, the storytelling session will satisfy up to seven diverse needs of parents, library staff and preschool children.

MARKET TARGETING

Market targeting involves the evaluation, selection and concentra-

127

tion on those market segments which the library has determined that it should serve. There are three strategies for doing this: undifferentiated marketing, differentiated marketing and concentrated marketing.

Undifferentiated marketing

In undifferentiated or mass marketing the library focuses upon what needs are common to all people. Services are provided which appeal to the broadest number of users. These services could be lending services, interlibrary loan services and reference services. In concentrating on these basic services, the library attempts to achieve excellence. Undifferentiated marketing is often pursued in times of financial constraint, when additional or specialist services are curtailed, and basic services consolidated. Costs associated with providing specialist services can be saved, but whether this is an effective strategy when pursuing a societal marketing concept is debatable.

Differentiated marketing

In differentiated marketing a library decides to operate in at least two segments of a market and designs separate services and programmes for each. In public libraries this may entail having a children's specialist, a youth services librarian, a business specialist librarian, a local history librarian, a librarian for the aged, as well as subject specialist librarians in particular subject areas. Each would manage a variety of programmes to suit the diverse needs of different library users. The aim of this approach is to provide services catering for specific needs which will strengthen the library's overall identity in the community and increase its use. However there are costs associated with this. Specialist services involve additional staff, administrative and promotional costs.

In differentiated marketing some library services may be heavily promoted, these are called saturate segments. Others may be designated as hold segments. In this case services are offered but not heavily promoted.

Concentrated marketing

Concentrated or niche marketing occurs when the library or information centre concentrates upon a small number of submarkets. Instead of spreading itself thinly, being all things to all people, the library or information centre provides in-depth services in a few areas, serving a small percentage of the marketplace.

The library or information centre purposefully determines a small number of target markets and sets out actively to serve these areas only. Through its concentration in particular areas the library or information centre achieves a strong market position because of its greater knowledge of its market segments' needs and its subsequent reputation. A special library or information centre may decide to concentrate upon a selective dissemination of information service and a high-speed reference service. This would be written into its goals and objectives, all staff would be aware of these priorities within the information centre or library and their primary duties would centre around these. Values such as efficiency, speed and individual needs would form part of the library's corporate culture.

A concentrated marketing strategy may be used when establishing a new library service. After determining several target markets and having regard for financial resources and the level of staff expertise, it may be decided that to concentrate upon serving a few market segments well is preferable to trying to spread the market base too thinly. The establishment of a new library or information service requires procedures to be put into place, staff to be trained, policies and routines to be established. This all takes time. To begin operations with a wide market base most likely will not be the most effective strategy to adopt. Later, when all operations are running smoothly, a decision can then be made as to whether to broaden the base. This is called a segment 'roll out' strategy.

No one strategy is superior to the others. In adopting a particular target strategy, the library or information centre manager must base his or her decision upon the type of library; the financial, technical, human and information resources available; the availability of competitive services; user and potential user needs, and the types of services having the potential to be offered. The library or

129

information centre manager must then decide which strategy is the most attractive given the constraints and opportunities of the library's or information centre's external environment, and its own strengths and weaknesses.

EXCHANGE SYSTEM ANALYSIS

Underlying the marketing concept is a system of exchange. The potential for exchange exists when two or more parties possess something of value which may be exchanged. This may be goods, services, money or goodwill. The simplest exchange is between two parties, and such an exchange may be seen in a public library where a library user will exchange money for a photocopy of a page from a reference book. Libraries and information services also offer other services in exchange for monies received from rates and taxes. Here, no direct exchange takes place between the user and supplier, rates and taxes being paid to the parent organization. Library and information centre staff exchange their knowledge, skills, time and energy in return for money (wages or salaries) and other fringe benefits from the employing organization.

Multiple-party exchanges occur when three or more parties are involved in exchanging something of value. In the case of the storytelling session in the public library, the parents require that their children meet others of the same age, engage in a learning process and be happy. They are exchanging their time for social and educational processes for their children. They also require that the library staff are friendly and that the library is clean and safe. In this instance they are exchanging monies paid in rates for services and safety. The children who attend want to have fun, maybe learn something and therefore obtain their parent's approval. They are exchanging their time for their parent's love and acceptance. The library, in holding the storytelling sessions, wishes to promote the library as a fun place and as a lifelong institution for information and self-education. The storytelling session must meet all of these needs in the exchange processes.

IMAGE ANALYSIS

Image studies measure the perceptions which people hold about an organization. They are important for a library or information centre because they determine what people respond to, which may not necessarily be the same as what the library really does. All libraries and information centres need a positive image in order to attract funds, potential staff members, users and maybe volunteers for certain programmes. However, the library's image will differ according to particular groups, their main interests and the way in which they perceive the services offered. Young adults will, for example, have a totally different perception of a public library than an elderly person or a preschool child. Stakeholders may perceive the library in more financial or functional terms than users who value its services.

The library's or information centre's image is the sum of the users', stakeholders', and non-users' beliefs, impressions and ideas of it. The library's community can have multiple attitudes, some of which will be positive, whilst others may be negative. Different sectors of the library's community should be surveyed in order to determine its image and profile. This will include surveying stake-holders, users and non-users regarding their attitudes and awareness in an effort to ascertain a spectrum of responses within each dimension. This can be done by asking two simple questions for which multiple choice answers are provided on a rating scale (Figure 8.1). The various sectors to which members of the community belong should be identified by the asking of a simple question to ascertain their relationship to the library. For example, are you a councillor, user, non-user ratepayer? A code should then be applied to identify that group's responses for follow-up activities. The responses are then plotted on a matrix graph (Figure 8.2).

Quadrants B, C and D in Figure 8.2 indicate the need for some development of the library's image. In order to do this, the library or information centre manager needs to have a mental picture of what he or she would like their organization's image to be. This is then compared with the existing image of the library or information centre. The image gap is the difference between the desired and actual images.

Different sectors or groups have different images of the library or information centre, but it may not be necessary to target all sectors or groups in trying to change the library's image. The matrix graph will identify both those groups most in need of targeting and

---

CITY OF NOAH

Image Analysis Survey

1. Community sector [_____] (staff use only)
(Please assign the appropriate identification code in box provided)

2. How familiar are you with your local library?

_____ Never heard of it
_____ Heard of it
_____ Know a little about it
_____ Know a fair amount about it
_____ Know a great deal about it

3. How favourable is your attitude to the services it provides?
(Please tick the most appropriate response)

_____ Very unfavourable
_____ Somewhat unfavourable
_____ Indifferent
_____ Somewhat favourable
_____ Very favourable

Thank you for your participation in the survey.

Figure 8.1   Proposed questions to ascertain a library's image

Favourable attitude	B. Good position but awareness of services is not high. Library needs to promote its activities.	A. Good position. Library should seek to maintain this position.
Attitude of users to the library	D. Bad position. Library needs to rebuild its image and increase its profile.	C. Bad position. Library needs to rebuild its image and correct its profile.
Non-favourable attitude	Low familiarity	Familiarity of users with library service High familiarity

Figure 8.2   Matrix graph of library's image

those groups for whom the library's current image should be maintained in its present position. Changes in image may be to make the library or information centre appear to be more efficient or useful to the funding or governing bodies, or more relevant to certain sectors of the community.

CONSUMER SATISFACTION STUDIES

Consumer satisfaction studies provide an indication as to whether existing library or information centre users are satisfied or not with current services. Consumer satisfaction studies are themselves a marketing tool as they can be used as an argument to maintain existing funding levels if the results are good, or for increased funding if the results show that user expectations of services are higher than those which are being provided.

However, it may be that if the studies determine that expectations for the services are higher than that which is being provided, the public may have an image problem. The public may be demanding more than can be provided within existing levels of funding, in which case it will need to be educated either that its expectations are beyond the limits of funding, or that it must pay higher rates or taxes to fund the additional services. The reality–expectations gap is the difference between the level of an adequate service and the level of a service to meet real expectations.

A matrix graph can be provided to help the library determine which services need improved performance and continued service (Figure 8.3). The graph determines those services which need improvement according to their performance rating and importance. Services are plotted along the two axes and this provides an indication of which services need attention. Services falling in quadrant A are important services which are being well provided. Services in quadrant B have possibly too high a performance level for their importance. The library staff can afford to pay less attention to these services. Services which fall into quadrant C have only a low priority and performance is deemed as low. These services may be the first to be abandoned if resources are few, in order to concentrate on those services in quadrant D. Quadrant D includes those services which are acknowledged to be important,

133

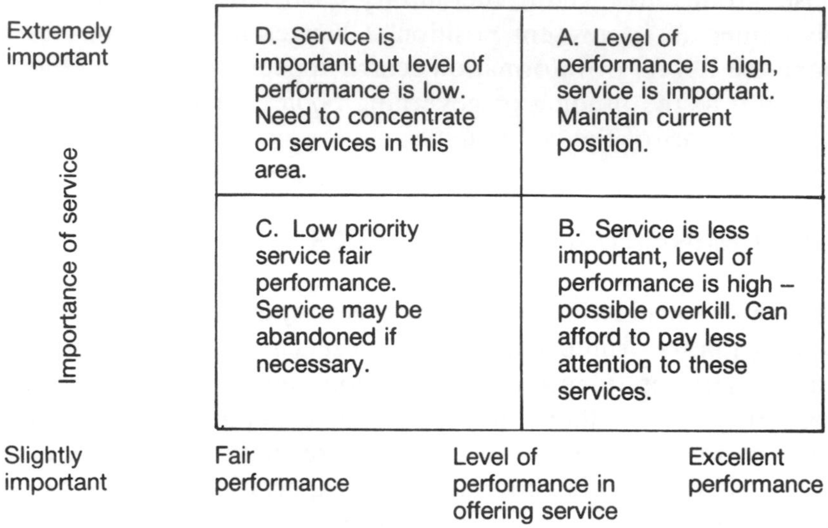

Extremely important	D. Service is important but level of performance is low. Need to concentrate on services in this area.	A. Level of performance is high, service is important. Maintain current position.
	C. Low priority service fair performance. Service may be abandoned if necessary.	B. Service is less important, level of performance is high – possible overkill. Can afford to pay less attention to these services.
Slightly important	Fair performance	Level of performance in offering service Excellent performance

Importance of service (vertical axis label)

Figure 8.3   Matrix graph to determine level of performance and importance of services

but where the library or information centre is performing badly. Library staff need to concentrate their resources in this area. Need and competence of staff may be substituted for importance and performance when deciding upon new services to introduce or when rationalizing existing services.

COMPETITIVE PORTFOLIO ANALYSIS: PRODUCT OR SERVICE PORTFOLIOS AND LIFE CYCLES

The product life cycle and the product portfolio matrix are being used to make strategic marketing decisions in commerce and industry. Whilst they are based upon products rather than services, their general concepts are useful for library and information centre managers as they help to distinguish which services have potential for growth. Growth or decline in services affect budget allocations, technology, staff levels and the future direction of the library's or information centre's services.

134

The product life cycle is based upon the concept that products or services, like living things, have a finite life span. The basic proposition is that market growth and competitive characteristics change from one stage of the product life cycle to the next. These changes have important implications for marketing and planning strategies (Figure 8.4).

The introductory stage of a library or information service is usually marked by slow growth in use, heavy advertising and promotion. Staff must develop the service to suit user needs, and much enthusiasm is needed. In the growth stage, there is an increase in use of the service which is still promoted quite heavily, and staff may have to fine tune the service further to suit user needs. The maturity stage is characterized by such services being seen as standard, a slowdown in growth and the spending of less time and money on advertising. In the decline stage, fewer people use the service, it is often superseded by other more appropriate services

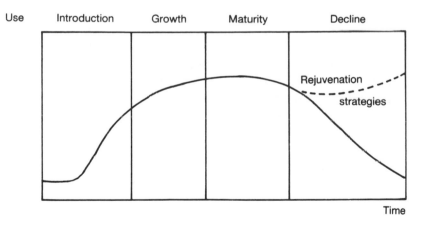

Figure 8.4   Product life cycle

or deemed to have a low priority and plans are made to terminate it.

The life cycle concept has some drawbacks. Sometimes the stages in the life cycle cannot be clearly separated and it may be difficult to distinguish into which stage of the life cycle the service falls. For library services, the maturity stage is the dominant stage and most services fall into this category. It is also often difficult to predict when the next stage of the life cycle will begin or how long it will last. Rejuvenation strategies may be used to stop the decline in the life cycle.

Information technology is likely to have a significant impact upon the life cycles of library and information services in the future. As information technologies become even more advanced and sophisticated they will have the effect of shortening the life cycles of library and information services, since new and better ways will be found to deliver services or access information, thereby rendering the existing services obsolete. This is already being seen in the impact of compact disc technology upon online information services. The end result of this impact is that library or information service managers will need to pay more attention to the product–service life cycle in the future.

Whilst the product–service life cycle focuses upon growth dynamics, the product portfolio matrix emphasizes market growth (attractiveness) and relative competitive position (strength) of products or services. As libraries and information centres are asked to become more competitive, and as the threat of privatization looms larger, the significance of the product (service) portfolio matrix will increase.

The most widely used matrix is that developed by the Boston Consulting Group. Known as the BCG portfolio matrix, it classifies each business unit according to its potential for growth and its relative competitive position. In libraries and information centres, services may be substituted for business units. The BCG matrix classifies products/markets into four groups and uses circles, with areas proportional to the sales volumes for each, to give a visual image of an organization's current products. In libraries or information centres, usage rates could be substituted for sales volumes to provide an image of its current services (Figure 8.5).

According to the BCG matrix, products which have a high market

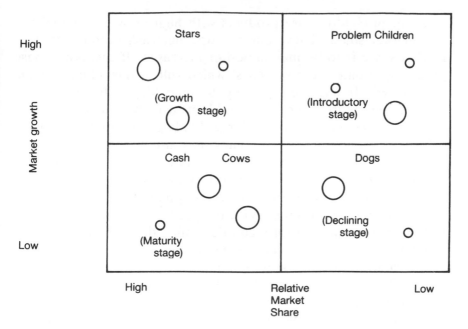

Figure 8.5 The Boston Consulting Group portfolio matrix

share and high growth (stars) are roughly self-sufficient in terms of cash flow. They have the highest profit margins. In terms of library or information services, these are important services and should be expanded if possible. Eventually the 'stars' will become 'cash cows' as they reach the maturity stage of the product–service.

'Cash cows' are valuable assets; they have a high share in a low growth market. As products they generate more cash than is necessary to maintain their market position and should be protected at all costs. In libraries or information centres, 'cash cows' would equate with established services which have a high rate of usage and which have little competition. They are valuable services and the marketing strategy should be to maintain their market share. 'Cash cow' services maintain the value image of the library or information centre and help to ensure its continued success and survival.

'Dogs' are products with low market share and slow growth. Their outlook for the future is usually bleak. 'Dogs' in libraries or information centres comprise those services which are declining in use and are often superseded by new and better services; alternatively, they are services which have failed to reach their potential.

137

'Problem children' are products with high growth potential but low market share. They require large net cash outflows if their market share is to be maintained or increased. If successful these products become the new 'stars' which will in the future become 'cash cows'. If unsuccessful they become 'dogs'. In libraries or information centres, 'problem children' usually equate with new services which require fairly large funding allocations for their establishment and promotion. They may also be services which do not perform well. There can be a variety of reasons for their poor performance; they may have been inadequately managed, or have had inappropriate marketing strategies applied to them.

By displaying these services on the product portfolio matrix, the library or information centre can determine their services' use and standing, and then link them to the product–service life cycle and its associated marketing and planning strategies.

The BCG matrix is useful in that it recognizes that products (services) have differential growth rates and emphasizes the relative share of market held by products (services) in the same stage of growth.

USE OF THE COMPETITIVE PORTFOLIO ANALYSIS IN MANAGING LIBRARY STOCK

In a multi-branch public library system the concept of the product life cycle can be used to extend the life of the stock by identifying the point in time when stock can be transferred to another branch library. Certain types of stock are either more popular or are used more than others. Fiction books, for example, have different life cycles. Some authors' works are more popular than others and their books quickly become worn out, whilst others have a limited market appeal and become read out.

A book with a limited market appeal will have a rising issue rate when it is first introduced into the library. At some point the issue rate will begin to fall as the product (book) passes through the maturity stage into the decline stage. If, at this stage, the book is transferred to another library it will be subject to a rejuvenation strategy. A new audience (users) will be found for the book and the product life cycle will begin again, prolonging the life and value of the book.

The BCG portfolio matrix is an important tool for assessing the quality of stock on the library's shelves. 'Best sellers' are 'stars'. They become 'cash cows' when their original price has been justified by their large issue rate, or when their presence on the shelves of the library creates an image of the library having good, current stock. 'Dogs' are stock which sit on the library's shelves because no one wants to read them. All libraries have some 'dogs'; the result of a mistake in stock selection, when the market for a item has been misjudged, or the blurb was misleading. 'Problem children' comprise the stock which contains valuable information but is often overlooked by users or library staff because of format, appearance, or lack of knowledge of the contents. 'Problem children' stock can become 'stars' through education of library staff or library promotions which display such stock in interesting ways. If left alone they will become 'dogs'.

DIVERSIFICATION AND SERVICE REJUVENATION

There comes a time when it appears that a library or information centre can no longer expand its services in its basic market. Growth has stabilized through the market being saturated and, if growth is to continue, new services or markets must be sought. The library or information centre has four options in this case: to remain in a

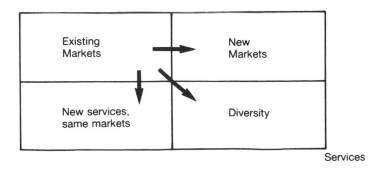

Services

Figure 8.6   Diversification strategies for libraries or information centres

stable situation and accept the status quo; to look for new markets; to diversify into new areas; or to provide new services to its existing markets (Figure 8.6).

Changes in consumer behaviour, competitor behaviour, technology or government policies may also influence the library or information centre to adopt one of the above strategies.

Similar options arise for library and information services. Rejuvenation strategies may be used to recover some of the services' lack of use over time or stop the decline in the product life cycle by either applying recapturing strategies, redesigning the service, refocusing or recasting it (Figure 8.7).

	Unmodified	Modified
Previous/ present users	Recapture Markets	Redesign Markets
New/ different users	Refocus	Recast

Figure 8.7 Rejuvenation strategies
Source: Lazer *et al.* (1984: 21–8). Copyright (1984) by the foundation for the School of Business at Indiana University. Used with permission.

Recapturing strategies

Recapturing strategies attempt to revive the old market. They concentrate on previous and existing users without modifying the service. Displays in libraries which promote existing services are in some sense recapturing strategies.

Redesigning strategies

Redesign involves marketing a modified version of a service or part of the library's stock which has been declining or has previously been abandoned. The original reasons for user rejection may no

140

longer prevail and it may be possible to rekindle interest among present users. In libraries and the publishing industry, redesign often occurs when particular authors go out of fashion but are brought back into vogue in new formats such as glossy paperbacks. Television and the film industry often act as the catalyst for redesign of the library's stock, creating demands for authors who have been unpopular for some time.

Recasting strategies

Recasting strategies are used in marketing a modified service to new users. The object is to capitalize on the organization's strengths and experience, although some adjustments to the service and market have to take place. An example of a recasting strategy in a public library may be where the population has aged; and storytelling sessions, once aimed at preschoolers have taken on a slightly different format and are now used as bibliotherapy with the aged.

Refocusing strategies

Refocusing involves marketing an abandoned or declining service to new users. Such an example may be marketing a local history collection, which may have been established through demand for school project material, to the local newspaper for a series of articles on local identities or places of interest. Such a strategy may result in greater usage of the service by the general public.

The library's decision to rejuvenate or diversify services will be based upon its resource requirements and capabilities. The potential of the rejuvenated or diversified services to contribute to the profile and value of the library or information centre, the cost involved and predicted extended life-span on a cost–benefit basis must also be assessed. In selecting the most appropriate strategy, the extent of service modification and degree of marketing effort needed to stimulate demand need to be evaluated.

REFERENCES

Kotler, P., FitzRoy, P. and Shaw, R. (1980), *Australian Marketing Management* (Sydney: Prentice Hall).

Lazer, W., Luqmani, M. and Quraeshi, Z. (1984), 'Product rejuvenation strategies' *Business Horizons*, November–December, pp.21–8.
McCarthy, E. J. (1971), *Basic Marketing: a managerial approach* (4th edn.) (Homewood, Ill.: Irwin)

PART IV
STRATEGIES FOR
STRUCTURAL PROCESSES

Introduction

This section aims to acquaint the reader with the processes which support the library or information centre by providing the coordination required for it effectively and efficiently to achieve its goals and objectives.

Chapter 9 describes the different organization structures which can be found in libraries and information centres. As these structures establish the patterns of relationships and responsibilities between departments and individuals they need to be carefully planned. Whilst there is no single best way to plan the design of an organization, the most effective organization structures bring together library programmes and activities to support the goals and objectives of the library or information centre. Various formal groups or committees can be found in organizations to further the coordination process. The use of these is also discussed in this chapter.

Structural coordination is achieved through line and staff departments. Line departments achieve the goals and objectives by delegation, command and work assignments within the organizational hierarchy. Staff departments influence the work of the line departments through advice, recommendation and suggestion. Line and staff functions, authority and conflicts are explored in Chapter 10. The concepts of unity of command, scalar principle and span of control which also influence the hierarchical structure and relationships are also described.

Chapter 11 considers the topic of communication. Good communication is a necessary ingredient for successful planning, organizing, decision-making, controlling, motivating and leadership functions. The process of communication is described providing the background for the rest of the chapter.

Communication can be considered to operate at two levels – at the level of the individual and at organizational level. Interpersonal communication can be enhanced with an awareness of such influencing factors as stereotyping, self-image and attitudes to others, and by developing good listening skills.

Communication at organizational level can occur in a variety of forms;

written, electronic, oral and non-verbal communication. Formal and informal channels of communication exist in all organizations. The extent to which these are used in libraries and information centres depends upon their type, size, complexity and corporate culture. These factors are also explored in Chapter 11.

Communication skills are exceptionally important for librarians and information professionals, not only as a function of management but also as the medium through which the library serves its client base. Chapter 11 explores the ways in which communication skills are used in libraries and information centres, including the various uses for different types of written reports and methods of holding effective meetings.

Finally, the chapter explores the communication processes which can be used to explain the organization's corporate culture.

9 Organization structures

INTRODUCTION

An organization structure is related to communication, coordination and control. A good organization structure provides for efficient work and communication systems as it establishes the patterns of relationships and responsibilities between departments and individuals within the library or information centre and its parent organization.

Formal structure is identified by:

1. the pattern of formal relationships and duties as found in organizational charts and job descriptions;
2. the way in which various tasks, activities and responsibilities are allocated to various departments and individuals through specialization;
3. the way in which these separate activities or tasks are coordinated by integration, grouped according to departments, and the departments themselves grouped into the total organization;
4. the power, status and hierarchical relationships within the organization, associated with authority;
5. the planned and formalized policies, procedures and controls which guide the activities and relationships of people in the organization through its administrative system.

Together these ensure that employees fully understand their role within the organization and what is expected of them.

DESIGNING THE ORGANIZATION STRUCTURE

An effective organization structure should reflect the goals and objectives of the library or information centre. Similar programmes and activities should be identified and grouped into units or departments which provide the best means of control and coordination to support these goals and objectives. This may be a complex task requiring considerable managerial effort in identifying the correct combination of programmes and activities. For instance, a decision may need to be made as to whether the library or information centre is structured according to the physical or technical tasks such as technical services or reader services in achieving the library's mission, or whether it would be better structured according to the end-user and by subject specialization. The two organization structures and related activities would differ accordingly.

An organization structure should also reflect the pattern or network of relationships and communication channels between various positions and position holders. Organizations possess both formal and informal structures, the formal being defined by management decisions and the informal developing out of the interactions and sentiments of the particular individuals comprising the organization.

The library or information centre's organization structure should be dynamic in its design, since change is a continuous feature of any organization. Internal and external forces constantly impact on existing structures, producing the need for change. As organizations grow and develop, different structures become necessary to meet the challenges of increasing size, advancing technology and changing environmental conditions.

The processes of planning, policy-making, setting objectives and problem-solving are inextricably linked with organization design. Without an effective organization structure, communication and coordination vital to the planning, problem-solving and decision-making functions cannot take place. The organization structure also identifies levels of management and hence those responsible for the different levels of objective-setting, programme implementation and associated problem-solving. Those at the top of the hierarchy will be responsible for planning and policy-making for the total organization. Those lower down in the hierarchy will find that their objective-setting tasks and problem-solving will relate specifically to their own areas of authority and responsibility.

148

ORGANIZATION CHARTS AND VERTICAL AND HORIZONTAL LINKAGES IN ORGANIZATIONS

An organization chart is a graphic presentation of the organization's structure. It may depict individuals, units or departments (see Figure 9.1). It should provide employees with information about their position in the organization, their relationship to others, their tasks and responsibilities, and to whom they report.

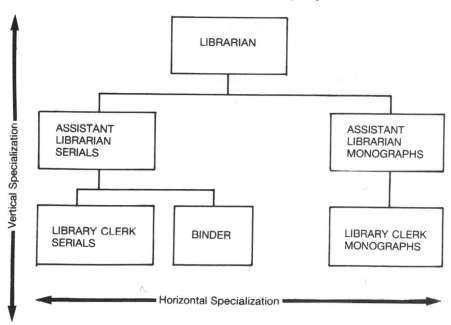

Figure 9.1   An organization chart at individual level showing vertical and horizontal specializations

The vertical lines in Figure 9.1 identify the hierarchy of authority, who reports to whom and the responsibilities of managers. In an organization chart, authority flows down and out. It does not return to the original line of authority.

Sometimes the status of an organization unit is misunderstood because of its location on the organization chart. The belief is frequently held that the higher on the chart the unit is represented, the greater its status and authority. This is not true. The importance

149

of an organization unit is determined by the line of authority and the number of managers that authority passes through before reaching the final authority.

DIFFERENTIATION AND ORGANIZATION STRUCTURE

As libraries and information centres grow in complexity, differentiation occurs. The primary purpose of differentiation is to subdivide the organization structure into departments so that managers can concentrate on their particular areas of expertise to ensure that their activities lead to the survival of the organization in the environment. 'Areas of expertise' can be related to knowledge of particular geographical locations, functional technologies, technologies and contents of products, or needs of particular types of users (markets).

The type of differentiation, according to function, location, product (service) or user will depend upon the environment. The library will adopt the differentiation which is most likely to succeed, considering the internal and external environments.

Some means of coordination has to be achieved to ensure that the decisions and activities in departments support the corporate goals and objectives. The degree of coordination between the departments will be affected by the external environment. As uncertainty increases, the need for coordination and information exchange between the various departments increases. This also affects the degree to which each department can remain interdependent.

Function organization structure

Differentiation or departmentalization according to function occurs when the organization's activities are divided into the primary functions to be performed. It is particularly appropriate for small organizations which base their growth on a single product or service within one market area and where functional expertise, efficiency and quality are needed. The function structure is most effective in a relatively stable environment.

Departmentalization according to function in a library or information centre has traditionally been based upon the transformation

150

processes of acquiring, organizing, lending and using materials, with small overall administrative functions providing coordination. This arrangement has the advantage of specialization and the concentration of similar activities within a departmental unit. It groups particular skills, knowledge and actions together to work on common problems. Employees have a very clear idea of their tasks which are often consistent with their specialist training.

Function structures place emphasis upon expertise within functions and departments without looking at the overall organization's goals. It is the type of differentiation which is most likely to develop subcultures. Members of each department adopt the values, goals and orientations of the particular function through their specialized skills and differences in goals and orientation. Even with task forces and integrators, the primary allegiance of employees will still be toward the goals of their own departments rather than cooperation with other departments.

Locality organization structure

Departmental structure according to locality is a common method of organizing geographically dispersed services. All organization activities performed in a particular geographic area are brought together and integrated into a single unit on the assumption that efficiency will improve. The pattern is typified by the establishment of regional offices. It is necessary in situations where organizations expand on a geographical basis, lessening the amount of control afforded by the head office or control headquarters. In special library or information centres, this occurs with the establishment of branch libraries to serve offsite facilities.

Product organization structure

Departmentalization according to product is a generic term used to describe the differentiation of libraries based on their resources, services or markets. It is an appropriate way to group activities when libraries offer many resources, products or services which are different in technical make-up, production, process or market distribution.

Specialization occurs according to the organization's output – that is, according to either or both products or services. Product differentiation is often found in academic libraries where the organization structures are designed to support the management of different types of resources (audio-visual materials, serials, books and so on) or subject specialization in which staff are involved in acquiring, processing and providing user services in specific subject areas. The product structure allows specialists to acquire in-depth knowledge and expertise of the material or subject area involved.

User organization structure

The grouping of activities to reflect the user is common in public libraries. Users are the key to the way many public libraries are grouped because of the varied demands placed upon them and the range of services which such libraries have to offer to a broad cross-section of the community with diverse needs and of diverse age groups.

Departmentalization according to users provides the means to meet the needs of specific markets. It allows for specialists to achieve in-depth knowledge of market needs. Individuals with a department can each build up one another's knowledge, training and experience. It focuses on the success or failure of particular services to user groups.

Hybrid organization structures

Many libraries or information centres do not have a pure product, function, locality or user structure: they are often a mix. Libraries often begin with a function structure, but as they grow in complexity and specialization develops, they begin to differentiate according to product and user – examples being an audio-visual librarian or a children's specialist librarian.

Matrix structures

Matrix structures compromise between traditional function structures and autonomous project groups centred around a particular product or service. They give simultaneous priority to both functional activities and products or services. In times of extensive

152

and rapid environmental change they provide for continuous information processing and coordination between both vertical and horizontal directions.

Matrix structures are geared to the traditional need to specialize activities into function departments which develop expertise and provide a permanent home base for employees, and the need to have units which integrate the expertise of specialized departments or individuals on a programme, project, product or systems management basis. They provide significant economies of scale in the use of the internal resources through flexibility in the use of staff and equipment. Matrix structures are geared to changing managerial requirements in research and development, or in large-scale and complex projects.

This type of structure requires a special leadership style leaning heavily towards open communication, an informal rather than a bureaucratic approach and a management system which fosters open discussion of problems. Success depends upon the manager's ability to persuade or influence other project members rather than formal authority, and upon employees adapting to work for two bosses. Unless managers and operating personnel are trained and educated to work in developing organization designs, they can suffer frustrations, emotional disturbances and loss of motivation. Working in an environment characterized by change as projects are started and completed is not so comfortable and secure as performing a continuing function in a more stable, standardized work-flow situation. Conflicts inevitably arise and the employee who is working for two bosses becomes caught in the conflict and may be expected to resolve it. Matrix structures often increase conflict and power struggles within the organization. They result in many meetings to discuss and coordinate activities and to resolve issues before major conflict occurs.

OTHER ORGANIZATION GROUPS

Project groups

Project groups are established for the duration of a particular programme. Group members can be drawn from within the organization

153

and from outside. Each group member from within the organization works for both a project group manager and a function manager. Dual command responsibilities may also be assigned to managers – for example, function control and project control. The chief executive heads up and balances the dual chain of command. Project groups are used in libraries or information centres as part of participation-in-management programmes. They are used to plan major changes and to design programmes which may influence large numbers of staff, and/or where the expertise of staff performing different functions or at different levels is needed.

Project groups provide flexibility for the organization in that they usually have a sunset clause attached, and are only in existence for the duration of a particular project.

Boards

Boards are a type of committee found in many organizations, especially public ones. Most private companies have a board of directors elected by the shareholders to oversee and guide top management. They hold the final responsibility for the organization. Boards hold regular meetings to ratify policies and consider reports from standing committees, and so on.

Ad hoc committees

This is a committee created for a relatively narrow, short-run, yet generally extremely important, purpose. An *ad hoc* committee meets irregularly. When its purpose is fulfilled it is normally dissolved.

Standing committee

A standing committee, as its name implies, is relatively permanent. The membership of such a committee is long-term and stable. Some standing committees, such as a budget review committee, deal with the same set of issues on a continuous basis. Others, such as a library management committee, deal with a variety of problems. Executive committees are standing committees which comprise top management and which are primarily concerned with strategy and policy. Standing committees meet regularly and usually before the board meeting in order to place recommended actions before the board.

Task forces

These are similar to the *ad hoc* committee and project groups. They have a relatively narrow purpose and a limited time horizon and are concerned with the integration or coordination of activities between units. The matters for consideration usually determine the regularity and length of meetings.

FACTORS AFFECTING THE CHOICE OF ORGANIZATION STRUCTURE

The organization structure is not an end in itself but simply a method of grouping activities to facilitate the achievement of the organization's goals. The selection of the type of departmental strategy depends upon the type of situation facing the organization. Because of the relative advantages of each type of departmentalization, most complex organizations use several of the integrating strategies and grouping activities.

The complexity of the organizing problem, the impact of the external environment and the principles of division of work are the basic concepts that management has to comprehend in order to provide an appropriate organizational structure. Dividing the work to meet the environmental needs is the initial step. The next problem of relating subordinates to supervisors and department to department involves coordination based upon the concepts of unity of command, span of control, delegation of authority, and integrating facilities.

There is no single best way to design an organization. The most successful organization design is one in which it and its sub-units 'fit' the technological and environmental demands and the needs of the corporate plan. Organization designs have changed over time. The classical theorists may have been correct in their approaches to unity of command since they were dealing with organizations in a stable environment; relatively little differentiation was required and the necessary integration could be done through rules and management hierarchy. However, in today's world of technological and environmental change, flexibility is required. The degree of variety and diversity in the environment is also an important influence on the choice of organization design, since it increases the need for differentiation; yet distinct functional specialists are likely to be in conflict with each other. Therefore integrating processes and structures, such as project teams and matrix structures, are needed.

INTEGRATION IN ORGANIZATIONS

The integration of work activities in organizations is achieved through communication, coordination and control. Communication involves the transfer of information both vertically and horizontally. Coordination links the different activities of departments and managerial levels into a coherent pattern designed to meet the corporate goals and objectives. Control is the process of ensuring that the coordinated activities comply with the corporate objectives.

Effective communication provides the basis for the coordination and control of activities. Individuals and departments need to be aware of what each other is doing.

The organization design or structure formally specifies or dictates who may (or may not) communicate with whom. An organization's lines of authority show the pathways through which messages have to flow. The lines that connect the sub-units in an organization's structure operate in both directions because communication occurs up and down the organization hierarchy. However, the same kinds of information are not communicated in each direction. Instructions and commands flow down the hierarchy, whilst referrals, reports and information flow upward. Coordination travels horizontally between peers and departments. More detailed information relating to forms of communication in libraries can be found in Chapter 11.

ORGANIZATION STRUCTURE AND CREATIVITY

Organization structures can either inhibit or encourage creativity. Organic and extremely decentralized organizations, in which small

156

project teams are found, foster an atmosphere in which new ideas and fast action can flourish. Bureaucratic organizations with strong lines of authority often prevent initiative and innovation.

Organization structures also influence the behaviours, communications and interactions of the individuals in them. A structure which provides for the sharing and testing of ideas amongst people is a necessary prerequisite for creativity.

Successful organizations are designed to encourage innovation and change. The product form of structure gives each unit a specific focus, so that innovation and creativity are rewarded.

10   Strategies for the structural coordination of libraries and information centres

INTRODUCTION

Structural coordination in libraries and information centres is achieved through line and staff departments.

Line departments (operating units) are those concerned with the achievement of the organization's objectives through the hierarchical delegation of authority, command, work assignments and supervision of others. Line managers have the ability to exercise control and use sanctions.

Staff departments (service units) influence the work of others through advice, recommendation or suggestion. They are not part of the traditional hierarchy of line departments, and can cut across all levels of hierarchy to provide advice, among other things, where and when needed. As they usually report direct to the executive, it is possible to use their knowledge without sacrificing the executive's coordinating function; thus the integrity of the line organization is maintained.

Several other concepts influence the hierarchical relationships. These are unity of command, the scalar principle and span of control.

LINE AND STAFF DEPARTMENTS

Line and staff functions

Staff functions have developed as organizations have become more complex. They provide the means by which staff with knowledge

158

and technical expertise in a particular area of specialization can be of assistance to the whole organization, frequently providing authority and influence without disturbing the traditional line function.

Staff departments assist line departments in solving special problems which require technical expertise and detailed attention. Staff people are experts in given fields and line managers rely upon them for advice. Staff specialists investigate issues and prepare and process data which line managers need for decision-making. They provide ideas and support the efforts of line managers.

Staff functions are usually separate from line management and, as they may interact with all levels of the hierarchy, a decision has to be made as to what authority staff personnel should be given. They can rarely direct others, exert control or use sanctions; the final responsibility for actions resides with line management.

Line and staff authority

Line authority is the basic and fundamental authority in any organization. It is the ultimate authority to command, act and decide in matters affecting others. It is the authority which sanctions or approves, directly or indirectly, the activities which take place in the organization. It is also the authority which channels and directs the responses of others and which requires them to conform to decisions, plans, policies, systems, procedures and goals. Line authority is not merely the right to decide, but also the right to direct. The authority to direct or to give ultimate sanction and approval to the activities of employees in an organization is an executive prerogative only. Non-managerial workers may decide, plan, organize or control their own jobs only within their scope of authority; they do not have the right to extend their decisions or commands to others.

The primary purpose of line authority is to make the organization work. It provides both the basic decisions involved in operating an enterprise and the initiating force for all kinds of actions. It makes the leadership process effective by establishing authentic channels of communication, and serves as a means of control by setting limits to the scope of authority of individuals.

Staff authority is a complex and difficult concept. It is best defined as authority whose scope is limited (by the absence of the right to direct or command) to auxillary and such facilitating activities as planning, recommending, advising and assisting. Staff authority is subordinate to line authority, as its purpose is to facilitate the activities being directed and controlled by line management. Its most outstanding characteristic is the absence of the right to command. The staff executive cannot command others outside their department's realm; they can only exercise and command authority over members of their own department.

Advice is a function of the staff department, but it is not restricted to just staff. Line executives also advise and recommend in performing their work. Since orders cannot be issued to actuate ideas, the staff unit's work is achieved by planning, thinking, studying, informing, recommending and suggesting.

There is, however, a continuum of authority that staff units do have in that, as already noted, many staff activities are advisory in nature. The manager is free to seek (or not seek) the advice of staff specialists (see Figure 10.1).

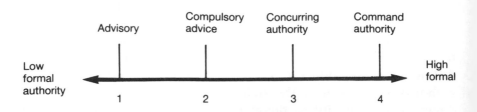

Figure 10.1 Continuum of authority for staff units

In the case of compulsory staff advice, the manager must at least listen to the appropriate staff agency, but need not follow their recommendations. This ensures that the manager makes use of the specialized knowledge of the appropriate staff agency. An example of this can be found in the recruitment of new library personnel: the personnel officer may offer his department's services and be included at the interview stage, but the final decision is made by the library manager.

Concurring staff authority requires that line and staff managers agree on a particular course of action to follow. This procedure expands the staff manager's authority, and restricts the line manager's decision-making discretion to areas where there is agreement on a particular course of action. Such a situation occurs in the development of a training programme where library staff and personnel staff are involved.

The strongest form of staff authority occurs when line departments grant limited command authority to staff departments, permitting them to give orders and expecting that other organizational units will comply. In most organizations, the personnel department has functional authority over many personnel practices in all departments throughout the organization, particularly where employees' safety is concerned.

Line and staff conflicts

Authority problems between line and staff units have created much friction and conflict in organizations in the past. There are a number of reasons why this should occur.

Generally, line people are more oriented towards advancement with the organization, whilst staff people work towards advancement in their profession. The former see their future in terms of loyalty to the organization, the latter to their profession. This difference in commitment and loyalty to the organization can lead to a conflict of interest.

Often there are differential role expectations. This is a type of interdepartmental conflict, since the staff department has an identity and separateness from the line, yet needs to persuade line departments to its point of view. This can produce a clash of domains of authority, expertise and activity. New specialities may also threaten old specialities.

Staff units are usually located higher in the organization and are often called upon by top management to make reports and analyses of operating divisions. Thus they acquire informal command authority. These staff functions are often perceived by line management as attempts to control and check on line units.

Specialists may be resented by line executives because of their advanced training, and other ways in which they differ from managers, who have usually achieved their positions through work and internal promotion. Overbearing attitudes on behalf of some staff personnel may intensify these feelings.

Staff personnel may become impatient to put their ideas into action through their own enthusiasm. In their intense efforts they may lose their sensitivity to tactful and diplomatic persuasion. They may appear to become empire-builders. Line management may resist change, particularly if the ideals are pushed too hard and too fast with the result that line management does not understand what the staff personnel are advocating. Line management may resent the loss of functions which can be transferred to staff executives.

Line executives are often charged with the responsibility of high productivity and low costs, whilst staff executives are often associated with high-cost units and higher salaries for little apparent tangible outcomes. They appear to those who do not understand or detect the benefits to be 'money wasteful'.

UNITY OF COMMAND

Early management theorists maintained that the concept of unity of command was one of the underlying principles of management. Unity of command states that an individual should have only one boss. Whilst it is recognized that this is a logical extension of the hierarchical form of organization structure, it does not always fit in unison with more modern types of organization structure, such as matrix structure. However, this concept is still necessary to provide for effective and clear delegation of authority in organizational structures which are hierarchical in nature. Confusion over who gives orders and who implements them is minimized when a chain of command is established.

SCALAR PRINCIPLE

The scalar principle refers to the chain of direct authority from manager to subordinate throughout the organization. The basic idea of the principle is that every employee should know his or her areas of responsibility, and no one individual should report to more than one superior. If this principle is followed, subordinates know who delegates authority to them and to whom matters beyond their authority must be referred.

SPAN OF CONTROL

Span of control is a concept related to the horizontal dimension of an organization structure. It deals with the number of subordinates who report directly to a superior. The concept holds that the larger the number of subordinates reporting directly to a manager, the more difficult it is to supervise and coordinate them effectively. Traditionally, the number of subordinates reporting to any one manager has ranged between 4 and 12. Generally, the more structured the task, the more subordinates may be contained in the span of control.

Other factors which determine the optimum number of subordinates that a manager can supervise effectively are the competence of the superior and subordinate; the degree of interaction between departments being supervised; the similarity or dissimilarity of activities being supervised; the extent of standardization, rules and procedures within the organization; the incidence of new problems in the supervisor's department; and the extent to which the supervisor must carry out non-managerial work.

Whilst a rigid concept of span of control is unrealistic, group cohesiveness is best with approximately five members. A small group does not provide sufficient interaction for cohesiveness, and a larger group tends to break down into subgroups or cliques. Small groups tend to generate higher member satisfaction than do large ones, largely because of the opportunity for participation by those members who want it. As groups become larger the demands on the leader become more exacting and complex and require the leader to become more directive. Thus leadership is needed because of the difficulties of coordinating the efforts of the larger group.

Large spans of control are feasible where the ability of the supervising person is great and where subordinates can carry out their responsibilities with a minimum of direct supervision by a higher executive. A high calibre manager with high energy and intelligence can absorb the extra pressure and deal effectively with the increased relationships; a relatively large span of control can be successful under his or her direction. The span of control can be even larger if, in addition, the subordinates they supervise possess a large degree of competence and have high levels of intelligence, energy, and ability, or if the work to be supervised consists of routines and mechanical processes. 'Flat' organizations usually have large spans of control with few levels of supervision.

11 Strategies for communication in libraries and information centres

INTRODUCTION

Communication is a fact of life. All human interaction is dependent upon communication for the exchange of information and the conveyance of ideas. Information or ideas do not themselves constitute communication. They must reach and be meaningfully understood by the other party to be part of the communication process. Communication occurs when the messages flowing between two parties have arrived at a stage where the images and ideas, which each is trying to pass to the other, have the same meaning to the receiver as to the sender.

Communication is the process by which the management functions of planning, organizing, decision-making, controlling, motivating and leading, are carried out. It is a two-way process. Correct information must be communicated to managers at all levels to enable them to make decisions. Managers must also communicate their needs, philosophies and decisions to others.

Feedback is a necessary part of communication. Until feedback is received, the manager does not know how an employee or associate is feeling, nor can he/she assess the performance of the individual and if necessary what corrective action to take. Employees also require feedback in order to allow them to take their own corrective action.

THE PROCESS OF COMMUNICATION

Communication is a process which takes place and is interpreted at the level of the individual. This is true even if the individual is acting

165

on behalf of, or interacting with, a machine, group or organization. In some situations, such as in the negotiating process, individuals may be communicating the views of others in their messages, but they will still perceive incoming messages initially from their personal viewpoint.

The key elements of the communication process are a source, a message, a receiver, feedback and noise. The source is the person or element who is responsible for encoding an intended meaning into a message. This may be the person who translates his or her thoughts (the message) into a language, such as French or English, with the hope that it can be understood by the other person(s). The receiver decodes the message into a perceived meaning. If both parties speak the same language and share a joint perception of the message then they are communicating. Feedback from receiver to source may or may not be given, but if it is, it serves either to confirm the message or to show that the message has not been

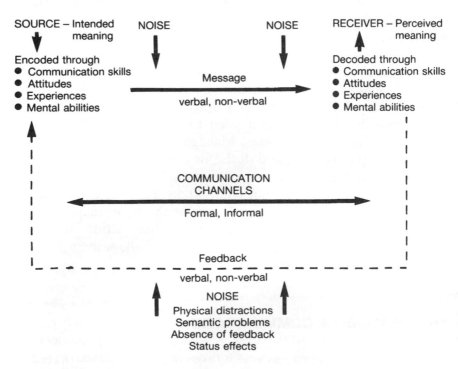

Figure 11.1 The communication process

received correctly. In the latter case another message reinforcing the context of the first one is usually sent. 'Noise' is anything present in the perceived signal that was not part of the originally intended message. It may originate from the sender or the receiver, or it may be the preoccupation of either party with some other pressure which may prevent them from fully understanding the implications of the message, which will thus be obscured (Figure 11.1). Noise distorts the original message.

Messages may be sent over more than one channel at a time. Whilst it may be unusual for two people to continue to speak to each other at the same time, it is usual for non-verbal communication to be transmitted between two people concurrently. This is often unconsciously acknowledged and interpreted by the other person, who may change or adapt his or her next verbal message as a result.

INTERPERSONAL COMMUNICATION

Self-image and attitudes to others

It is helpful when communicating with others to appreciate and understand the complexity of interpersonal communication. The interpersonal aspect of communication has been described by Lippitt (1982: 88–9) and involves the searching and understanding of the self and others' self-image, needs, values, expectations, standards and norms and perceptions. Self-image involves the perceptions of an individual about him/herself, or the group to which he/she belongs. The concept of group can be expanded to include a nation. Self-image takes into account ego, pride, traditions, ambitions. Needs reflect requirements in order that psychological or physiological yearnings are satisfied. They include love, security, recognition and success. Values reflect subjective ideas held dearly. Expectations are anticipated outcomes, desired or otherwise, which are likely to be the consequence of actions or the lack of actions. Standards are found in fixed norms which reflect cultural background and experience. Perceptions are preconceived ideas which may or may not distort an individual's views.

To this may be added a background of stored information,

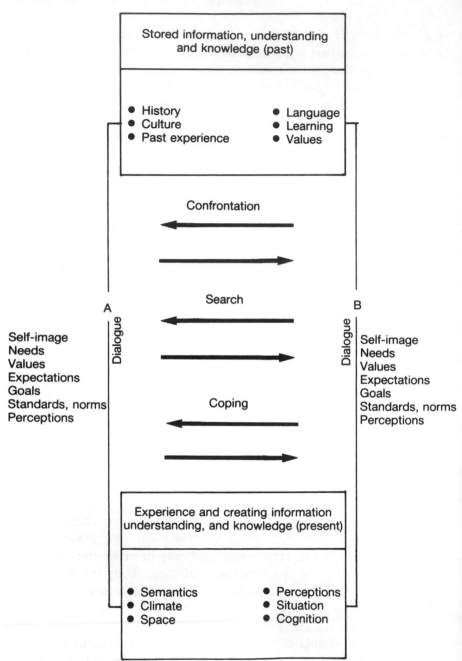

Figure 11.2 The process of interfacing
Source: Lippitt (1982: 89) Reprinted by permission of Prentice Hall, Inc., Englewood Cliffs, New Jersey.

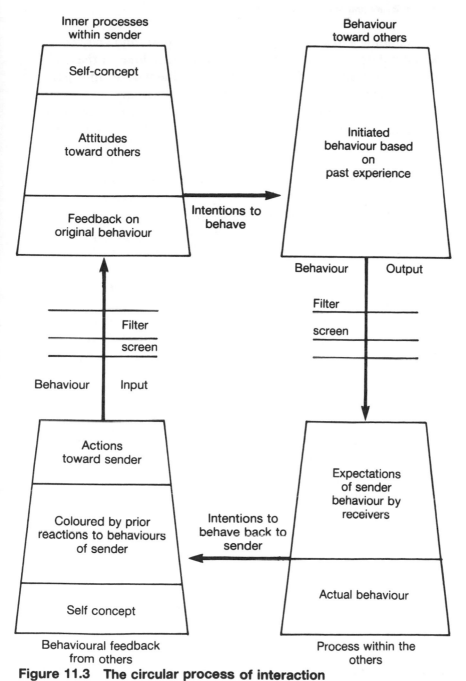

Figure 11.3 The circular process of interaction

Source: Lippitt (1982: 89) Reprinted by permission of Prentice Hall, Inc., Englewood Cliffs, New Jersey.

understanding and knowledge based on the past, and an experience, understanding and knowledge of the present. None of these can be mutually exclusive, and all interact to influence the interpersonal communication process at the time (Figure 11.2).

Lippitt (1982: 89–90) describes interpersonal communication as also being a circulatory process. The individual has a picture of him/ herself and an understanding of the kind of person he or she is. This is known as their self-image. Individuals also possess a set of attitudes towards the person(s) with whom they are communicating, which can either be positive or negative. As a result of the self-image and set of attitudes, intentions to behave in a certain way are formed. These intentions will be coloured by past experiences in similar situations, and perceptions of the attitudes of the other(s) towards themselves. Receivers filter the behaviour as it is being received according to whether they like or dislike the senders. The receiver also has some prior expectations as to how the sender should be behaving. Incoming behaviour will be evaluated as to whether it meets these expectations. As a result of the evaluation, the receiver will respond to the sender. The original sender also filters the incoming behaviour according to his/her prejudices, attitudes, etc., and the process begins again (Figure 11.3).

Effective interpersonal communication may be achieved by focusing upon concrete information rather than being vague or abstract. The actual behaviour of an individual should be focused upon, rather than their personality. Opinions should be formed upon descriptive actions and not judgemental ones or inferences. The emphasis should be upon developing alternatives and the sharing of ideas and information, rather than the giving of advice.

Managers will find that their interpersonal communication skills can be enhanced by being accessible to those who are working on a given situation or who will participate in it, and by defining each individual's or group's areas of responsibility. Goals should be kept clearly in mind and others should be helped to do the same. The manager should develop trust between all concerned and be frank with employees on plans and problems. Above all, effective listening skills should be developed.

To communicate better, individuals or groups must understand each other better. Interpersonal communication can all too often be based upon a subjective analysis of the other person(s) rather

170

than the objectivity of the message conveyed. This factor is an extremely important one for library managers and information professionals to be aware of, as by the nature of their work their communication role is far more widespread than the average manager.

Listening

A good communicator is also a good listener. Poor listening is one of the most inhibiting features for the communication of ideas. A library manager who is a good listener can gain invaluable information from subordinates in solving job-related problems.

A manager who commands effective listening skills will help to create an atmosphere of understanding and respect. As a result, employees will often be more willing to cooperate. Effective listening requires the individual to listen to what is being said in terms of what is being meant. Key words, inferences, prejudices, provide meaningful detail which explain underlying thoughts. Effective listeners also remember what has been said and the context in which it was said. They will try to understand the viewpoint of the other party, even though it may be a contradiction to their own ideas or values.

Hearing is not listening. Listening involves interpreting non-verbal communication signals such as mood, aggression, nervousness and incorporating these into the verbal message which is received.

Listening skills can be improved through practice, training and concentration. Good listeners do not interrupt or attempt to finish others' sentences. They are patient, allowing the other party plenty of time. They try to put the other party at ease and make an effort to remove or minimize distractions. Active listening allows the listener to place themselves in the other party's position and look at things from their point of view. Effective listeners ask pertinent questions thereby providing a feedback mechanism to the other party demonstrating that the listener is listening to what is being said. Finally, good listeners never show anger or criticize the other party. Listening skills can lead to a more productive work environment through increased motivation and understanding.

171

Stereotyping and halo effect

Stereotyping involves forming generalized opinions of how people of a given sex, religion or race appear, think, feel and act. It is an attempt to classify or categorize individuals so that they lose their individuality and are in turn assigned the characteristics of an entire group of people.

Stereotyping affects the interpersonal communication process because it keeps individuals from understanding one another. Stereotyping is 'noise' which prevents one party from hearing the message which the other party is sending and which colours attitudes and prejudices.

The halo effect is a tendency to judge an individual favourably, or occasionally unfavourably, in many areas on the basis of one strong point on which the other party places high value. Halo effects can have positive or negative consequences for the other party. It affects the communication process in that anything which they say is consistently interpreted in either a positive or negative fashion.

Formal and informal channels of communication

Both formal and informal channels of communication are used in libraries and information centres. The extent to which formal and informal channels of communication are used within libraries and information centres will depend upon the type, size, complexity and corporate culture of the library organization. If the library is large then library managers and information staff will communicate both formally and informally within the library's lateral and hierarchical structure; and outside of the structure to the policy-making bodies, stakeholders, users, colleagues in other libraries and members of other institutions which interface with the library in its external environment.

If the library is small, and the librarian's or information professional's role is a singular one or shared with few others to provide an information or research service to an organization, then there will be little or no need for formal intradepartmental communication. However, interdepartmental communication with external bodies such as described above will continue to be both on a formal and informal basis.

172

Generally speaking, the larger or more complex the organization the more formal will be the communication processes. The organization's external environment and corporate culture will also influence the formality of its communication systems. Rapidly changing, complex external environments call for organic-type organization structures. Communication is generally less formal and more open in cases like these. Bureaucratic-type structures operate in simple and stable environments: there is time for procedures and regulations to be followed and so communication is much more formal. The corporate culture of the organization will also dictate whether communication must follow clear lines of authority, or whether it is open and free-flowing.

Formal channels of communication

There are three kinds of formal channels of communication; downward, upward and horizontal.

Downward communication. Downward communication is frequently used in organizations. It is used by management for transmitting policies, procedures, corporate goals and objectives, directives, and so on to subordinates. Downward communication should also occur in the strategic planning process, when implementing change and in decision-making. It can be found in written form in policy or procedure manuals, corporate plans, appraisal forms, job descriptions and memoranda. Oral forms of downward communication are contained in addresses or speeches, meetings, appraisal interviews and general, yet formal, discussions or conversations. In many cases downward communication does not occur by itself, ideas and information are passed upward in return.

Downward communication requires diplomacy and tact in an endeavour to decrease latent or real hostility towards management. Downward communication should always be open and timely. Subordinates should know of events which are likely to occur before they occur, not as they occur or afterwards. Openness and timeliness generate trust.

Indoctrination is sometimes used to tell employees about events which the organization thinks is important. Company newsletters and memoranda, and company events such as the annual corporate

173

dinner or staff Christmas party are examples of indoctrination. To be effective the messages portrayed must be sincere and backed up by action.

Upward communication. Upward channels of communication send information from the subordinate to the supervisor to provide feedback for management both orally and in the form of reports or memoranda. Upward communication should be encouraged, as it provides feedback on how well employees understand downward communication. It should be allowed to occur freely and continuously, not just when management wants to hear it. Upward communication can also occur in the form of requests for clarification on issues, policies or procedures and in decision-making.

Upward communication may be distorted in a number of ways. Subordinates will usually screen out any unfavourable or negative aspects when communicating upwards, in an attempt to impress their superiors. Unfortunately, some subordinates try to enhance their image by highlighting others who have not contributed as well. The supervisor needs to be aware of this. Sometimes the original message will be clouded by the employees' personal anxieties, aspirations, beliefs or values. Employees may deliberately withhold, distort, or manipulate communication in an attempt to force an issue with management through the use of coercive power.

Horizontal communication. Horizontal channels of communication flow across lines of communication. They are used between people of the same level, with colleagues in other libraries and with library users. Examples of formal communication methods to users are in the provision of overdue notices, selective dissemination of information services, or reservation advice notices.

Communication horizontally, within both libraries and parent organizations, is found in the form of memos and reports. Paperwork is exchanged between departments and individuals about problems, decisions which have been made or activities which may affect them. Copies of correspondence or reports are often circulated between departments and individuals for information purposes. Communication on paper is usually one-way. Unless the receiver makes a special effort, little feedback or discussion takes place. This is the same for electronic communication systems such as electronic mail and other office communication systems.

Direct contact between individuals is usually the most efficient form of horizontal integration. Face-to-face situations are preferable to telephone conversations, as they allow for non-verbal communication as well as verbal communication. Direct contact can be scheduled through appointments and meetings.

Informal channels of communication

Informal communication is a natural phenomenon of human nature. It arises from the social relationship of people, unlike formal communication which is structured by hierarchies, work relationships and work practices. Informal communication supplements formal communication; in the absence of good official communication, informal communication may supplant it. Informal communication channels distribute information which may not have been communicated officially. The 'grapevine' is the most widely recognized form of informal communication. It is fast, highly selective and discriminating. It provides management with insights into employee attitudes, helps spread useful information and provides a safety valve for employee emotions. But whilst rumour and hostility, which often make up the grapevine, may help certain people psychologically by releasing emotions, they can disturb many others. Grapevines may also spread false rumours. This is particularly dangerous given the fact that they cannot be controlled by management, as the grapevine has no permanent membership.

Informal communication is used to a large extent on the information desk and at the issue desk. Whilst, initially, formal communication is used to ascertain user needs and exchange ideas on existing or suggested services, the librarian and user will begin to understand each other on a more personal basis after a period of time. As both the users and the librarian or information specialist become more familiar with each other, formal communication may give way to more informal communication patterns in some areas.

Sometimes the lines which distinguish the purpose and use of informal and formal communication become hazy. In situations where the library or information service exists to provide information or research services to an organization, the users of the library will be its management and staff. In this situation, the librarian or information specialist will become used to communicating upwards, downwards and laterally through the hierarchy, formally and informally about managerial or organizational matters with the same people as he or she will provide with information as library users in a professional capacity.

COMMUNICATION SKILLS IN LIBRARIES AND INFORMATION CENTRES

Communication skills are extremely important for librarians and information professionals. Not only do librarians have to communicate with each other in issuing or responding to directives and in carrying out the functions of management; they also communicate continually with library users. In addition, the very nature of their job requires them to assess, select, process and disseminate vehicles of communication in the form of books, films, cassettes, online catalogues, CD-Roms, and the like, and provide information services to their users. They must be experts in recognizing the most appropriate vehicle with which to provide or communicate information to a large number of people, whose communication skills both as senders and receivers will differ widely. They must continually update their knowledge about new and emerging communication techniques which will make their tasks more efficient and effective.

Communication is used in the planning process to obtain information relating to the internal and external environments of the library or information centre. Top managers communicate with individuals and groups both from within and outside the library to gain such information for the needs assessment and situation audit, using reports, personal contacts and meetings to do this. Mid-level managers discuss the implications of managerial policies and overall goals with top management and, in turn, their strategies for implementation with first-line management.

By its nature, the corporate planning process involves staff at all levels. In creating a positive environment for its implementation which dispels fears and encourages initiative and innovation, an open communication system throughout the entire organization is needed. The corporate plan itself is the vehicle by which the library's or information centre's mission, corporate goals and objectives are communicated to employees at all levels and also to those outside the organization.

The finding of methods to improve efficiency involves discussion and the sharing of ideas and information on the part of all concerned. Communication between all parties is also the basic ingredient to participative decision-making.

The tasks of lobbying, marketing, promoting, negotiating and liaison require an effective communicator. High-level communication skills are often needed when carrying out these activities. The effectiveness of these activities relies upon the library or information centre manager having an in-depth knowledge and understanding of their organization. Such information can only be obtained through the communication process.

The manager is the key communicator of library policies. Responsibility for their correct interpretation rests with management. Policies are communication tools as they provide the answers to routine questions.

A major part of management's time is directed to ensuring adequate funding in order that the library or information centre can carry out its goals and objectives. Library managers must constantly demonstrate, through various communication channels, that their resources are being efficiently and effectively utilized.

An effective manager or supervisor will always clearly communicate to subordinates what is expected of them and what they are responsible for. This may involve them either physically demonstrating the task or providing an actual example of what good performance looks like. Good work should always be rewarded. An effective manager should always communicate his/her feelings about the performance as and where it happens. By expressing how they feel and by active listening – that is, by expressing how they think that the other person is feeling – effective managers convey the correct feedback.

Feedback should take the form of encouragement where possible, but with quick, specific, pertinent reprimands where required for incorrect performance. In correcting behaviour, library managers should deal with one aspect of behaviour at a time and should never attack an individual's value system. In this way corrective action can be taken so as not to damage the relationship between the subordinate and the manager.

Mintzberg's (1973: 92–3) 10 management roles all rely upon communication. As a figurehead, leader or liaison person, the manager is involved in interpersonal communication. As an information monitor and disseminator, and as a spokesperson, the manager has to actively seek and transmit information to others. In their decision-making role, as the entrepreneur, disturbance handler, resource allocator and negotiator, the manager needs effective interpersonal communication skills to obtain and impart information.

Communication is also the basis upon which users' or clients' information needs are satisfied, through the correct interpretation of their requests for information. Information needs are often satisfied by communicating with inanimate objects such as computer terminals which are linked to national or international databases or to a CD-ROM or video disk. Librarians or information professionals, when carrying out a literature search, make the natural transition of enquiring (encoding terms or ideas) on a terminal to a database, often on the other side of the world, reading (decoding) the resultant message and then turning to discuss (communicating) the resultant information with the person sitting next to them. They have switched from communicating with people to machines and back to people, and from communicating with someone next to them to a database on the other side of the world, possibly without even realizing the implications.

Technology allows libraries and information centres to handle or communicate large amounts of data over long distances on an immediate basis for instant action-taking such as ordering books and related materials. It facilitates the communication process in that it allows communication to occur in situations beyond the physical or mental capacity of an individual.

Mathews (1983: 22) draws attention to the temporal context of communication. She advocates that library staff should be rostered to work directly with the public during their best 'communicating' time. There are 'morning' people and 'late starters'. Desk duty rosters should be assigned on the basis of allowing library staff to interact with the public at a time when their communication skills are at their peak. Staff will then feel more comfortable working with the public and this will have a positive effect upon their approach to work and their interaction with the public.

LIBRARY AND INFORMATION CENTRE REPORTS

Library and information centre managers are called upon to write and submit reports on a regular or irregular basis, the purpose of which is to communicate to top management or boards or committees at the ownership level information upon which informed decisions can be made. In their role as information disseminators, library and information centre managers must either write or commission annual reports, monthly or quarterly reports, reports relating to specific issues, submissions and budget papers.

Annual reports

At the end of the financial year, which may be tied to the calendar year or the business financial year, library managers will be involved in either organizing their own library's or information centre's annual report or providing copy for the organization's annual report. Sometimes they will need to do both. Large and medium-sized libraries tend to produce an annual report of their own.

The annual report serves to provide an account of the library or information centre's activities for the year. As it contains statistical data it is used by other librarians as a source with which interlibrary comparisons can be made. It is also a public relations exercise in which the achievements of the year are reported and may additionally be viewed as the document which accounts for the use of public funds or investments and provides feedback to the ownership level and to the public. Attention is often drawn in the report to problems which prevent the organization from carrying out all of its activities, eg: lack of funding. Annual reports are published at the end of the organization's financial year in order that activities (outputs) can be related to use of funds, staff, etc. (inputs), and information is provided which acknowledges the organization's level of performance. Usually annual reports are circulated to other related organizations and considerable prestige is attached to their contents and format.

179

Annual reports usually provide a financial statement showing the source and use of funds, a list of key managerial positions, holders of such positions and their qualifications, an organizational chart, statistics including comparisons of the previous year's figures, measures of performance and accounts of activities within the organization.

Monthly reports

The library or information centre manager may also be called on to present regular monthly or quarterly reports. These are regarded as providing feedback to top management or the ownership level on a regular basis and contain statistical information and reports on library activities. Often issues of concern can be raised through these reports and attention is thereby drawn to such issues for further action.

Reports on specific issues

Regular reports are supplemented by reports on specific issues. These include papers for discussion and/or action, requests for the introduction of additional services or changes in service level, requests for changes in policy or reports relating to future planning. Reports such as these vary in length from half a page to several pages long. They begin with a summary of the reasons for the report and contain details of background, progress to date, legal or resource implications and recommendations. Specific reports are usually written by mid-level management from data collected in-house and from external sources and are written for top management or the ownership level in order that appropriate action can be authorized and taken.

Budgets

Budgets are a form of report in that they identify the requirement for, and the proposed use of funds. They communicate the need for funding, priority services and major areas of expenditure to top management, employees and stakeholders.

Submissions to outside bodies

Often library and information centre managers are called upon to draft submissions to government bodies or similar types of organizations relating to external issues which have or will have an impact upon their services or functions. Examples of which could be implications of a proposed new copyright legislation or the effect of reduced funding upon the library's services. These submissions are drafted by the library manager on behalf of the organization to communicate its stand or opinion on a particular issue. As the report is prepared from the organization's point of view, being its official communication on the subject, it may need to be ratified by top management or the ownership level before being forwarded to the appropriate body.

MEETINGS

A meeting is a communication process which brings together a group of people with a common interest, to accomplish some purpose or goal. The sharing of knowledge and experience allows participants to be involved in planning, decision-making, problem-solving, negotiating, evaluation, consultation and/or information dissemination.

Meetings can be held on a routine basis to provide information and allow for feedback or *ad hoc* when involved in planning or problem-solving. Library and information centre managers will both hold meetings with their staff and attend meetings called by those in a higher level of the organization hierarchy or by persons from external organizations with whom they deal. In addition, they will probably belong to professional bodies which will also hold occasional meetings.

Handled effectively and efficiently a meeting will result in creative thinking, multiple thought input, enhanced group cohesiveness, commitment, cooperation and communication leading to better decision-making in solving problems. Handled ineffectively or inefficiently a meeting will result in stifled creativity, aggressiveness, attacks on others, breakdown in communication leading to the

181

creation of more problems, lack of productivity and a great deal of time wasted.

Framework for effective meetings

The purpose or goal of the meeting should be well defined and an agenda drawn up which reflects that purpose. This will provide a sense of direction for participants. A good detailed agenda should prepare those attending for the tasks which they need to accomplish during the meeting. The agenda should provide details of date, time and place of the meeting. Time refers to both the starting and ending time as open-ended meetings invite time-wasting procedures. It is also useful to label agenda items according to their desired outcome, for example, 'for discussion', 'for decision', 'for information'.

The agenda should be circulated in advance to those attending allowing time for perusal and background work to take place. It is also important that any necessary background material – for example, reports, statistics, proposals, and so on – accompany the agenda when it is distributed.

It is important carefully to select the participants in order to ensure that all those who need to participate in the decision-making process are present; that those who attend have something to contribute through relevant knowledge or appropriate level of expertise; and that those attending also communicate and contribute to the meeting in a positive, creative and open fashion. To ignore any of these factors may hinder the productivity and effectiveness of the meeting. If the wrong people attend they will stifle creativity and waste their time and that of others. If too many people attend or if those who are not directly involved with the matters on hand attend, there is also the risk that too much time will be spent explaining the background information or issues will become side-tracked.

In some types of meeting the make-up of the committee will determine who should attend. For example, the members of the library's finance committee will automatically attend any finance committee meeting by nature of their positions. In other instances, particularly if it is an *ad hoc* meeting, the chairperson will have a right to stipulate who is to attend. The ideal number of participants in a meeting will generally range between four and eight. This number ensures that all participants can contribute their views. Any less than this number may result in not all of the relevant issues being explored; any more will result in too much diversity and a lack of control and input. The pace of the meeting should not be too slow, waffling and sidetracking should not be allowed.

In order to facilitate open discussion and ensure the full participation of all those attending, it is essential that the person in the chair displays leadership qualities which foster open communication and overcome any potential personality problems. Individuals should not be allowed to dominate meetings. Effective meetings foster team spirit, allow members to accumulate a body of wisdom and experience otherwise denied, open minds, and create flexibility in thinking. To achieve this calls for a democratic style of management and a knowledge of group dynamics in order to steer the participants in a creative fashion in the desired direction. A skilled chairperson will be able to persuade participants to think again and get proposals accepted where less experienced colleagues may fail. Bearing in mind that people will more willingly support decisions they have helped to make, this is important.

All decisions made at the meeting should be recorded, together with details as to who is responsible for follow-up actions, what these actions are and when they should take place.

Purposes of meetings

Meetings are a useful tool in decision-making when a decision requires judgement rather than calculations or expertise, or when a pooling of ideas improves the chances of a good decision. They are also important where it is necessary to get the participants' acceptance of the decision (Figure 11.4).

Meetings should not be called to solve routine problems or where it is difficult to demonstrate the correctness of any one particular solution to others. Neither are they useful as a vehicle for briefing subordinates about issues upon which they have little control or which are not work-related. While a manager may feel that it is an effective use of his or her time, their subordinates will usually resent what seems to them a waste of time.

Sometimes meetings are useful to establish regular contact

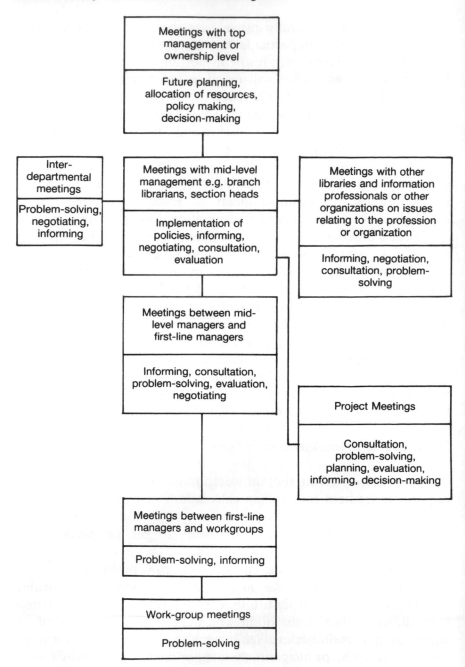

Figure 11.4   Purposes and types of meetings held in libraries and information centres

between departments, which ensures that they all move in the same direction to achieve the organization's corporate goals. A strong case can be made for allowing managers from other parts of the organization occasionally to attend library or information centre meetings and share in the decision-making where their input and experience could be valuable.

Occasional meetings between different specialists and people of different levels may also bring together people who differ in their thinking. Mutual understanding and cooperation may grow from this. Meetings attended by different levels of management can improve relationships, boost productivity and allow direct communication between senior and junior people. Less experienced members will greatly benefit from the knowledge and expertise of the more senior members, whilst senior members in their turn should obtain valuable feedback as to the beliefs and values which flow through the organization.

In libraries and information centres meetings are frequently called at lower levels in the hierarchy to inform subordinates, for problem-solving purposes and/or to allow an avenue of feedback from subordinates to management. The upper levels of management meet mainly for planning purposes, to allocate resources and make decisions on a corporate basis.

Meetings may be held for political reasons. This is inadvisable as the motives will quickly be recognized by the more experienced attendees and the meeting's value consequently diminished. Examples of such instances are as image-building exercises, to demonstrate conspicuously that things are happening in the area or to impress the boss.

The meeting environment

It is important that meetings are held in non-threatening environments. If people from a variety of organizations or departments are meeting, it is often best that this be on neutral territory. The room and seating arrangements will make a difference to the outcome of the meeting. A round or oval table is better for problem-solving and group discussion; participants should be comfortably seated in a business-like manner with room to move and ability to see clearly all members. There should be no noise distractions or interruptions although, in the case of long meetings, breaks should be scheduled with refreshments of non-alcoholic beverages. The size of the room should give the impression of being comfortably full but not crowded. Too large premises will be threatening and stifle discussion. Attention should be given to seating arrangements so that people likely to be in conflict or confrontation with each other are not placed opposite each other.

COMMUNICATION AND CORPORATE CULTURE

The corporate culture of an organization is a consequence of the communication processes within it. The culture is learnt and maintained through the interaction of the people in the organization. People interact by exchanging words, tones and pitches and non-verbal behaviours such as gestures, appearances, postures and special relationships. These interactions form patterns which, after repeated use, become accepted as norms and values. Meaningful behaviour patterns are passed on to others through modelling, instruction, correction and their wish to comply with norms.

Cultures are also sustained and transmitted through the communication processes of languages, storytelling about the heroes and villains of the library's past, and through rituals and ceremonies. Managers consciously and unconsciously signal values and goals to library staff through statements, metaphors and physical symbols. Logos represent company symbols and communicate values created specifically for employees and customers. Employees identify with the symbols and feel an integral part of the organization.

The consolidation of all cultural forms is to be found in rites and ceremonies. In performing the activities of rites or ceremonies, people make use of other cultural forms - customary language, gestures, ritualized behaviours, artifacts and settings. This heightens the expression of shared meanings appropriate to the occasion. Events such as receptions, annual dinners, board meetings, Christmas functions, retirement functions, award presentations, professional conferences, are rites in which the corporate culture is displayed. They are efficient and effective methods of communicating and instilling beliefs into an organization.

Corporate stories, legends, slogans, anecdotes, myths and fairytales are all important as they convey the library's or information centre's shared values. Anecdotes and stories provide the opportunity for people to share their experiences. The significant stories are those told by many people. These are the ones which are active in the cultural network and which provide evidence of the corporate culture.

Stories of 'heroes and villains' will provide an insight into corporate values and the personal qualities of employees who are likely to be successful or unsuccessful. The attributes of those heroes who are in high esteem will emulate those qualities likely to be found in successful employees of the library or information centre. 'Villains and outlaws' are those whose values or attributes were opposed to those of the library or information centre. They provide the corporate guidance of 'what not to do'. Villains are remembered long after they have left the organization for their 'sins'. They are the outlaws.

Communication rules are also part of the corporate culture of a library or information centre. These are tacit understandings about appropriate ways to interact with others in given roles and situations. They are generally unwritten and unspoken. As prescriptions for behaviour, they function to coordinate, interpret and justify interactive behaviour and act as self-monitoring devices. They provide guidelines as to what is acceptable interactive behaviour within the library or information centre.

BARRIERS TO COMMUNICATION

The existence of various avenues or media for communicating does not always ensure that communication will take place. The communication process may fail for a number of reasons.

A major barrier in communication is that no two individuals are alike. Individuals have different perceptions of people and situations which are governed by their past experiences, values, knowledge, attitudes, expectations and self-image. This may result in an inability to build a two-way communication process.

There will also be differences in listening abilities, which will be coloured by natural tendencies to judge and evaluate both what is

187

being said and the person saying it. This will lead to differences in interpretation of the message.

Often there is a lack of distinction between information and communication and a lack of clarity as to who needs the information. Relevant information may not be able to be synthesized due to the overabundance of irrelevant information. Being over-informed is as inhibiting as being underinformed.

Problems may be oversimplified in the message or deliberately generalized, distorted, or omitted. Alternatively, the receiver may be insensitive to the problems expressed in the message and so not listen properly to what is being said.

REFERENCES

Lippitt, G.L. (1982), *Organizational Renewal: a holistic approach to organization development* (2nd edn.), (Englewood Cliffs, N.J.: Prentice Hall).

Mathews, A.J. (1983), *Communicate: a librarian's guide to inter-personal communications* (Chicago: American Library Association).

Mintzberg, H. (1973), *The nature of managerial work* (New York: Harper and Row).

PART V
STRATEGIES FOR TECHNICAL EFFECTIVENESS

Introduction

In this section, the reader is introduced to various issues which relate to the management of technology in libraries and information centres and its impact upon human resources and organizations generally. Technology is an all-embracing term covering the equipment, knowledge, systems and methods used in transforming inputs to outputs. Therefore, all of these aspects are considered in this section.

Management procedures for the systems analysis, design, tendering, evaluation and installation of library automation systems have been deliberately omitted from this text as it is felt that these topics are more than adequately covered elsewhere in the literature. However, a list of recommended texts on the topic of library automated systems has been included in the reading list relating to this section.

Chapter 12 introduces the reader to the issues which arise out of the use of technology in libraries and information centres. Particular attention is paid to the issues which arise out of the introduction of information technology, a part of which includes library automation systems. To many people, the word 'technology' immediately encapsulates an image of a computer screen; however, as previously mentioned, the definition of technology is far more extensive. It is therefore important that, in addition to planning for information technology, attention is also paid to the planning of library sites, internal layout, job design, library operations, capacities and quality control, as these all influence the transformation processes.

Joan Woodward found that the correct assimilation of organization structure, leadership style, tasks and personal relationships with certain types of production technologies led to successful organizations. The concept of production technologies can be related to the characteristics of the various departments within libraries. Readers may find that some of Woodward's findings can be used to successfully manage the individual characteristics of departments within libraries.

Success in the use of technology is influenced by, and also influences, the corporate culture of the library or information centre. Different types of libraries emphasize the importance of different tasks, which in turn affect the values which pervade the library. In addition, information technology can affect an organization's corporate culture. These matters are also considered in Chapter 12.

Chapter 13 introduces the reader to concepts of task differentiation and its influence upon individual and group values which can in turn lead to conflict. It is often a source of puzzlement why librarians and other people with a professional background have particular difficulties in dealing with treasurers or administrators within their organization. This chapter attempts to explain the basis for some of these differences. An understanding of these can help to reassure the librarian that some of the difficulties which they encounter are based upon values and professional ethics rather than personal dislike for the other person.

Finally, Chapter 14 deals with management information systems. A management information system is an important tool for any library or information centre. Such a system need not be an automated one; a manual system can well satisfy the need of a small library or information centre. Management information systems assist the library in maintaining its competitive advantage and can be used to monitor the performance of the library or information centre.

12 Managing technologies in libraries and information centres

INTRODUCTION

Technology comprises the tools, equipment, knowledge, systems and methods used in transforming materials and other inputs needed by libraries into outputs as finished products or services. Technology can be subdivided into material and non-material technologies. Material technologies refer to tangible implements such as CD-ROM technology; hardware, software and peripheral devices associated with integrated library automation systems; other personal computer applications such as spreadsheets, word-processing, etc; binding machines and other tools and equipment. Non-material technologies pertain to knowledge, skills, processes, education and methods.

As libraries and information centres deal mainly with information, the majority of their technical applications will be in the collection, handling, storage and dissemination of information, or information technology.

Planning for information technology requires a systematic approach and is part of the strategic planning process. Such a process requires the support and involvement of both top management and the users. Increasingly, the information technology planning process is integrated with the corporate planning process. This arises out of an awareness that information is a valuable organization resource which can assist in the formation of value-added services and help the library or information centre to survive in a changing environment.

Different technologies are used in different types of libraries and different departments within libraries and information centres. This affects their management styles, organization structures, control and communication systems and procedures. Technology also affects the corporate culture and value system. Different values will be attached to different technologies. This will affect staff selection, staff training, task emphasis and budget allocations.

EFFECT OF TECHNOLOGY ON THE LIBRARY

The introduction of modern technologies, particularly information technologies, has had far-reaching effects upon organizations such as libraries and information centres. The rate of technological change is likely to increase still further in the future so it is important that library and information centre managers are aware of the impact of the technologies upon their organization. In addition, they must develop the skills to manage the opportunities and threats presented by these technologies. The management of technology is not a specialized task for technical experts. It is a top-level management task as it affects a very broad range of personnel and requires high-level decision-making to ensure its effective use.

Information technology provides for the creation of new job opportunities and job enrichment for some, and retrenchment and fear for others. The introduction of integrated library automation systems and other information technologies have created shifts in demand for certain categories of skills, and shifts in the job emphasis of certain levels of staff. There is a growing demand for library staff with information technology management skills. Whilst some staff have been freed from tedious, repetitive or monotonous tasks and are now generally able to concentrate upon more meaningful tasks, others have found that their tasks have become more unimaginative leading to less job satisfaction. Different management styles may be needed to compensate for these situations.

The introduction of any new technology into a library or information centre can lead to uncertainty and change. Inevitably this creates fears, stress and strain which then lead to industrial problems if they are not correctly managed. Fears of job loss, changing work patterns, loss of personal work relationships through relocation, job re-classification and the need to learn new skills at an advanced age can be reduced through good communication and effective management.

194

Occupational Overuse Syndrome (injuries caused by repetitive actions such as long spells at a keyboard without frequent breaks) and eyestrain are two physical complaints which can occur if proper work scheduling does not take place. Good communication and educational processes which provide increased understanding of their causes will decrease the possibility of their occurrence and alleviate some concerns.

Information technologies create new areas of responsibility for managers. Issues such as the protection and security of data stored on systems and the safeguarding of personal information pertaining to library membership details require consideration. Whilst it is true that this type of information has always been gathered by libraries, the ability to both manipulate and extract data has been made easier and faster by information systems, thus rendering it more vulnerable to wrongful use.

PLANNING FOR TECHNOLOGY

The purpose for the introduction of any new technology should be to assist the library or information centre to achieve its mission statement and corporate goals. This may be accomplished by solving existing problems or by automating existing manual processes which lead to beneficial outcomes such as improved productivity, faster service or staff savings. Above all, the technical operations of a library or information centre should support its corporate plan.

A systematic approach to technological planning, be it information technology or any other technology, should be followed. Those involved in the planning process must have a good understanding of the corporate goals and critical success factors of the library or information centre and how technical strategies can support these. They must also have a clear understanding of the operational processes and/or problems facing their library in order to seek the appropriate technical solutions. The technology plan must be fully justified and approved by top management prior to the commencement of any action which incurs either an organization commitment or an allocation of funds.

195

Information technologies

Emerging technologies, particularly in the field of information technology, mean that a variety of technological applications are available. For example, electronic mail, voice mail, videotex, expert systems, relational databases offer different solutions to different problems. The integration of data, voice and image, together with flexible communications and networks, support a creative approach to information-handling. It is important that all avenues of technology are explored before one particular technological solution is chosen to improve the library's service or solve a problem.

An information technology corporate plan should be produced to complement the library's corporate plan. This plan outlines the facilities, materials, equipment, personnel and strategies needed to provide the library's services. The services, themselves, should be designed to complement the mission and goals of the library or information centre, the service mix being developed through the library's marketing activities.

In producing the information technology corporate plan, a feasibility study should be undertaken to determine the human impact of the new technology on users and staff; the productivity of the proposed processes, resources or equipment; the reliability of supply and operations of the resources and equipment; and the legality and safety of the proposed technology.

The effective use of the planned information technology depends upon the provision of appropriate technical and supervisory training to all potential users and the involvement of those users in the design, development and implementation stages.

Safety is important. It refers not just to the occupational health and safety of employees and other users of the technology, but also to environmental impacts where they might exist. The concept of occupational safety is raised, for example, when a well-known brand of keyboard equipment, thought to be associated with Occupational Overuse Syndrome, is competitively priced. The library or information centre manager must choose between meeting a budget allocation of limited funds and a potential, although not proven, occupational danger to their staff.

In procuring information technologies the library or information centre manager needs to obtain the best quality for the best price

196

or terms of payments. Materials and equipment need to be delivered on schedule and in good condition. Reliability, after-sales service and support are also important. Products may meet *de facto* industry standards but may, or may not, be compatible with the parent organization's technology. This may be important for the library or information centre where compatibility of information systems, such as word processing, is needed for the transfer of documents and reports. Systems should also be user-friendly and adaptable to change to meet emerging requirements.

Library sites

The selection of a site for a library or information centre is one of the most important issues in planning. Often a site for a public library is selected and earmarked many years before the library is opened. In other cases, such as a special library or information centre, the development is a natural occurrence in the growth of an organization, as differentiation and specialization occurs. The selection of a site for a library or information service should take into account its proximity to users and such competitors as other libraries. Access to appropriately qualified human resources, availability of transport, land or leasing costs and community factors need also to be taken into consideration.

Internal layout

The layout of the library or information centre and the technical processes involved have to be planned. In doing so, labour and equipment need to be utilized efficiently, and the movement and handling of materials should be kept to a minimum. Work space should be used sparingly yet efficiently, minimizing potential hazards and danger spots. It is important that the design of the library is kept flexible in order that future requirements for change can be accommodated. Above all, the environment of the library or information centre should be aesthetically appealing, allowing for a high quality of working life. For example, printers should be equipped with acoustic hoods and located away from work areas where concentration is required.

Job design

The design of layouts and technical processes determines how services are produced. Job design fits people to both the technology and the job through a series of tasks. Job design requires that movement from one physical area to another is kept to a minimum; that technical processes follow in a logical sequence; and that output is not delayed through waiting for another process to be completed. Adequate terminals, power outlets, data lines, and so on should be provided to support given tasks.

The right people should fit the job and the organization. The job analysis determines the personal attributes, skills and knowledge required to perform the tasks involved. The corporate culture of the library or information centre will determine the most appropriate personality, values and outlook of individuals to fit the organization and its activities.

Operations

The routine operations of the library or information centre need to be planned. Inventory policies have to be established. In libraries this is achieved through stock selection and other policies which determine what items are purchased and in what format. Demands for services are met by scheduling: for instance, staff are rostered on issue and enquiry desks; morning tea and lunch breaks are scheduled amongst staff; opening hours are determined by considering potential demands for library services at certain times of the day. Operations within the library also need to be scheduled. The tasks of ordering, acquiring, applying a bibliographic description and processing an item for loan must follow one another. This may require coordination between departments.

Capacities

Planning should also take place for capacities. This includes the physical capacity of the library's or information centre's floor or shelf space to hold the required materials in their different formats; the physical and psychological capacity of staff to perform all the necessary tasks; the technological capacity of the equipment, materials, and so on to perform the required functions; and the financial capacity of the library's or information centre's budget to fund the required services.

Quality control

Product and quality controls are needed to determine how the technological, human, information and financial resources are being used. Quality standards need to be determined as well as how they are to be met.

PRODUCTION TECHNOLOGY AND ORGANIZATIONAL DESIGN

Production technologies relate to the methods used in carrying out the various tasks of the library or information centre. They are linked to organizational design in that successful organizations are those in which the structure, leadership style, tasks and personal relationships fit the production technology being used. Different technologies can be found in various types of libraries and within sections or departments of libraries or information centres. This calls for the employment of different management styles, tasks and structures.

The Woodward studies

Joan Woodward (1958) studied 100 manufacturing firms in Britain first-hand to learn how they were organized. She observed their structural characteristics (span of control, levels of management, management and clerical ratios, worker skill level), management style (communication methods, use of sanctions) and type of manufacturing process and related these to the organization's commercial success.

She classified organizations into three groups:

- Group 1   Small batch unit production.
- Group 2   Large batch and mass production
- Group 3   Continuous process production

199

Organizations in Group 1 tended to produce simple units to customers' orders, manufacturing and assembling them to meet specific needs. Custom work is the norm, and the technology relies heavily on the human operator. Predictability of outcome is low. Group 2 organizations are characterized by long production runs of standardized parts, as customers do not have specific needs. Group 3 is an entirely mechanized process. There is no stopping or starting, the process is continuous. The organization has high control over the processes and outcomes are predictable.

Using these classifications, Woodward (1965) was able to show that management levels increased as the technical complexity increased from unit production to continuous process. The span of control, formalized procedures and centralization was high for mass-production technologies but low for other technologies. The management system in unit production and continuous process technologies was organic in nature, whilst in mass production the management system was bureaucratic with standardized jobs and formalized procedures.

Production technologies can be linked to characteristics within libraries or information centres and their departments. Routine technologies such as shelving or issuing items require little education or experience. Non-routine processes, such as those involved in providing a reference or information service, require formal education and job experience. Routine technologies are also characterized by extensive standardization, formalization and a division of labour into small tasks. Most serials acquisitions departments in large libraries will display these qualities. Departments with less routine tasks will have less formal structures and less standardization.

Span of control is influenced by task complexity and professionalism. Highly professional staff require less supervision because this is compensated by their expertise and codes of ethics or responsibilities. The more complex the task the more supervisor involvement is required, which leads to a smaller span of control. Routine tasks require less involvement, and the span of control can be larger.

Communication increases as task variety increases. In routine situations, rules and procedures are used to make decisions; in non-routine procedures discussions are used as part of the decision-

Table 12.1

A framework for fitting technical processes with the managerial and organization structural subsystems

	Large Batch, Mass Production	Small Batch, Unit, Continuous Process
Managerial Subsystem	Autocratic – psychologically distant Fair – distant leader–member relationships Delegation of authority and responsibility Power centralized to management Power and discretion at lower levels – small	Democratic – psychologically close Good leader–member relationships Permissive and participatory management style Power decentralized Lower levels participate in decision-making
Structural Subsystem	Large batch, mass production units Highly centralized, formalized procedures Supervisors control activities Standardized jobs – structured tasks Standardized activities Emphasis on efficiency and quality of output Span of control high Routine technology is characterized by standardization, division of labour into small tasks and formalization	Small batch, unit, continuous process Decentralized, less formalized procedures Unstructured tasks Less formal structures and less standardization Quality of output is important More complex and non-routine tasks – less span of control
	Mechanistic	Organic
	Emphasis on written communication Vertical/written communication Responds to crisis	Emphasis on verbal communication Vertical communication where tasks are less analysable Horizontal communication All issues considered
	Less demand for skilled workers Require little education or experience	High demand for skilled workers Requires qualified staff – formal education and job experience

making process. Coordination also increases as task variety increases.

Library and information centre departments should be designed according to the requirements of Woodward's technologies (Table 12.1). For example, reader services departments may be viewed as utilizing small batch or unit technologies in that each library user or information-seeker is handled on an individual basis. Technical services departments may be regarded as using large batch or mass production technologies as they process a number of items at a time by routine methods. The span of control, management style, communication and control methods should complement the technology being used in the department.

TECHNOLOGY AND CORPORATE CULTURE

Task environment

Different types of libraries serve different markets. Each market operates in a different environment, has different clientele with different needs and time horizons. This causes libraries or information centres to place different emphases upon services. An information centre may place an emphasis upon research and information provision, whilst a public library may wish to emphasize its lending services, its local community information service, or its children's services. These emphases are linked to an internal emphasis on certain tasks, training, the budget and to corporate values.

In the first instance of the information centre, timely and comprehensive information is needed. Much time is spent searching online databases and compact disks for information and arranging the facsimile transmission of articles. Values of speed and accuracy, comprehensiveness and currency of data are incorporated into the information centre's corporate culture. The material technologies comprise facsimile machines and terminals with access to international or national databases and constitute prominent items in the information centre's budget, as they are the means by which demands for service are met.

Staff are given training in online searching and, here, the corporate values of accuracy and comprehensiveness are stressed. The

provision of information becomes a priority task with other maintenance tasks taking second place. Within the maintenance tasks,
those which act as the means by which information can be obtained
quickly are given priority. All staff are aware of what is valued and
where priorities lie and this knowledge is incorporated into their
daily decision-making.

The public library may emphasize its fast issue procedures and
therefore choose an automated library system which will aid this.
Clerical staff are aware that the serving of people on the issue desk
takes priority over some other tasks, such as the shelving of books.
Values of speed and accuracy are attached to these tasks. In terms
of the local community information service or the children's services, professional staff are chosen who have the necessary attributes, skills and expertise to promote and conduct such services.
Values of helpfulness and empathy prevail. Budgetary allocations
may be higher in these areas than in other service areas.

In larger libraries, different values may be seen in different
departments. An acquisitions department may have values of reliability, response times, accuracy and cost savings. Cataloguers may
value comprehensiveness, standards and precision. Reference staff
may value speed, accuracy, helpfulness and empathy. Library and
information centre managers should be aware of these differences
in values or sub-values brought about by the technologies of
different departments and should appoint staff whose attributes and
personality complement the dominant values.

Information technology environment

Information technology can affect the organization's corporate
culture. When personal computers, databases and information
systems are compatible throughout the library or information
centre, users can share information and ways of looking at it. When
each department 'owns' its own system, information is not shared
and subcultures arise: conflicts then develop over rights to ownership of information.

Information is a powerbase. The withdrawal or absence of it can
be used to isolate individuals. Management information systems can
be used to increase the power of selected people in the organization
by giving them access to information that no one else has. Personal

computer systems are particularly prone to allowing individuals to withhold information from others.

Information systems interact with the political environment of the library or information centre to improve or hinder the user's ability to make decisions or change organizational dependencies. The corporate culture can be influenced by who controls the system and who has physical possession of the hardware.

The influence of information technology upon corporate cultures in libraries can best be illustrated by considering the historical development of library automation. Library automation systems were first introduced into libraries to solve specific problems such as the handling of acquisitions. Gradually, more systems were introduced to solve problems associated with circulation or serial control, but these systems still worked in isolation from each other. This perpetuated mechanistic practices as they fostered clear lines of authority and ownership of particular functions. The manager of each department had control over what processes were automated and how they were conducted.

The concept of database management systems cut across organization lines as they shared data. This led to more organic practices being developed in libraries and increased cooperation between departments. The introduction of subject specialization was made possible as staff could be involved in the selection, acquisition, bibliographic control and user services whilst operating from the one computer terminal.

Unrestricted databases and widely available query facilities have also provided the opportunity for system users to interact with other functions within the organization.

Future trends towards networking and information-sharing raise questions about openness and ownership of data. Libraries and information centres whose corporate cultures have organic tendencies are more likely to cooperate in networking arrangements than those whose cultures are more mechanistic or closed.

REFERENCES

Woodward, J. (1958), *Management and Technology* (London HMSO).
Woodward, J. (1965), *Industrial Organisation: theory and practice* (London: Oxford University Press).

13 Managing expertise in libraries and information centres

INTRODUCTION

Larger libraries and information centres are made up of people whose functions and purposes differ widely. There are task differentiations of a clerical, professional and administrative nature, people who plan and those who execute, and differentiation according the subject specialization or the technology involved. In addition, most libraries belong to a much wider organization where further differentiation of both tasks and outlook occurs. An understanding of these differences can be personally reassuring as it assists the librarian or information professional in recognizing the source of much conflict in organizations.

Differentiation is demonstrated in the organization structure and in job descriptions. It is also seen in the social roles of employees, the distribution of power, control and reward systems and the communication process in general. Differentiation leads to the rise of subcultures and the presence of different values not just between departments, but also between different types of staff. It may also lead to intergroup conflict.

DIFFERENTIATION IN ORGANIZATIONS

Values

One major difference in values occurs between professional and administrative staff. Examples of this will often be seen when comparing library staff (clerical and professional) to the administration staff of the organization to which the library belongs.

Professional staff usually place an emphasis on the professional quality of their work, often staying after-hours to complete important tasks. Administrative staff will generally do no more or less than what is required.

The majority of actions and decisions of professional staff are determined by a professional code of ethics, whilst the actions of administrative staff are determined by their role requirements. This will often cause each to view the other party with suspicion as their motives for actions and values will differ.

The task environment

Library and information centre staff usually work as a team and have a strong identity with the library. This is the result of the task structures within libraries, individuals' dependence upon each other to get things done and, often, the physical separation of the library from the office environment. As a result, library staff may be perceived as being 'different' by administrators who work to preserve the organization's hierarchy.

Outlook

By their nature, librarians and information specialists are cosmopolitan people. Their strong sense of professionalism leads them to the view that they are librarians or information professionals working for an organization – that is, they usually have a low identity with any one particular organization as their career development lies within the profession. Administrators are local people. They are primarily organization people, who just happen to be in the role of an administrator. They are trained internally by the organization and judged accordingly, and their career development lies in promotion up the organization's hierarchy. This often leads to conflicts of goals arising between librarians and administrators.

Methods of assessment

The standards of training of librarians and information professionals and their subsequent expertise and competence is set by the library

206

or information service profession. In addition to their judgement by the profession, the librarian or information professional often needs to conform to internal organizational standards. Their annual performance appraisal will be usually based on these standards rather than their professional ones. If the values and norms differ widely between the two, this will place the librarian or information professional in a conflict situation which may affect their motivation.

Culture

Members of the library profession have a culture of their own in that they will use a common language, display symbols such as their diplomas and degrees, and often hold the norms and values of their professional association. The use of certain professional phrases may be threatening to administrators if they are uncertain of their meaning. Likewise, many backroom library tasks, and the terminology used to describe them, differ from those of administrators. This can lead to a misunderstanding of the reasons for certain library tasks and the attitude that librarians are highly-paid people who 'stamp out or read books all day'.

Motivation

The strong sense of identity with the profession leads to other behaviours and attitudes. Motivation is often found in the value of the service rather than in professional gain. This will again differ from that of administrators. Librarians will often require a high degree of freedom and autonomy in their areas of work, due partly to their physical separation from the general office environment and to the nature of their tasks.

Recognition

Recognition of professionalism is often found in the writing of papers for professional journals. This may not be recognized to the same degree by the employing organization where recognition is achieved through the organization's regulations and achievement of its internal goals.

Career development

The differences in outlook between professionals and administrators or non-professionals will have implications for their career development, training and reward systems. The internal career path needs may differ for the professional and for the non-professional or administrator. Usually the only avenues of promotion within organizations are to administrative or managerial positions. This may be contrary to the needs of the professional librarian who will find the additional administrative responsibilities unwelcome. Managers need to arrange for career paths for specialist librarians who wish to continue working in their area of expertise but require recognition and rewards for their achievements.

Because knowledge is a professional librarian's or information specialist's greatest asset, he or she needs to keep up-to-date with professional issues. Their training and staff development requires that they attend courses, conferences and meetings outside of the organization. They may require the organization to fund their attendance at such activities and allow them time to attend.

Reward systems

Reward systems will also differ for professional staff and non-professional or administrative staff. Professional staff are usually motivated by improved work conditions, opportunities for professional contact and autonomy in the workplace, rather than by money or status.

The library or information centre manager should be aware of differences in values between professional staff and administration staff and attempt to explain these differences in order to minimize conflict. Failing the opportunity to do this, the recognition of these differences may help to explain situations which occur from time to time. Within their own staff hierarchy, the library manager should minimize such conflicts through open communication and provide for appropriate career development, staff training and reward systems.

SUMMARY

Differences in value occur between professional and administrative staff through varying work emphases, codes of ethics, tasks, work orientations, training standards, identities and sources of motivation. These affect the way professionals and administrators view each other and have implications for the management of various categories of staff.

14 Management information systems in libraries and information centres

INTRODUCTION

A management information system (MIS) is a set of formalized rules and procedures designed, maintained and used by people with the help of information-processing technology, for the purpose of providing information to fulfil management needs. It provides for decision-making by synthesizing and organizing data.

A management information system captures data and information from many sources internal and external to the organization. This is used to guide and support rapid and effective decision-making. The complexity of the data and/or information included in the management information system will depend upon management's perception of the system and its usefulness.

Decision support systems are higher developments of management information systems. They provide specific answers to management problems through computer simulation and gaming techniques – for instance, the comparison of costs of maintaining an interlibrary loan system versus the cost of buying and processing every item requested.

MANAGEMENT INFORMATION SYSTEMS

A management information system is a single source from which the manager can obtain specific information. It may be described as a collection, storage and presentation system. It provides a single, responsive, automated mechanism for delivering information from multiple sources to the manager in a usable form.

Whilst management information systems operate within the technical subsystem of libraries and information centres, they are relevant to the management functions of communication, decision-making, planning, controlling and measuring the performance of human resources and the operational functions within libraries and information centres.

Typical management information systems establish or enhance control points within technical processes. They provide for control of information which was not previously available and for information-sharing across departments. Often they reduce the time taken to perform certain tasks, allow other tasks to be executed which previously would have been too time-consuming (for example, a 'what if?' analysis), and generally improve the standard of reporting mechanisms.

Attributes of a management information system

To be effective, a management information system should display the attributes listed below.

Accessibility

The management information system should be made available to managers at all levels within the library or information centre. Information stored in the system should be able to be retrieved easily and speedily.

Comprehensiveness

The system should be as comprehensive as possible. However, in reality this will depend upon top management's perception of the usefulness of the information which can be included in such a system. Figure 14.1 illustrates a comprehensive management information system for a public library.

Accuracy

A management information system should contain accurate data.

211

Generally two types of errors occur – errors of transcript and errors of computation.

Appropriateness

In designing the management information system, the information needs of all managers must be considered in order to ensure that the data and information contained in the system is appropriate. A delicate balance between paucity of information and information overload is needed. Irrelevant information is both costly to research, enter and store, and costly in time for the system users who will have to sift through the information at hand in order to identify the appropriate data or information.

Timeliness

Information and data must continually be updated to reflect the latest trends or situation audit. Out-of-date information is inaccurate information and has no place in a management information system.

Clarity

Information should be free from ambiguity. The purpose for, and sources of, the information or data which is stored on the system should be immediately obvious to the user.

Flexibility

Reference has already been made to the fact that the information stored on the system will be used by more than one level of management. The information must therefore be adaptable for use by more than one user.

Verifiability

The information contained in a management information system should be able to be verified. Sources of external data should be cited.

212

Freedom from bias

As the information or data contained in the management information system is to be used to facilitate decision-making, it is important that it is free from bias. The information should not be entered or modified after entry in such a way as to influence the users towards a particular course of action.

Quantifiability

A management information system should only contain data or information which has been obtained through formal communication channels and can therefore be suitably verified. It should not contain information which has been obtained through informal communication channels such as *ad hoc* telephone conversations or rumours.

Classifications of management information systems

The information or data contained in management information systems can generally be classified according to function and time-scale. This is demonstrated in Figure 14.1 where a management information system for a public library has been grouped according to the various functions to be found in a typical public library environment. It should be noted, however, that information produced for one function is often required for several other functions.

The other classification of information is according to timeframe. Information can be classified for historical, control and planning purposes. Information which reflects past periods and is used for comparative purposes or to provide background information is classified as historical information. Control information reflects the current period and is likely to be used at the operational level to determine performance and provide for decision-making on operational issues. Planning information is used for strategic management purposes and relates to possible future trends. This type of information is more likely to be used in decision-making by top management.

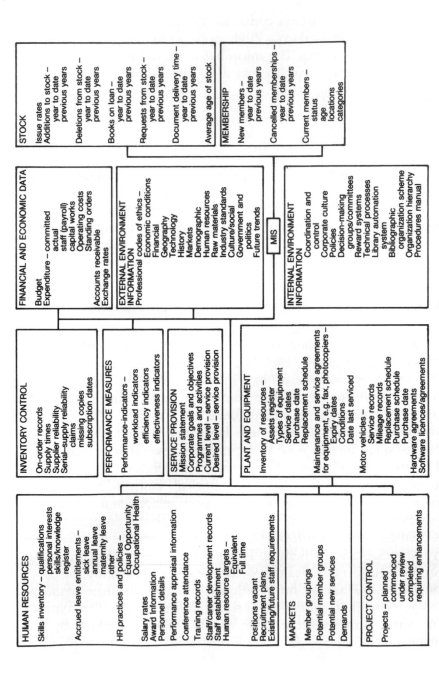

STOCK

Issue rates
Additions to stock –
  year to date
  previous years
Deletions from stock –
  year to date
  previous years

Books on loan –
  year to date
  previous years

Requests from stock –
  year to date
  previous years

Document delivery time –
  year to date
  previous years

Average age of stock

MEMBERSHIP

New members –
  year to date
  previous years

Cancelled memberships –
  year to date
  previous years

Current members –
  status
  age
  locations
  categories

FINANCIAL AND ECONOMIC DATA

Budget
Expenditure – committed
  actual
  staff (payroll)
  capital works
  Operating costs
  Standing orders
Accounts receivable
Exchange rates

EXTERNAL ENVIRONMENT INFORMATION

Professional codes of ethics –
  Economic conditions
  Financial
  Geography
  Technology
  History
  Markets
  Demographic
  Human resources
  Raw materials
  Industry standards
  Culture/social
  Government and
  politics
  Future trends

INTERNAL ENVIRONMENT INFORMATION

Coordination and
  control
Corporate culture
Policies
Decision-making
  groups/committees
Reward systems
Technical processes
Library automation
  system
Bibliographic
  organization scheme
Organization hierarchy
Procedures manual

MIS

INVENTORY CONTROL

On-order records
Supply times
Supplier reliability
Serial–supply reliability
  claims
  missing copies
  subscription dates

PERFORMANCE MEASURES

Performance-indicators –
  workload indicators
  efficiency indicators
  effectiveness indicators

SERVICE PROVISION

Mission statement
Corporate goals and objectives
Programmes and activities
Current level – service provision
Desired level – service provision

PLANT AND EQUIPMENT

Inventory of resources –
  Assets register
  Types of equipment
  Service dates
  Purchase date
  Replacement schedule

Maintenance and service agreements
for equipment, e.g. fax, photocopiers –
  Expiry dates
  Conditions
  Date last serviced

Motor vehicles –
  Service records
  Mileage records
  Replacement schedule
  Purchase schedule
  Purchase date
Hardware agreements
Software licences/agreements

HUMAN RESOURCES

Skills inventory – qualifications
  personal interests
  skills/knowledge
  register

Accrued leave entitlements –
  sick leave
  annual leave
  maternity leave
  other

HR practices and policies –
  Equal Opportunity
  Occupational Health

Salary rates
Award information
Personnel details

Performance appraisal information

Conference attendance

Training records

Staff/career development records
Staff establishment
Human resource targets –
  Equivalent
  Full time

Positions vacant
Recruitment plans
Existing/future staff requirements

MARKETS

Member groupings
Potential member groups
Potential new services
Demands

PROJECT CONTROL

Projects – planned
  commenced
  under review
  completed
  requiring enhancements

Figure 14.1   A management information system for a public library

Uses of management information systems in libraries

An important use of a management information system is to provide information which assists in the evaluation of the performance of the library or information centre. Evaluation processes rely upon management having accurate and timely information about programme inputs and outputs.

A management information system can be used to provide supporting information to determine:

1. efficiency: is the library doing things right?
2. effectiveness: is the library doing the right things?
3. competitiveness: is the library heading in a direction which is consistent with the environment (that is, does the library have a strategy, and is it certain that it is the correct one)?

Data, identified in the form of a performance indicator can be collected from various sources, stored in the management information system and used to verify performance of the library or information centre.

It could be stated that the effective and efficient provision of library services for the user is very much related to the internal performance of the organization's resources. To illustrate the use of a management information system in monitoring the performance of resources, the following examples are chosen from the human resource module of the management information system:

A library's output performance is directly related to the motivation and performance of its human resources. A high staff turnover rate which is monitored by the management information system and identified as occurring in a particular department or in a particular category of staff can indicate poor performance on the part of the employer. A high turnover rate of clerical staff may indicate that the management practices do not assist in providing for career progression or personal development and/or training opportunities.

Staff who suffer from poor esteem are unlikely to be creative or resourceful in their work and, as a result, the performance of the library with suffer. Conversely, a highly motivated staff will challenge existing ideas and systems for the betterment of the service, provide new strategies to provide competitive advantage and find

215

ways of creating value-added services out of existing routines. Through the identification of poor human resource management, corrective measures may be taken which will in turn improve the library's output performance.

Management information systems facilitate the collection of data from one source which can then be used for other purposes. Performance appraisals are not just annual opportunities to praise or reward good performance, to correct faults or to identify areas for personal development and training; they serve other functions which are often overlooked. The annual performance appraisal provides the opportunity to identify the organization's underlying subcultures and to determine individuals' values and beliefs. If this information is entered into the management information system and subsequently analysed, subcultures which undermine the chosen corporate culture can be identified and measures taken to correct the situation.

Staff training and development is critical to a library's performance. Emerging and existing needs should be logged in the management information system and attendance at conferences monitored against these. Particular areas to pay attention to are areas of overintensity or inbalance of training (both at subject level and make-up of staff – that is, professional versus support staff). The library's critical success factors should also be monitored against content of the training sessions to ensure that these are covered.

By providing the means to collect, store and manipulate information, management information systems can be used to identify issues and provide necessary input to facilitate effective decision-making.

DECISION SUPPORT SYSTEMS

Decision support systems focus attention on key decisions and decision-making tasks, with the specific aim of improving the effectiveness of the library manager's problem solving processes. All management decision-making should be logged in a decision support system which defines each problem as it was perceived, the information known at the time, the commonly held assumptions, some debatable issues, and the final decision.

Information in the decision support system should be retrievable

216

in as many ways as possible to facilitate faster and better decision-making in the future. A secondary outcome of extensive facilities for the retrieving of information will be that middle-level managers will better understand the reasons for decision-making if they have access to information about the processes involved.

Decision support systems are used at strategic management level. They do not generate monthly reports, but look at macro-level decision-making needs. For example, they can be used to determine the level of the following year's budget, or to support decision-making for determining the future direction of library services.

PART VI
STRATEGIES FOR MANAGING
THE PSYCHOSOCIAL ENVIRONMENT

Introduction

The psychosocial environment consists of the interpersonal relationships which exist in organizations. Successful organizations are those in which there are positive relationships between, and within, all its levels. This section aims to provide background information to the dynamics of interpersonal relationships and some means by which a positive psychosocial environment can be fostered within a library or information centre.

Within any organization, groups are formed. These do not necessarily have to be formalized; informal groups of people will form naturally, emerging out of some aspect of common interest. Chapter 15 introduces the reader to the concept of group dynamics.

The ability to understand the underlying purposes for the formation of different groups, together with the processes associated with the formation of such groups, will assist the library manager to recognize affiliations between individuals which may either be constructive or destructive for the library.

A second purpose for understanding the stages of group development is that each stage needs to be managed very differently. The introduction of any new project or programme will most likely result in the formation of a new group to serve in some capacity. An understanding of how to manage the stages of group development can enable the project to progress more smoothly.

A knowledge of group norms, member roles and group cohesiveness will assist in the understanding of the complex process of interpersonal dynamics, and sometimes provide a rational explanation for what can seem to be perplexing behaviour between individuals.

Most people will have been subjected to power, influence and authority in the course of their work or studies. However, it is sometimes difficult to establish how or why certain powers are more influential than others. An understanding of the uses of power is important for even if a librarian is not in a position to exert much power himself, he or she should be aware of the use of power by others, particularly when it directly affects him or her. Chapter 16 describes five different bases of power, some of which can be derived from position, whilst others are from personal

221

sources. The uses of these powerbases in libraries and information centres is discussed.

There are also many ways in which influence can be used within organizations and in personal relationships. Some are more effective than others in particular situations. The effective use of different types of influence in library or information centre situations is also discussed in Chapter 16.

Finally, the topics of authority and delegation are introduced. Many people are confused by the concept of authority as it may not always be accepted. Its acceptance is governed by such factors as leadership, situation, expertise and compliance. The bases for authority and delegation are described in order to provide the reader with a better understanding of how they can be used effectively.

Chapter 17 provides the reader with some strategies for personal networking and an understanding of organizational politics. Library and information centre managers are going to become involved in organizational politics even if it is at a passive or observation level. Organizational politics sometimes affects decision-making processes and an awareness of political groups and/or alignments within the organization will help to provide an understanding of why certain events occur.

Political behaviour within organizations is an expression of personal or group power and influence. Political behaviour always occurs for a reason, be it to further personal or departmental gain, as a protection from others or simply to exercise power. Most of the strategies which are used are ethical, but inevitably there are occasions when they are not. Chapter 17 describes several political tactics (both ethical and unethical) which are used in organizations.

In order to be an effective manager, the librarian or information professional must create networks both internal and external to their parent organization. These networks will allow the librarian to establish alliances with key people who will be important for their personal career development and in undertaking their duties at work. Belonging to the right network within the parent organization opens 'doors' and can provide much needed support at crucial times such as budget allocation time or when critical decisions need to be made. Networks maintained outside of the work organization can provide valuable external information for decision-making and contacts for interlibrary cooperation and so on. There is a section on how to establish networks and a description on the different types of networks which can be found in the organizational context.

Political arguments on matters which affect the library or information centre sometimes have to be presented on paper in the form of a report to the executive decision-making committee. In many instances, the librarian will not have the opportunity to attend these meetings to reinforce verbally the contents of the report, so their act of persuasion will be in the report itself and in the prior lobbying of key people with the potential to lend support for their cause at the decision-making meeting. Chapter 17 briefly describes how to present arguments on paper and how to lobby effectively.

Negotiating is a process which is used to reach a common agreement on matters where there are both common and conflicting goals. Chapter 18 considers different strategies which can be used for effective negotiation on matters which affect the library and its staff. The various negotiating stages are described and ideas are presented to assist in successful negotiation practices. As negotiation is related to personal interests, problems inevitably arise. The reasons for these problems occuring are described and solutions given as to how they can be overcome.

Chapter 19 introduces the reader to the topic of leadership, which is important in any organization. Not all managers are leaders and there are leaders who are not managers. Leaders have to be in possession of certain skills and use them effectively. The use of these skills in the context of libraries and information centres is described. Also described are several leadership theories to provide the reader with some background information to the concept of leadership.

The topic of motivation is considered in Chapter 20. A successful library or information centre manager is able to motivate his or her staff and is one measure of a manager's performance as a leader. However, managers will only be able to motivate their staff where the staff perceive that their individual efforts will lead to personal gain or positive outcomes. Motivation is a complex issue and, as such, has been explained by a variety of theories. Some of the more popular theories are considered in this chapter.

Conflict is a natural occurrence in any organization. Whilst it can be destructive if not handled correctly, conflict is usually a healthy sign of competition. There are many reasons for its occurrence and these are explored in Chapter 21.

Conflict may also arise at a personal level which may or may not be related to the work environment. The library or information centre needs to be aware of when to step in to help resolve the conflict in these situations so that the self-esteem and/or privacy of the individual is maintained. Personal conflict may not be immediately obvious to the manager; although, often, the individual will react out of character. Several symptoms of inner conflict are described in Chapter 21 to alert

223

the library or information centre manager to the potential existence of personal conflict amongst their employees.

Finally, the processes for managing and resolving conflict are described, together with interpersonal conflict management styles.

The final chapter in this section on psychosocial environment within organizations deals with the topic of managing stress. Stress is the human system's response in adjusting to demands or life events and is not harmful until it becomes constant or excessive. The topic of stress management is increasingly being seen as an important issue within organizations. One reason for this is that vulnerability to the negative effects of stress differs widely between individuals. A better understanding of the sources of stress can help reduce employee absenteeism and increase productivity, as well as provide for an enhanced quality of working life.

Vulnerability to stress also changes according to events, moods, experiences and age. These concepts are all explored in order to increase the library manager's understanding of the topic and so help reduce their own and their staff's vulnerability to the negative effects of stress. Potential stress factors in the workplace are described. The chapter also considers some strategies which can be used to control stress arising from both organizational and personal demands.

15 Group dynamics

INTRODUCTION

A group is a collection of people who regularly interact with one another over time in the pursuit of one or more common goals or purposes. There are four basic components of a group: a group needs at least two people to exist; the individuals must interact regularly in order to maintain the group; all group members must have a common goal or purpose; and there should be a stable structure.

A collection of people waiting to have their books and other items checked out at the issue desk is not a group even if their common purpose at the time is to borrow materials from the library. People must interact and influence each other in some way to be considered a group. However, social interaction is not the only characteristic needed to form a group. If the same collection of people become hostile after waiting five minutes at the issue desk whilst the clerk on the desk chats to an acquaintance on the telephone, their interaction with each other by way of comments and non-verbal communication such as raised eyebrows or hands on hips constitutes social interaction in an attempt to collectively rectify the situation. However, the lack of a stable structure finally determines that this is not a group as it is doubtful whether all the members of the queue would ever meet again. In the unlikely event that the members of the library forming the queue then formed themselves into a protest committee, to protest about the lack of service in the library, to the parent organization at some later date, this would constitute a group as all the four conditions would be met.

Groups appear both formally and informally within libraries, information centres and their parent organizations. The organization hierarchy will determine the make-up of the formal work groups, whilst other formal groups will be formed on a task group basis. Groups will also form within organizations on an informal basis, related to individual psychological need, activities and interests.

Groups develop through a four-stage process of forming, storming, norming and performing. As they develop, they assume the characteristics of group cohesiveness, group norms and member roles. Each are important and need to be expertly managed as they can either be productive or destructive to the library or information centre.

Intergroup conflict can be a necessary activity within a library or information centre. However, if it begins to have adverse affects upon the organization as a whole, steps should be taken to minimize or remove it.

TYPES OF GROUPS IN ORGANIZATIONS

Groups appear in various forms within organizations. There are

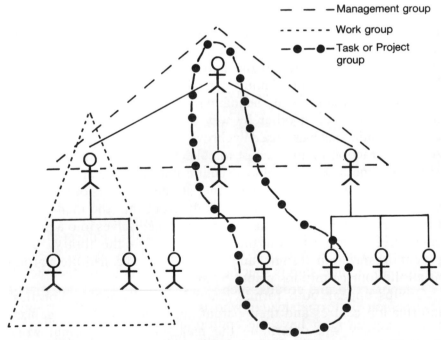

Figure 15.1   The organization as an interlocking network of formal groups

226

formal and informal groups, psychological groups, work groups and task groups.

Formal groups

Formal groups are created by the organization to accomplish a number of tasks within an indefinite or definite timescale. They are to some extent determined by the organizational chart and may comprise work groups consisting of the library manager or information professional and their immediate subordinates or project groups designed for a specific purpose. Formal groups are created through formal authority for a purpose. They have clearly distinguishable superior–subordinate relationships and are often identified on the formal organization chart as branch libraries, departments or divisions, the branch librarian, departmental or divisional head being formally designated as the leader of the permanent work group. (Figure 15.1).

Work groups

Work groups are the most recognized form of formal groups. They are functional groups in that they perform a number of functions for purposes specified by the organization. Work groups remain in existence after they achieve their current objectives, and they are the formal groups which operate as a department or branch library.

Task groups

Task groups are created by the library or information centre to accomplish a relatively narrow range of purposes within a stated or implied timescale. They are formal groups with a 'sunset clause'. *Ad hoc* committees and task forces are examples of task groups. The group membership is specified by the library's management.

Temporary formal groups, such as task forces, have a designated chairperson or formal leader who is accountable for the results. Such a person must have the appropriate interpersonal skills and be prepared to accept responsibility. Like the permanent group head they should review progress at regular intervals and provide

227

performance feedback to members of the group. The fact that they are not a designated formal head of a department does not excuse them from being prepared for the work which needs to be accomplished.

Management groups

In most libraries and information centres there will also be a management group consisting of top and mid-level management who will be involved with long-range planning and policy-setting within the library itself. Such an example would be the principal librarian and the heads of technical services, readers' services and administration sections. The mid-level manager then forms the link between the management group and the work group at the operational level, as he or she belongs to both groups.

Informal groups

Informal or interest groups exist for purposes which may or may not be relevant to the organization. These groups emerge within

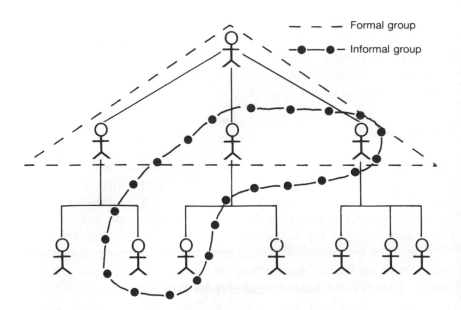

Figure 15.2 Formal and informal groups existing in organizations

organizations without being formally designated by someone in authority for a specific purpose. Each member chooses to participate without being told to do so. The activities of the group may or may not match those of the organization. Informal groups can be a powerful organizational force with which the library or information centre manager must contend (Figure 15.2).

Informal groups can coexist with formal groups in an attempt to overcome bureaucratic tendencies and to foster networks of interpersonal relationships which aid workflows in ways that formal lines of authority fail to provide. They also help individuals satisfy needs which are left unmet or thwarted by formal group affiliations.

By paying attention to the formation of informal groups and understanding the support mechanisms which they provide, library managers may identify certain security or affiliation systems missing in the formal structure. The identification of informal group leaders may provide valuable insight into the politics and leadership existing within the organization. Once identified, library managers may be able to channel the activities of informal group leaders presently working against organizational policies into creative, positive outcomes.

Psychological groups

Psychological groups occur where members are aware of one another's needs and potential resource contributions. Informal groups can usually be classed as psychological groups, but this is not always the case for formal groups. Often at the first meeting of a library task group the members may not be aware of the potential of the other members and where their expertise and values are shared. Members may be aloof until they become aware of some shared meanings and each other's needs. As they become aware of each other, they grow into a psychological group achieving high levels of interaction and mutual identification in pursuit of a common purpose.

INVOLVEMENT OF MANAGEMENT IN GROUPS

Managers can be involved in groups in different capacities – maybe

229

as ordinary members or leaders of a formal group. They can also be part of an informal group network. As leaders they can play the role of a supervisor or a chairperson.

STAGES OF GROUP DEVELOPMENT

Groups will function in libraries and information centres for a number of reasons. The organization will create formal groups such as work groups and task groups to accomplish the corporate goals and objectives. Upon commencing employment with a library or information centre, employees are allocated to a work group, which may comprise the library staff or, if it is a one-man-band, the librarian will belong to a larger work group. Individuals will volunteer or be co-opted to serve on *ad hoc* committees and task forces.

Individuals will also join psychological or informal groups. The reasons for doing this include interpersonal attraction, an interest in the group's activities, such as sport or chess, or an interest in the group's goals, such as environmental conservation.

After a group has been created, either formally by the organization or by group members, it will spend much time developing. There are four stages of group development: forming, storming, norming and performing.

The forming stage

The forming stage occurs as individual members of the group become acquainted with each other and begin to test which interpersonal behaviours are acceptable and which are not. Group boundaries and group rules are defined. The real task of the group is clarified.

The storming stage

The second stage (storming) is usually highly emotional involving high tension among members and periods of hostility and infighting. Each member wishes to retain their individuality and may resist the structure which is emerging. Interpersonal styles are clarified and

230

negotiations take place in an effort to find ways of accomplishing group goals whilst satisfying individual needs. Gradually a group leader emerges. Attention is paid to items which prevent the group's goals from being met.

The norming stage

The third stage (norming) begins the integration process. Each person begins to recognize and accept his or her role and those of others. The group becomes more cohesive, adopting group norms which serve to regulate individual behaviour in order to achieve the group's goals. The group begins to be coordinated and teamwork emerges. A leader is selected, harmony is emphasized and minority viewpoints are discouraged.

The performing stage

Performing is the final stage of group development. The group is totally integrated and is able to focus on the situation at hand. It functions well and can deal with complex tasks through the interaction which occurs. The structure is stable and members work as one unit.

These stages do not occur as discrete steps but are usually quite discernible because of their distinct activities.

GROUP CHARACTERISTICS

As groups develop they assume certain characteristics. These can be described as group norms, member roles and group cohesiveness.

Group norms

Group norms are standards of behaviour which the group adapts for its members. They are informal rules which enhance the group's structure and reinforce a certain degree of conformity among group members. Norms differ from organizational rules in that they are not written. They are subtle standards which exist and regulate group behaviour.

Group norms are established during the third stage of group development. They are created through a series of actions by members of a group and the other members' responses as a group. The way in which the responses are made provide the basis for the norm. The norms which produce outcomes where success is greatest are those which survive. The norms are reinforced through their successes in positive problem-solving and in integration. Gradually there becomes an assumption that, if a norm is followed, success will result, and so norms are followed unconsciously.

Norms help groups avoid chaos and influence their performance. For instance, in libraries or information centres, performance norms can be identified as honesty, pride of work or professionalism. A performance norm is a key characteristic of a work group and may have either a positive or negative influence on both the group's and the library's productivity. Library and information centre managers should be aware of the norms operating in their work groups and try to introduce positive, productive performance norms. Positive performance norms can be achieved by rewarding desired behaviours; by training and orienting new employees to adopt the desired behaviours; by recruiting employees who appear to have the desired attributes and behaviours; and by monitoring performance and providing feedback regarding the desired behaviours.

Member roles

The individuals within each group maintain different roles. A role is a typical behaviour which characterizes a person in a social context. As groups develop, the various group members will play different roles in the social structure of the group. This is known as role differentiation.

There are several terms which are used to describe various roles. An expected role is that which the other members of the group expect from an individual. The perceived role is what the individual perceives the role to mean. The enacted role is what the individual actually does in the role. This then further influences the expected role. By rights, these three roles should be congruent; this is not, however, always the case.

232

Role ambiguity

Role ambiguity results when there is some uncertainty in the minds of either an individual or members of the group as to precisely what their role is at any given time. If an individual's conception of his or her role is unclear this can lead to role ambiguity even if this is clear to others. The use of job descriptions in libraries and information centres helps to overcome role ambiguity in an organizational sense.

Role conflict

Role conflict occurs when the appropriate behaviours for enacting a role may be inconsistent with the appropriate behaviours for enacting either another role or other requirements of the same role. The expectations of each role may be quite clear and the expectations be compatible for each role, but the roles themselves may be in conflict. Role conflict is generally categorized into two varieties. Interrole conflict is found where there are incompatible demands of two or more different roles being played by the same person. The need for the librarian to act as an administrator and positively consider the issue of privatization may cause a role conflict. The second variety of role conflict may be found in an intrarole conflict. In this case, contradictory demands within a single role are received by an individual. Such an example may occur where the chief librarian may instruct the branch librarians to cancel all storytelling sessions as a result of a council resolution. The branch librarians would argue that as the storytelling session had educational value beyond the interaction or recreational role, and that the chief librarian should get the resolution overturned.

Person–role conflict occurs where a person is asked to fulfil a requirement which is against their personal values, attitudes or needs. Such an example may be where the librarian must avoid acting as a censor and so is forced to stock material which is in conflict with some very strong personal views.

Role conflicts may sometimes be eased by reducing the importance of one of the roles, or by compartmentalizing the two roles so that they do not overlap. This is important as role conflict has been linked to stress, rapid employee turnover and poor performance.

Role overload

Role overload occurs when expectations for the role exceed the individual's capabilities. Individuals are required to perform more roles – say, as a decision-maker, as an information disseminator, as a negotiator and as a peace-maker – than they originally envisaged or have the capacity for. Role overload should not be confused with work overload.

Role underload

Role underload occurs when an individual feels that they have the capacity to handle a bigger role or greater set of roles than is assigned to them. Role underload may be overcome by assigning additional roles or by delegating tasks and responsibilities.

Both role overload and role underload can be the outcome of a position being filled by someone who was incorrectly advised about the job at the interview. An unrealistic assessment of a position during the interview situation may lead to role overload or role underload and its subsequent job disenchantment, dissatifaction, poor performance and a high staff turnover.

Group cohesiveness

Group cohesiveness is the extent to which members of the group are attracted to each other and to the group as a whole. Highly cohesive groups are those in which members are attracted to each other, accept the group's goals and help work toward meeting them. Cohesion is likely to be higher in groups where members share similar attitudes, socioeconomic backgrounds and needs. Small library work groups are usually cohesive because they share common professional values and attitudes.

Not all cohesive groups are productive for the organization. Some groups can do considerable harm if their goals are contrary to those of the parent organization. However, where groups are closely knit and have supportive management, their productivity is increased. Library and information centre managers should increase or decrease their work group's cohesiveness according to whether they

234

are productive or harmful. Group cohesiveness can be increased through intergroup competition, through personal attraction amongst those of the group, by rewarding the group rather than the individuals, by frequent interaction and by agreement on the group's goals. Group cohesiveness can be decreased by competition within the group or by the domination of one party, by disagreement on the group's goals and by group size.

GROUP SIZE

As the size of the group increases, the number of possible relationships between its members increases. This leads to the need for increased communication and coordination amongst the group members. It also leads to the development of subgroups which may be damaging to the overall group's cohesiveness and its associated productivity. Smaller groups enable members to interact more frequently and increases their cohesiveness. The optimum number for a group is five people.

INTERGROUP CONFLICT

Intergroup conflict occurs when members of a group perceive that they are being prevented from achieving their group goals by the actions of another group. Most intergroup conflict occurs in organizations between departments. For example, library staff may feel that they are prevented from giving a good service to members because of requirements by the finance or treasury department that all fines and charges are documented in a very time-consuming fashion.

Conflict may also occur between hierarchical levels over issues of power, authority and control. Proposed takeovers or mergers of departments will lead to conflict on both a hierarchical basis and on a horizontal basis for power and control.

Due to the differences in technologies, values, work tasks and subordinate attributes of departments within large libraries, some interdepartmental conflict or rivalry will be ongoing. Such conflict will be productive by increasing group cohesiveness and output and

235

is a necessary part of subcultures within organizations. However, when conflicts emerge above the subculture level and become destructive managerial action should be taken.

In a major conflict situation, the cohesiveness of each department will increase, whilst communication between the conflicting departments will tend to decrease. The group which loses the conflict will find that it will also lose its cohesiveness. It is advantageous that, with a major conflict involving departments, the issues are resolved quickly and in a way that each party gains or a win–win situation. This can be achieved by setting a superordinate goal – that is, one which has to be achieved by the cooperation of both groups or by skilful negotiation.

16 Power, influence, authority and delegation

INTRODUCTION

Power, influence and authority are behavioural processes which allow managers to achieve their goals through the actions of others. Power is the ability to influence others, and it is legitimized in authority.

French and Raven (1959) have defined five sources of power: three are derived from organizational sources whilst the other two are derived from personal sources. Reward, coercive and legitimate powers are the three powerbases which are derived from positions within the organization. Expert and referent power sources are personal power sources.

Successful managers have a good understanding of the various power sources and follow a contingent approach in their use. Managers need to use all of their power sources to ensure the cooperation of individuals in order to achieve the organization's goals.

Influence is the behavioural response to the use of power. Several forms of influence based upon the five power sources can be found in libraries and information centres.

Authority is institutionalized power. Library and information centre managers possess official authority based on their position and personal authority based on their expertise. There can also be authority of a situation, where a sequence of events allows an individual to initiate the compliance of a request in circumstances where they would not normally be able to do so.

Authority can be delegated. The delegation process allows the giving of responsibility and authority to others to execute a job. However, the other party is still accountable to the manager for the outcomes. The final responsibility and authority still rests with the manager.

Some managers are reluctant to delegate for a number of reasons. If they fail to delegate, they will often be overloaded with work and unable to perform their most important tasks successfully. Delegation is also a necessary source of staff development and motivation.

POWER

Power is the potential of one unit to influence another in relation to any one or more aspects, such as behaviour or attitude. The exercise of power may precipitate either willing or unwilling, conscious or unconscious compliance.

Power bases

Library and information centre managers derive power from both organizational and individual sources. These are called position power and personal power. French and Raven (1959) have defined five different bases of power:

- Position power   –   reward power
                               –   coercive power
                               –   legitimate power
- Personal power   –   expert power
                               –   referent power

Reward power

Reward power is measured by the extent to which a manager can use extrinsic and intrinsic rewards in order to control others. The most common way of using reward power in libraries or information centres is to offer tangible rewards to subordinates. This is contingent on the subordinates perceiving that the manager has sufficient authority to be able to offer rewards. Requests should also be perceived by subordinates as feasible, proper and ethical, and the incentive sufficiently attractive and at a level which could not be attained by another, less costly, course of action. For instance, if an assistant librarian asked a clerk-typist to work one hour late one night to type a report in exchange for two hours off during the following day, the request would be considered in the light of whether the assistant librarian had the authority to grant the two hours off, or even to ask the clerk to stay behind in the first place; whether the staff roster situation and personal workload made it feasible to have two hours off the next day; whether the activities already planned for that night were of sufficient importance; and whether someone else was available to work late.

Coercive power

Coercive power is the extent to which a manager can deny desired rewards or administer punishments in order to control other people. Effective managers try to avoid coercive power except when absolutely necessary as it is likely to cause resentment and erode their referent power. Subordinates may react to coercion with hostility and aggression. There are some situations where coercion is appropriate such as punishments for the violation of professional ethics. Coercion and punishment are only effective when applied to a small percentage of subordinates.

There are usually other alternatives to the use of coercive power. Subordinates should always be kept fully informed of rules and policies and the penalties for their violation. Work performance should be consistently monitored and corrective action administered promptly. Any warnings should be administered in private and appropriate punishments handed out.

Legitimate power

Legitimate power is the extent to which a manager can use a subordinate's beliefs or values that they have the right to request it and to which the subordinate has the obligation to comply. Legitimate power is found in authority. Legitimate requests are found in a branch librarian directing a library clerk to answer the telephone or in the chief librarian requesting that branch librarians submit their budget papers by the following week. Requests should be made politely, confidently and clearly, with their underlying reasons explained. Formal orders and directions should be given through proper channels of communication; compliance should be insisted upon and verified regularly.

Expert power

Expert power is the ability to control another's behaviour through the possession of knowledge, experience or judgement which the other person does not have, but needs. Most lecturers in library or information studies demonstrate the possession of expert power over their students. However, possession of superior expertise is not sufficient for all managers or lecturers to influence subordinates. It is also necessary for the subordinate to recognize the manager's or lecturer's expertise and perceive them to be a credible source of information. This may be achieved by promoting an image of expertise through the display of diplomas on their office walls; by acting confidently and decisively in a crisis; by keeping informed and informing others by presenting papers at conferences; and by maintaining their own credibility by avoiding threats to the self-esteem of others.

Referent power

Referent power is the ability to control another's behaviour through their wanting to identify with the power source, their admiration of the manager or through their wanting to receive the manager's approval. Role models have referent power as they engender a feeling of personal affection, loyalty and admiration on behalf of the subordinate.

Within libraries or information centres personal loyalty to a manager often develops over a long period of time. A library or information centre manager is likely to have loyal, devoted subordinates if they show consideration for their needs and feelings, and if they treat everyone fairly and equally. Personal interactions with subordinates which reinforce their positive work applications will increase the referent power of the manager.

Counterpower

Power sources can be neutralized by counterpower. Subordinates

240

may influence the manager by exercising a restraint on the manager's use of power. This counterpower of subordinates is often seen in union action where employees engage the services of an outside body to negotiate on their behalf with management. Subordinates will rarely need to use direct threats as modern management techniques stress the use of non-coercive powerbases.

The use of power by managers of libraries or information centres is not restricted to their subordinates. Power and counterpower sources are used with superiors, peers in other sections of the organization, the subordinates of peers, suppliers of resources, library users, the library stakeholders, its competitors, unions and government agencies. Successful managers use the power they develop in their relationships, along with persuasion, to influence people on whom they are dependent to behave in ways that make it possible for the managers to get their jobs done effectively.

Acquiring power

The most common four ways of establishing power in relationships with others are to develop a sense of obligation in others; to build a reputation as an 'expert' in certain matters; to foster others' unconscious identification with them or their ideas; and to maintain the belief that others are dependent upon them. These are examples of referent, expert and position power sources.

Managers who are successful at acquiring power are sensitive to what others consider to be legitimate behaviour in acquiring and using power. They have a good understanding of the various types of power and methods of influence. They are sensitive to the different types of power and their effects on different people. Professional staff, for instance, will be more influenced by expert power than coercive power. Successful managers are aware of the various methods of influence, what each method can accomplish, and the costs and risks involved.

Successful managers follow a contingent approach in their use of power. They develop all types of power to some degree in order that the correct type can be used in the right circumstances. However, restraint and self-control are necessary to ensure that power is not used impulsively.

Power is an important part of the management process. Managers

241

are typically dependent upon others, many of whom are not in their direct control. They must be in a position to use power to ensure the cooperation necessary for them to achieve their work goals.

INFLUENCE

Influence is a behavioural response to the exercise of power. When power sources are activated, they can be influential in that they get someone to do something in the required way.

Uses of influence

Legitimate request

There are many uses of influence within organizations, some of which are more meaningful than others (Yukl, 1981: 12–17). One of the most common forms of influence to be found in libraries or information centres is the legitimate request. When a librarian requests an assistant to check the bibliographic details of a book the assistant will normally comply, because the assistant sees the librarian as having the authority or right to request such an action. The requests are usually made within the work-role setting and are viewed as legitimate.

Instrumental compliance

Instrumental compliance is based upon reward power and is used when a person is induced to alter their behaviour by the offering of a tangible reward. Instrumental compliance can be used when correcting the faults or mistakes of library staff, or during the annual appraisal interview where it is linked to annual increments in salaries.

Coercion

Coercion is based upon coercive power and is found in explicit or implicit threats to ensure compliance. Threats of dismissal or strike action are examples of coercion. To be effective the individual who is doing the coercing must be perceived as being able to carry out the threats.

Rational persuasion

Rational persuasion occurs when a party is convinced to change their mind, or that the suggested behaviour is the best way for needs and goals to be satisfied. Logical arguments are used to persuade the other party that the proposals are justified and that they will be successful. Rational persuasion requires that the persuader fully understands the other party's needs or perceptions of the situation, since the persuader does not offer any tangible controls on the outcomes. Rational persuasion can be used in libraries to change decisions.

Rational faith

Rational faith is based upon expert power. The agent's credibility or expertise is sufficient to influence the other party to take a particular course of action. Rational faith is used in libraries when a user takes home a novel which has been recommended by the librarian as a good book. The user may not be aware of the author or their work, but will read the book on the recommendation of the librarian.

Inspirational appeal

Inspirational appeal occurs where a person will carry out an activity not for tangible rewards but because they 'feel good'. The agent is persuaded that there is some value which is sufficiently important to justify the behaviour. Inspirational appeal may be used to influence or convince a librarian that they should hold an honorary position in a professional library association.

Indoctrination

Indoctrination establishes certain values and beliefs in people which leads to behaviours which support the organizational goals and which are held by the organization's members. It is usually carried

243

out in libraries and information centres in a passive way as part of the induction process. In competitive, profitmaking organizations indoctrination can follow a much more severe course in that new employees could be forced to renounce any allegiances to previous organizations.

Information distortion

Information distortion influences a person's impressions and attitudes as it limits or censors the information that they receive. The target person is influenced without being aware of it. Information distortion takes place in libraries and information centres when reports are edited or when information is withheld from those who need it. Subordinates may withhold information about certain problems from their supervisors in an effort to influence the supervisor's opinion of them.

Situational engineering

Situational engineering occurs when a physical or social situation is manipulated. A person's behaviour is influenced by his or her perception of a situation. If the situation is changed their behaviour can be altered. For example, a group of library clerks may complain to management and their union over what they perceive to be unfair work practices. If management then negotiates with the union for changes to these work practices in exchange for some other small concession, the library clerks may change their behaviour and accept the new situation.

Personal identification

Personal identification or emulation is based upon referent power. Individuals will either imitate the behaviour of an admired person or develop attitudes similar to those held by them. Role modelling is based upon personal identification.

Decision identification

Decision identification forms the basis of participative management techniques. If a person believes that he or she has had a substantial influence over the final decision, that person is likely to identify with the decision. As a result of this identification, he or she will be more strongly committed to implement the decision effectively.

AUTHORITY

As stated earlier, authority is institutionalized power. Whilst authority is based upon formal position and legitimacy, its acceptance is governed by factors such as compliance, leadership and expertise. Library and information centre managers possess official authority arising out of their position and, hopefully, personal authority deriving from their intelligence, knowledge, skills and expertise. These can be classified as authority of position, authority of knowledge and authority of situation.

Authority of position

Authority of position is that part of authority which is conferred upon individuals because they occupy a particular hierarchical position in an organization. The position and title are approximately indicative of the relative standing of the position-holder's authority compared to other individuals, even though it may not be a specific measure of the exact degree of authority. The true extent of the position-holder's authority is measured by the scope and range of their activities within the organization.

Authority of knowledge

In complex organizations, where specialization occurs, the specialist's knowledge confers on him or her a degree of authority over those not having the necessary knowledge to make a decision or solve a problem. This is known as authority of knowledge. This authority is independent of levels or positions and is therefore not necessarily attached to the manager or leader. A children's librarian will have authority of knowledge in areas of children's book selection and children's services.

245

Authority of situation

Finally, authority can exist in a given context, specific as to time and place. The use of authority under such conditions is determined by the elements of the situation. As an example, an individual who upon witnessing a fire in a library storage room rushes to the main area and shouts 'Fire', will initiate an activity amongst the people in the room which may not occur given a normal situation. The situation therefore provokes leadership behaviour and the acceptance of responsibility on behalf of an individual, who, though not in a position of authority, would assume authority in that particular situation by issuing orders.

The acceptance theory of authority explains why there are times when authority is or is not accepted in libraries. Managerial directives will only be obeyed when the subordinate truly understands the directive; when the subordinate feels capable of carrying out the directive; when they believe that the directive is in the best interests of the library or information centre; and, when the directive is consistent with their own personal values.

DELEGATION

Delegation is the organizational process by which top management makes it possible for others to share in the work to be accomplished. It is the process by which authority is distributed throughout the organization so that others may share the delegating manager's work and responsibilities.

The distribution of authority does not occur automatically; it occurs by deliberate design or plan. It is the delegation of authority which, together with the allocation of work, accounts for the establishment of an organization's structural characteristics. The responsibilities delegated are managerial in character; decision-making, planning, organizing, controlling, coordinating and leading within the role of their authority. For example, the director of a library service may not be responsible for the recruitment process of a library clerk at a branch library. This responsibility is delegated to the branch librarian, with the cooperation of staff management in the form of the personnel department.

246

The delegation process occurs in three stages. First, the subordinate is given responsibility for a job such as to write a report or to manage a branch library. Second, the person is also given the authority to do the job. The subordinate is given the necessary position power needed to execute the job. Finally, the subordinate is required to be accountable for their actions and outcomes to the manager.

Whilst the manager has delegated authority to the subordinate, they are still in possession of their own authority over the situation. They have neither more nor less authority than they did before they delegated it.

The same thing is true of responsibility. No matter how much authority a manager delegates, he or she still retains ultimate responsibility and authority for what happens in his or her part of the organization. Although authority and responsibility are interdependent, the delegation of authority does not involve the delegation of responsibility, in the sense that, once duties or tasks are assigned, the delegator is thereby relieved of them.

The people who are given authority must recognize the fact that they will be judged by their superior on the quality of their performance. They are still accountable to their superior. By accepting authority, people denote their acceptance of responsibility and accountability.

The delegators of authority have the task of evaluating their subordinates' performance, as they are still accountable for the subordinate to whom they have delegated authority. To require subordinates to submit their performance for review and evaluation is to hold them accountable for results.

Delegation improves decision quality and acceptance. It can lessen the load of higher levels of management and allows for quicker responses. Since the subordinate is often closer to the point of action and has more specific information than the manager, it allows for a better decision in less time. It is also a form of job enrichment and an effective method of managerial development and training, providing for internal promotion and career paths within the organization. Subordinates' jobs become more meaningful and challenging leading to increased levels of motivation. In times of economic restraint, where career paths are restricted, delegation serves as one way in which good library staff are retained by the library.

Whilst most subordinates will welcome delegation there may also be some resistance. Some employees do not wish for any more authority or responsibility than they have already, or do not wish to increase their already demanding workload. Others may lack self-confidence or have a low personal need for achievement. The amount of delegation which will be acceptable will vary according to the manager, the subordinate and the situation.

Unfortunately, some library or information centre managers do not delegate. A failure or reluctance to delegate is caused by a number of reasons. The manager may feel insecure or does not know what to do. They may lack confidence in subordinates being able to perform the task, although this is evidence that their training and staff development programmes are not performing effectively. Their insecurity may be further aggravated by a feeling that their subordinates have the potential to do a better job than themselves. They may also have a desire to maintain absolute control over the operations of the library or information centre.

Delegation, like other processes, can be learned. The most basic principle to effective delegation is the willingness by managers to give their subordinates real freedom to accomplish their delegated tasks. Managers have to accept that there are several ways of handling a problem and that their own way is not necessarily the one which their subordinates would choose.

Subordinates may make errors, but they have to be allowed to develop their own solutions and learn from their mistakes. Improved communication and understanding between managers and subordinates can also overcome barriers to delegation. Managers should learn the strengths, weaknesses and preferences of subordinates in order to decide more realistically which tasks can be delegated to whom.

The delegation process can be enhanced if the subordinate completely understands his or her responsibilities and role expectations. They should be given sufficient authority to carry out their tasks and their responsibilities and limits of discretion should be well defined. Assistance in the forms of psychological support, advice, technical information, should be provided and feedback given at regular intervals. The subordinate should be willing to accept their responsibilities and be encouraged to act on his or her own and make use of their newly acquired authority.

REFERENCES

French, J.R.P., and Raven, B. (1959) 'The bases of social power', in D. Cartwright (ed.), *Studies in Social Power* (Ann Arbor, Michigan: Institute for Social Research).
Yukl, G. (1981), *Leadership in Organizations* (Englewood Cliffs, NJ: Prentice Hall).

249

17 Strategies for personal networking and organization politics

INTRODUCTION

The involvement of the library or information service manager in personal networking both inside and outside of the parent organization and an awareness of organization politics is critical for the success of the library.

Political behaviour is linked to power, influence and competition and is a natural process within organizations. Most politics and competition are beneficial to organizations as they increase the motivation and output of the opposing sides. However, unchecked politics or political behaviour used to further an individual's needs at the expense of others can be detrimental to all concerned.

Whilst many people view political tactics as being unfair, many are indeed quite ethical. In deciding which tactics are ethical and which are not, their impact upon the organization and its members should be considered.

Networks allow library and information centre managers to function successfully. They provide information, support, and can positively influence outcomes. Networks are a closed-group pheno-menum: they protect their members and have norms and values which are never challenged. There are four types of networks based on a common purpose of power, ideology, people or profession. Upon joining an organization, the library or information centre manager should quickly establish a personal network in order to obtain information and support.

Not all political persuasion can take place verbally. Reports need to be written which argue various points of view or cases. The library or information centre manager should become skilled at presenting arguments on paper.

250

Lobby groups are a form of political group which attempt to impose their view or influence others. They may try to influence the library or information centre on some issues, or see it as a vehicle by which their cause may be further supported. Librarians will also be involved in lobbying in the course of their managerial tasks. They may lobby top management or those at the ownership level before important decisions relating to the library or information centre are made.

POLITICS IN ORGANIZATIONS

Political behaviour and politics in organizations are closely related to power, and influence. Jeffrey Pfeffer (1981: 7) defines organization politics as the activity by which individuals

> . . . acquire, develop, and use power and other resources to obtain one's outcomes in a situation in which there is uncertainty or discensus about choice.

Individuals will engage in political behaviour either to further their own ends; to protect themselves from others; to further goals which they believe to be in the organization's best interests; or to acquire and exercise power. Even if individuals themselves perceive politics to be unethical they cannot help but be occasionally involved, no matter how unwittingly, in political battles and political networks.

Power may be sought by individuals or groups. The quest for power will inevitably lead to competition which, if healthy and productive, will be beneficial to the organization and its members. However, when such a quest leads to disruptive, selfish or harmful behaviours, the outcomes may not be as beneficial.

Competition leads to differences of opinions and values, and conflicts over priorities and goals. It will be found in even the smallest library or information centre. Whilst there will be no internal competition in a 'one-man-band' library or information centre, the librarian or information specialist will compete for resources, using power, influence and politics on an organization-wide basis. Competition also leads to the formation of pressure groups, lobbying, cliques and cabals, rivalry, personality clashes and

251

alliances. All of these are evidence of organization politics. To believe that libraries or information centres are apolitical is very naive.

It is generally accepted that, to succeed, top managers have to be good politicians. The incidence of political behaviour is greater at the top levels of management as they strive to have their goals and values adopted by the organization. Strategic decisions made at top management level are often politically influenced. At lower levels within the organization, politics are most likely to be used by individuals to further their own ambitions – for example to obtain a promotion or salary increase.

Politics and competition are beneficial to all organizations as they usually result in increased output between the competing groups or individuals. However, unchecked politics can result in the organization losing its sense of direction, or in its spending too much time solving the resultant problems at the expense of pursuing its corporate goals and objectives.

Political behaviour used to further an individual's own needs may be damaging to others or the organization. An example of such would be an individual who influenced management's perception of a co-worker to the extent that the co-worker was viewed unfavourably for promotion. This is the negative side of political behaviour and should be counteracted.

Organization politics are also structure-related. Generally, bureaucratic or mechanistic structures will lead to politics relating to standards of control, rules, policies and procedures. The power of particular individuals to control and enforce adherence to these will lead to internal politics. Politics in organic structures will emphasize these aspects less, tending to be related to operating units, workteams and groups, and stressing trust and cooperation.

In diverse structures, politics will arise through misunderstanding and lack of knowledge of others' tasks and responsibilities. Libraries can often be seen as diverse structures with technical services being equated with mechanistic structures whilst reader services demonstrate more organic qualities. Thus reader services librarians who are used to dealing with diverse public demands often view technical service personnel as inflexible, bureaucratic and bogged down with unnecessary rules. Technical service personnel may likewise view reader services personnel with suspicion.

Political tactics

Organization politics are often viewed ambivalently, whilst political tactics are perceived by most as unhealthy and unfair. Not all political tactics fall into this category; many are ethical practices which can further the interests of the library or library manager to the benefit of the organization.

Once alerted, the library and information centre manager should readily be able to identify and maybe use intra-organizational politics for the benefit of his or her library. Becoming a 'political animal' takes considerable skill, and necessitates the exercise of caution because, if the tactics are used inappropriately, the exercise will almost certainly backfire. It is necessary, however, for the library or information centre manager to become skilful at identifying political tactics in order to recognize situations where politics are affecting them or their library.

There are several effective political tactics which are commonly used in organizations. Some of these are ethical, others are not (see Table 17.1).

In deciding which tactics are ethical or unethical, the impact of the political behaviour upon the rights of others should be addressed. If basic human rights are violated, the political tactics are, of course, unethical. The principles of equity and fair play should also be considered, both in terms of individuals and the organization. Often political behaviour is judged according to a utilitarian approach, being the greatest good for the greatest number. Where behaviours are viewed as unethical or illegitimate they should cease inmediately.

To ensure their survival within an organization, it is paramount that library and information centre managers identify the political behaviours of others and manage their own. It is also important that they be aware that, even if their actions are not personally politically motivated, others may assume that they are.

Several steps can be used by the manager or supervisor to minimize the political behaviour of subordinates where it can be seen to be detrimental to their position or that of the library or information centre. These include bringing disputes or disagreements into the open where they can be solved, and providing challenging situations and feedback to all.

253

Table 17.1
Ethical and unethical political tactics used and in organizations

Clean Tactics (Ethical)	Dirty Tactics (Unethical)
1. Establishing an alliance with others who are willing to support the preferred position or action. Others may include peers, subordinates and superiors – but it is important that the right allies are chosen – these should be people who have something to contribute and who can be relied upon. Arising out of such an alliance can be the formation of a power coalition.	1. Attacking or blaming others – creating a scapegoat by falsely attributing blame for negative outcomes to others. Holding others responsible for events they did not produce.
2. Choosing a powerful mentor. Having an influential mentor can be beneficial to one's career. Such a relationship can be an effective tactic to acquiring power as others view associates of powerful people as being powerful themselves – part of the aura is passed on. Powerful mentors can assist in the reaching of important goals by 'opening doors' or establishing networks. They can also provide protection and guidance when necessary, a valuable asset in the tough times.	2. Withholding or distorting information either restricts the flow of information to others or provides them with misleading 'facts'. Either action will hinder the decision-making process, create frustration and anguish for the individual or group, and often harm the organization as a whole.
3. Developing a base of support for one's ideas. In effect it enhances the individuals personal powerbase through the use of referent power. Once a base of support for one's idea is gained, the supporters will want to identify with the individual and their idea.	3. Use of hidden agendas. Announcing one agenda for meetings and then following a totally different 'hidden' one, preventing opponents from being adequately prepared.
4. Projecting a favourable image to management and others. People who demonstrate a high level of competence are viewed with having a considerable degree of expert and/or referent power through the 'halo' effect.	4. Spreading false rumours about individuals on a personal or behavioural basis.

5. Establishing control over access to information. As information is a vital commodity, anyone who has control over information flow, or access to information yields considerable power. This 'gatekeeper' function can be determined by organization structure and alliances or networks.

6. Praising others and ingratiating oneself with powers can create a referent power source.

7. Neutralizing opponents – co-opting enemies. Often people whose support is required but who currently stand in the way are co-opted into the group. Once they are made part of the group they become subject to its norms and adopt its values and goals.

   In meetings, those known to be opponents of an item on the agenda can be partly neutralized if they are seated next to the individual who is proposing the item.

8. Creating obligations and a basis for reciprocity. IOUs can be scattered by doing favours for others, assisting them with problems or supporting them against their opponents. All these actions will place them in debt. Effective users of these strategies will always get more than they give. The value of a favour may be worth more to the receiver than to the doer, the doer usually finding the favours smaller and easy to perform.

NETWORKING

To enable libraries and information centres to function successfully, networks should be established by the library or information centre manager within the parent organization, within the library and information profession and with members of external organizations, such as trade suppliers or politicians. Such networks will enable the library manager or information professional to establish alliances with key people who are likely to support preferred positions or actions. Networks are particularly important for 'one-man-bands', as these librarians work in professional isolation, yet rely on other libraries or librarians for professional information, advice and interlibrary loans.

Belonging to the right network will 'open doors'. Many legitimate political tactics rely upon networks. In belonging to others' networks valuable information is often obtained which would not otherwise be forthcoming. This will often lead to improved decision-making or allow corrective or appropriate action to be taken to avoid undesired outcomes. Networks provide support and can influence outcomes. This may be useful at budget time or when major decisions take place about the future role of the library or information centre.

Networking entails the development of formal and informal communication channels throughout the parent organization whereby information can be obtained and disseminated. It is a two-way process. It is important for managers to develop their own personal network of contacts within the organization to whom they may also go for advice.

In establishing their own networks, library and information centre managers may choose to occupy a central position, through which all information is channelled. This will allow them to exert influence over others and provide them with a power base.

Networks as groups

Networks are natural coalitions – that is, groups whose joint interests, viewpoints and preferences need to be protected. Within networks support and advice is freely and positively given, but networks are also a closed group phenomena, with those belonging

256

to the network holding sacred certain unchallengeable values and norms. Intra-organizational networks are often identified by common behaviour modes, certain dress codes and modes of thinking.

Practician-oriented networks

Networks are formed for a common purpose which benefits those who belong. They may be practician-oriented and comprise individuals who have similar training or professional interests. These networks provide true intellectual and professional stimuli for new ideas and innovations. In support of their ideals, they may attempt to influence other employees or organizations.

Power networks

Privilege or power networks comprise people who wield substantial influence or wish to be influential. These culture clubs operate through personal powerbases. Introductions to the group are either by invitation or through the 'old school tie network'.

Ideological networks

Ideological networks comprise different types of people who wish to pursue particular ideas. Pressure groups are an example of ideological networks in that they are formed to pursue particular social objectives.

People-oriented networks

The most common networks in organizations are the people-oriented networks which exist for the sake of their members. These are important for the library or information centre manager as they are valuable sources of information and support.

The gatekeeper

The entrance to the network is facilitated by identifying a gate-keeper, who is an influential member of the group. Personal sponsorship by a gatekeeper is important as this enables the person entering the network quickly to become acquainted with senior network members and enhance his or her channels of communication and success.

Establishing networks

Library and information centre managers should quickly develop their own personal networks inside and outside of their organization in order to satisfy their need for information and to establish their powerbase. The reason for doing this is that, upon joining any organization, the library or information centre manager is at first ineffective because they have not established their own internal organization networks. They do not know who they can trust, who to go to for accurate information, or who their allies or supporters are likely to be.

Whilst it is likely that they will have brought with them networks already established with people or organizations from their previous appointments, they will still need support, information and advice from within their own organization in order to deal with everyday internal matters. Until such networks are established, effective communication and decision-making cannot take place.

Library and information centre managers should establish their networks with thought. Members of staff operating in such key areas as finance, information systems and personnel and who are likely to provide support should be identified and personal contact made with them. It is often more favourable for the initial contact to be made on a face-to-face basis with the library or information centre manager explaining who they are and exchanging some of their work ideas and values. In the process of the exchange it will become clear whether common values are held, whether support may or may not be forthcoming and whether the individual may be regarded as a useful ally and member of a network.

In making the initial contact, close attention should be paid to the non-verbal communication processes as these will provide valuable information as to the actual support which may be given. This is one of the reasons for making the first contact in person as it could be that support was being offered but may not be forthcoming when needed. It is also seen as being friendly, polite and considerate to make the initial approaches in person.

In areas where vital relationships have to be established, and where initial reactions may not be as favourable as had been hoped, it is useful to continue to interact on a person-to-person basis where practical until such times as a firm relationship has been established. In so doing, the library or information centre manager is again able to make use of non-verbal communication, responding to signals to reinforce the positive side of the work relationship.

PRESENTING POLITICAL ARGUMENTS ON PAPER

Not all political arguments or dealings with people can be carried out on a personal or face-to-face basis. The ability to be present to respond to questions, reinforce arguments or apply political persuasion in response to verbal or non-verbal feedback is not always available. Such is the case where reports are submitted to meetings which the library or information centre manager is not in a position to attend.

In presenting arguments on paper it is important that each item is properly researched and portrayed in as simple a manner as possible with regard to appropriate detail and content. Reports are usually prepared for someone higher up the organization hierarchy to read. Their time will be precious. The more explicit and lucid the comments, the more favourably the report is likely to be received.

The contents of the report should anticipate and answer likely questions and be self-explanatory. Reports should include an introductory heading, an introduction, current information on the subject of the report, viable alternative courses of action, and a recommendation(s). The opening paragraph of the main body of the report should summarize any previous history or background and indicate why the report is necessary. The current situation should be described, providing up-to-date, relevant information in as precise and brief a form as possible. The alternative courses of action which are spelt out, should discuss the relevant advantages, disadvantages, costings and outcomes. A preferred option should be recommended with reasons where applicable.

LOBBYING AND LOBBY GROUPS

Lobbying is an attempt to influence decisions at the ownership level through persuasion and the provision of information. Occasionally the library manager or information professional will involve him or herself in lobbying as a political strategy, when the survival, stability or growth of the library or information centre is at stake.

Good communication channels between all levels of the organization will enhance the spread of information, although it may be necessary at times to supply additional information which will further the library or information centre's cause. When this is provided to higher levels, either verbally or in writing, in an attempt to influence the decisions it is known as lobbying. Lobbying is a legitimate practice if used positively and with care and thought.

The library or information centre manager will also be the subject of lobbying from lobby groups. Lobby groups which result from organized interest groups are features of modern democratic societies. It is the task of the library or information centre manager to balance the lobby group's concerns with the overall needs of the community to ensure that no one sector of the community influences the services or media selection to the detriment of others.

Lobby groups often see government as a pervasive and powerful source, influencing every facet of an individual's life. As most libraries or information centres belong to the public sector, libraries are seen to be influential too. Lobby groups may attempt to make the library or information centre an avenue by which their point of view is supported to the detriment of the opposing point of view.

Lobby or interest groups tend to constitute the principal potential avenue of influence outside of official government interaction. They need to be considered but not allowed to impose their requirements upon the organization. If possible, their energies need to be channelled in a direction which can help the library or information service.

REFERENCE

Pfeffer, J. (1981), *Power in Organizations* (Marshfield, Mass.: Pitman).

18 Strategies for negotiation

INTRODUCTION

Negotiation can be defined as a process with varying degrees of formality in which two or more parties try to reach common agreement on matters where there are both common and conflicting goals. The parties deal directly with each other in an effort to persuade or compromise as to a desirable conclusion given a set of circumstances. Successful negotiating requires experience on behalf of both parties, confidence and possession of high-level communication skills. Time and information are critical factors in successful negotiations.

EFFECTIVE NEGOTIATION

Whilst compromise is the cornerstone to negotiating, effective negotiation uses both compromise and collaboration. Collaboration enables the realization of common interests, whilst compromising conflicting interests. In libraries and information centres negotiation practices relate mainly to working conditions or implementing decisions.

Effective negotiating should result in shared meaning – that is, in a convergence of values, views, attitudes, styles, perceptions and beliefs. This results in a congruence of goals and objectives between management and staff which provide for common organizational identity. The success of negotiation depends upon the people who are involved. Outer-directed people, whose values, skills and attitudes are gained from outside of themselves, are easier to change attitudinally than inner-directed persons, who resist group pressure, do things their way, have a sense of independence, are entrepreneurial; all of which limits their sense of negotiation.

Not all conflicts can be settled through negotiation. It may be that some people's interests and reluctance are genuine and the information centre manager should be aware of this and possibly seek other solutions. It is pointless to attempt cooperation for cooperation's sake if the outcomes are likely to be less than those achieved by other methods.

Library managers or information professionals acting as negotiators have to strike a balance between being steadfast in their desires, yet sufficiently cooperative with the other party to allow negotiations to take place. This is particularly true when personal interests are at stake, as emotions are prone to be far more volatile in these situations.

Negotiation can be very much a personal process, even though the negotiator may be acting on behalf of other people. It is an exercise in predicting the other's position without the negotiator disclosing their own. However, there still needs to be some leeway to tantalize the other party into wanting to know more about what is being offered. The detection of non-verbal communication signals may provide valuable information in determining the other party's position.

Negotiation requires trade-offs between short and long-term gains. This is particularly true when negotiating the implementation of a decision, as it is inherent in this exercise that the two parties will need to continue to work with each other after the event.

When negotiation takes place at the stage when decisions are being implemented it is paramount that the affected party trusts the motives of management. Apparent honesty and openness is an important feature of the negotiating process. However, sometimes complete honesty runs the risk of exploitation by the other party. In such a situation, the preservation of a good working relationship is necessary, no matter the level or status of the parties concerned. Negotiators must be willing to give up more than they would like in order to obtain a result which is preferable in the long run. Negotiation will provide a result which is less than the perfect solution, but one that is more than that provided by the next-best alternative. Faces should be saved and the all-important working relationship should be preserved; the parties themselves may even have learnt a good deal more about each other as a by-product of the negotiating process.

THE PROCESS OF NEGOTIATION

The first stage

The initial meeting of the bargaining teams, be it at a meeting with employee and/or union representatives or the strategic decision-making body, is important. Its importance lies in the fact that it should establish the climate which will prevail during the ensuing negotiations. Tensions need to be relaxed so that common sense prevails, rather than outright confrontation. The atmosphere created in the first few minutes of the meeting or greetings stage is critical. Feelings are based upon non-verbal clues such as eye contact, posture and gesture, and by patterns of movement.

The physical properties of the negotiating room can affect the negotiating atmosphere. The shape and size of the table will either place participants in a compromising or contending position. Round tables are less threatening than square or oblong ones. Opposing parties will usually want to sit opposite each other. This allows them to pick up their opposite numbers' non-verbal communication signals and places each party in a competitive position. At times when a compromise is to be achieved, opposing parties may sit next to each other.

The first meeting is usually devoted to establishing the bargaining authority possessed by representatives on both sides if they are unknown to each other. A 'pecking' order will be established and personal interactions developed. In negotiating instances where all parties are known to each other this stage may be omitted. In the case of external people being involved – for example, trade union representatives – it is necessary to determine the rules and procedures to be used during negotiations. Where internal negotiations take place, the rules and procedures should be well known throughout the organization; their norms being part of the corporate culture.

The second stage

The second stage is characterized by each side attempting to consider the opponent's position without revealing its own. Each side will try to avoid disclosing their key important factors in the proposal in order to avoid being forced to pay a higher price than is necessary to have the proposal accepted. Negotiators will also attempt to get greater concessions in return for granting those requests which their opponents want most.

The proposals may be discussed in the order of their appearance on the agenda or in some other sequence. The sequence in which they are discussed may also be a subject for negotiation. If the discussion of the most important issues is deferred until last, this can often serve as a leverage for gaining agreement on more minor issues which precede the important ones.

The settlement

A process of haggling, bargaining, and settling then begins. The proposals are resolved at a stage when agreement is reached within the limits that each party is willing to concede. The agreement is then ratified. In settling and ratifying the agreement, all the points and concessions of the agreement are summarized and all actions accounted for. A document is produced which provides a record of what was achieved. Finally, responsibility is allocated to individuals or groups for the implementation of the agreement.

THE INFLUENCE OF THE PERSON AND ITS ROLE IN THE NEGOTIATION PROCESS

Good negotiators are experienced in negotiating processes. They have high aspirations, are articulate and have great presence and self-confidence. Their self-confidence arises out of their technical knowledge of the field in which they are negotiating and in their past negotiating experience. Successful negotiators are creative, yet determined and disciplined. They need a high frustration or tolerance level. Age makes a difference. In their early years of negotiating, negotiators tend to be very competitive, showing signs of aggression or abrasiveness. In their later years there tends to be a high tolerance of others. Ideally, the negotiator should be between these two stages – that is, experienced but still keen to be successful. Above all, the successful negotiator must enjoy negotiating and have an understanding of how to devise mutually beneficial alternatives.

To be effective, the negotiator should be able to identify both with their own role and that of the opposite number. Non-verbal communications are important here. The negotiator should also take steps to identify the apparent hierarchical structure of the opposing team. Above all, their opposite numbers should not be regarded as just mechanical representatives. All are there for a purpose, and each will have their individual purpose and strategies.

Sensitivity to the behaviours of others will help the negotiator in his or her task. Negotiators are better able to anticipate and evaluate how other persons are likely to respond to the offers being made if they are attentive to what they are saying, able to distinguish between what the other is saying and what they really mean, and translate their offers and demands into what is the real situation.

The role of a negotiator as an agent may range all the way from an emissary commissioned only to state the position, to a free agent with considerable latitude. This range of responsiveness is likely to affect the negotiation process. The more latitude, the stronger the effect of the 'person' variables. It could be expected that a person entrusted with the implementation of a decision which involved people's interests would have more latitude. Consequently, that individual's personality is going to be an influencing factor in the negotiating process.

IDEAS FOR SUCCESSFUL NEGOTIATING

Timeframes

One of the most critical aspects of the negotiating process is time, which can be either a constriction or an advantage. It is important not to let the opposing side know of any time constraints which the negotiator may have. Time pressures have two effects. First, as the

265

deadline approaches, decisions will be made faster, leading to one party losing their demand power. Second, to declare any time constraint may result in the other party holding out their real negotiating process until close to the deadline, in order to place the negotiator in a more vulnerable or critical position. The library or information centre manager should be patient, realizing that the other party must have a deadline too. As their deadline comes close there may be a shift in power back to the manager.

Information

Information is also critical to the negotiating process. The library or information centre manager should quietly and consistently probe the other party for information in a humble way. They should listen rather than talk, asking questions rather than answering them. It is useful to check the other party's credibility by asking questions to which the answer is already known.

Attentive listening and observation are critical. Often unintentional clues can be given out. Negotiators should have faith in their own problem-solving abilities.

Agendas

Momentum for results can sometimes be encouraged by placing easier items earlier on the negotiation agenda, so that both parties may be able to build upon their successes. A mediator may serve as a valuable communications link between parties, coordinating movement towards compromise. Trust, too, is important, but it is the absence of distrust which makes negotiating more effective.

The opening bid should be put firmly, without reservation or hesitation. For the 'sellers' it should be the highest defensible bid. For the 'buyers' it should be the lowest defensible offer.

Breaking deadlocks

If a deadlock is threatened there should be a break in the negotiating procedures. This can either be achieved by using a time break such as lunch or morning refreshments, or by talking about some

266

aspect other than that where a deadlock is threatened. A mediator or third party may also be used to help the negotiating process at this stage.

PROBLEMS IN NEGOTIATING

Stress and tension

The environment of negotiators has been likened to a fishbowl, with everyone interested in the negotiating performance. The face-saving techniques which are often used and the associated anxiety, enhances the stresses and tensions of those who are involved in the negotiating process.

High levels of stress and tension can have a debilitating effect on negotiations, as they may cause greater hostility among negotiators, leading to harder bargaining strategies resulting in less successful outcomes. Increases in tension beyond a certain point may make members of either party less capable of evaluating information and making the fine discriminations necessary in order to achieve a mutually satisfactory solution. It is important that library and information centre managers are aware of their personal stress levels when undertaking any negotiating procedures. They should monitor their tensions, looking for physical symptoms such as aggression or tension headaches.

Conserving the position

The psychological need to impress others and maintain a position of strength is poignant in negotiation. Taken too far, however, it is likely to lead to rigid and contentious demands which may spoil the negotiating process. Skilful negotiators like their concessions to be seen as a willingness to deal from a position of strength rather than a weakness, and also like their concessions to be allowed because of their competency as a negotiator. Effective negotiators believe that, through mutual sensitivity, they are capable of influencing their adversary's behaviour.

Some negotiators find it tempting to commit themselves to tough negotiating positions when discussions bog down in an effort to impose such a considerable cost to the adversary that they will yield under pressure. However, it is a mistake to assume that negotiators can be pressured into arriving at a settlement. The threat of an impasse being reached when time expires may be sufficient in itself for a result to be obtained closer to the time. To adopt the first attitude will result either in the perpetrator having to retreat to their former position, losing credibility in the process, or opening the way to subsequent exploitation by the other.

Emotions

The negotiation process is complicated by the fact that not all people are alike. Not everyone is a self-actualizer; not everyone wants to participate in the decision-making/negotiating process; some may even resist. Library and information centre managers will meet a multiplicity of emotions as they try to negotiate.

Complex situations

A host of different negotiating strategies to suit different environments and different kinds of conflict are necessary, yet if there is no one who is sufficiently knowledgeable or obligated from the other party then negotiation becomes very difficult. Ideally, when people's interests are at stake, the problem for the negotiator will not be so much lack of interest but the finding of a knowledgeable representative.

The complexity of the situation may cause different parties to develop different conceptions of the situation and therefore prefer a different structure for handling the negotiations. This will arise particularly if staff have not been involved in the decision-making process beforehand. An impasse may result from an inability to resolve the differences, and a mediator may be required to alter perceptions or definitions of purpose on behalf of either management or staff, thus delaying or putting in jeopardy the implementation of the negotiations.

REFERENCE

Pruitt, D.G. (1983), 'Strategic choice in negotiation', *American Behavioural Scientist*, **27**(2), November–December, pp. 167–91.

19 Leadership strategies

INTRODUCTION

Leadership is the process by which a person or a group tries to influence the tasks or behaviours of others towards a final and required outcome. It is a social influence process within organizations in that it motivates others to do something that is required to achieve corporate goals and objectives. Leadership differs from management in that management directs both human and non-human resources towards a goal, whereas leadership is only concerned with people.

The skills of leadership can be learnt, and are best developed in a corporate climate which fosters encouragement, cooperation, admiration, trust and loyalty and where there are role models to provide examples of effective leadership.

Not everyone is a leader. Leaders are those people who are able to use their technical skills, human relations skills or conceptual skills to influence others' tasks or behaviours. The relative importance of these skills depends upon the leadership situation and the level of management.

Leadership effectiveness can be measured by the extent to which the group or organization can achieve its goals. Effective leadership skills are needed to reconcile the goals of management and individuals with those of the organization.

Leadership theory has developed from the 'Great Man' concept and Trait theory to a contingency theory. The contingency theory determines that the environment, group cohesiveness, task structure, material technology, subordinate attributes, leader–member relations, subordinate expectations and degree of formalization in the organization's structure all influence the leadership process. Fiedler's model states that, according to the situation (position power, task structure, leader–member relations), the leader should be task- or relationship-oriented. On the other hand, House's Path–Goal theory states that the effect of leader behaviour on subordinate motivation and satisfaction depends upon the leadership situation, nature of the group tasks and work environment. Subordinate characteristics such as needs, ability to perform tasks and personality traits are also important.

Within organizations, leaders are also responsible for creating visions and values, for developing shared meaning between management and subordinates and for providing inspiration to achieve the organization's goals.

MEASURING THE EFFECTIVENESS OF LEADERSHIP

The most commonly used measure of leadership effectiveness in libraries or information centres is based upon performance – that is, the extent to which the leader's work group or branch of the library service achieves its own goals. These goals must, in turn, lead to the achievement of the corporate goals.

Performance is strongly linked to motivational issues. Individuals' goals and sources of motivation differ according to their level within the organization's hierarchy, and may or may not be congruent with the organization's goals. The leader's task is therefore to motivate all individuals and integrate each individual's goals with those of the organization.

The personal goals for top and mid-level management are usually related to the management goals. Their prime motivators are the higher-order needs for achievement, recognition and self-actualization. These needs are to be found in challenging jobs and the creative demands which lead to increased organizational performance.

First-line managers and their subordinates will be more likely to have personal goals which are related to the lower-order needs, such as good working conditions, fringe benefits, friendships at work, and good salaries. These goals may not always be congruent with the goals of management or the organization. However, if these needs are not perceived to be met, the performance of the library or information centre may suffer.

Effective leadership is demonstrated through skills which provide challenges and opportunities, secure appropriate resources and working environments, and, reconcile the goals of the organization, management and employees. Conflicting goals between management and employees, or inappropriate working environments will lower morale, lessen levels of motivation and, consequently, lower productivity. As a result, the organization may fail to achieve its corporate goals.

Tangible evidence of corporate goal attainment or performance for libraries or information centres operating within profitmaking organizations is found in overall profit growth, sales increase and increased return on investment. The extent to which the library or information centre efficiently and effectively provides information services which enables such growth to occur will act as a measure of the leadership capabilities of the library or information centre manager.

In non-profitmaking organizations leadership effectiveness is usually based upon comparative measures or subjective evaluations. Comparative measures are often related to budget expenditures such as cost per unit of output, or on market share ratio such as percentage of users in a particular market segment.

Objective measures of leadership effectiveness can be found in the way in which the managerial tasks of planning, goal-setting, problem-solving and coordinating are carried out.

Subjective evaluations of leadership can be undertaken by considering the way in which managers carry out their duties and how this is measured by their superiors, peers or subordinates. Superiors may measure the manager's attitudes and initiatives to problem-solving or methods of conflict resolution. Peers may measure their professional capacities and contribution to knowledge, whilst subordinates may measure the manager's decision-making style, the extent of their influence on others within the organization or the way in which the manager expresses his or her appreciation for additional work which has been undertaken.

Effective leaders clarify roles by defining duties and responsibilities. They also set and emphasize performance goals during the annual appraisal interview, and monitor these closely throughout the year. Supportive leaders who build subordinate confidence, share information and structure reward mechanisms to reflect the motivational needs of their staff are usually effective in raising the level of employee performance. However, these attributes are not effective in isolation of other leadership tasks. Effective leaders must also work to eliminate problems in the task environment, minimize conflict, smooth work operations, and obtain a satisfactory level of resources to enable the staff to meet the organizational goals.

Effective leaders act to inspire and stimulate individuals and groups which in turn leads to increased motivation and a higher level of morale. Through interaction and decision-sharing they develop teamwork and a positive and effective corporate culture. Effective leaders are also successful in improving the quality of management decisions and in increasing the readiness of subordinates to accept change.

LEADERSHIP THEORIES

Fiedler's contingency model

In the 1950s Fred Fiedler began working with some associates on a situational theory of leadership effectiveness. Fiedler concluded that a group's performance is contingent upon the appropriate matching of the leadership style and the degree of favourableness of the group situation for the leader.

Leadership style, according to Fiedler, was measured by a least-preferred co-worker (LPC) score, obtained by the leader's critical rating of the person with whom he or she least prefers to work. A low-LPC-scoring leader who rates most critically is task-motivated, whilst a high-scoring LPC leader shows sensitivity for their relationships with others in their ratings and is people-oriented. Criticality is not an overriding feature. In certain situations a task-motivated leader is required.

Task-oriented individuals need to get things done. They gain self-esteem from tangible, measurable evidence of performance and achievement. They are strongly motivated successfully to accomplish any task to which they have committed themselves, even if there are few or no external rewards. Task-motivated leaders feel most comfortable working from clear guidelines and standard operating procedures in situations over which they have little control. When these are missing, the leaders try to develop them by moving in and taking charge early to increase their amount of control in a situation, to the point where they do not consider the subordinate's interpersonal problems or conflicts. When they are in complete control of the situation and do not have to worry so much about getting the job done, task-motivated leaders tend to be considerate and pleasant. They are content to let their group handle the job, but tend to resist interference from those in higher levels of authority.

Task-oriented leaders are out of their element in moderate control situations, especially those with interpersonal conflicts. They are likely to concentrate so heavily on the task that they ignore group members' needs, as well as any conflicts that may exist. Hence the performance of the group may suffer.

People-oriented leaders are concerned with doing a good job, but their primary orientation is towards good interpersonal relationships with others. Their self-esteem is affected by how other people relate to them. They tolerate different viewpoints and are good at dealing with complex problems requiring creative and resourceful thinking. In stressful and challenging low-control situations, these relationship-oriented behaviours may become exaggerated. They may become so involved in subordinate consultation that they do not pay enough attention to the job. Group support becomes so important that they may be reluctant to put into action necessary job requirements which are known to be annoying to other members.

Fiedler's theory suggests that task-motivated leaders will be most successful in situations of high leadership control and in situations of low leadership control. They are likely to be less successful in situations of moderate control. The relationship-oriented leader is at his/her best in moderate-control situations where the leader's concern for interpersonal relations is appropriate. Relationship-oriented leaders are not successful in either high or low control situations.

Fiedler's model advocates that the most appropriate leadership style, either task-oriented or people-oriented, is determined by those factors discussed above. The model also suggests that group performance can be improved by modifying the leader's style, or by modifying the group or task situation. It is a situation-type leadership theory as the most appropriate leadership style is chosen according to the situation at hand. Leaders can use either style depending upon the situation to obtain the best results.

House's Path–Goal theory

Robert House developed his Path–Goal theory of leadership (1971: 321–39) to explain how the consideration or initiating structure behaviours of leaders influence the motivation and satisfaction of subordinates – in particular, their perceptions of work goals and personal goals.

House's Path–Goal theory links leader behaviour with subordinate expectations and valences, subordinate effort and satisfaction, and the characteristics of the task, environment and subordinates. Leader behaviour is described as being either supportive, directive, participative or achievement-oriented.

Subordinate expectations and valences are based upon the 'expectancy theory' in which the motivation of employees is explained through their consideration of the final outcome. Employees will decide upon the amount of effort to devote to a particular task or job depending upon the perceived likelihood of the outcome.

The perceived likelihood is referred to as the worker's 'effort–performance expectancy'. If the employee considers that desirable outcomes are likely to result from successful task completion, the level of motivation will be much higher when completing the task than if undesirable outcomes are foreshadowed. The desirability of each outcome is called its 'valence'.

Subordinate satisfaction or dissatisfaction is aligned to the intrinsic benefits and costs experienced by employees in performing the tasks. Intrinsic benefits are evident when the work is meaningful, pleasant and interesting. Intrinsic costs refer to psychological stress arising out of boring, tedious, frustrating or dangerous work.

According to House, the role of the leader is to increase the rewards to subordinates for successful task completion and to facilitate the task completion process by clarifying issues, reducing roadblocks and increasing the opportunities for work satisfaction. Leaders should also provide coaching, guidance and performance incentives where they are not provided by the organization.

The leader's behaviour will affect the subordinate's job satisfac-

274

tion and their motivation. It will also affect the subordinate's satisfaction with the leader. Supportive leadership behaviour is linked to consideration in that it considers the needs of subordinates and creates a friendly work environment.

Directive leadership behaviour is similar to initiating structure. The leader provides specific guidance, rules, procedures and schedules to employees which are followed to achieve preset goals.

Participative leadership involves employee participation in management. Subordinates are consulted for their opinions as part of the decision-making process.

Achievement-oriented leaders set challenging goals for employees. They emphasize performance improvement and display their confidence in their subordinates. Excellence is pursued.

The nature of the group task and environment are also important in determining the appropriate leadership style. Subordinate needs and their ability to carry out the tasks, the task structure, the material technology involved and the degree of formalization in the organization's structure are variables which will affect the outcome of specific leadership behaviour.

According to Path–Goal theory, directive leadership will increase subordinate effort and satisfaction when task demands are ambiguous and clarification does not come from elsewhere. In such a situation, leader directiveness compensates for lack of structure. In clear task situations, directive leadership has the opposite effect and is viewed as a hindrance by subordinates.

Supportive leadership, in situations where tasks are stressful, tedious, boring, dangerous, frustrating, or highly repetitive, can make conditions more bearable for subordinates. By showing consideration and displaying other supportive actions the leader will compensate for the unpleasant conditions, increasing both subordinate effort and satisfaction. However, in a situation where the task is interesting and enjoyable, supportive leadership will have little or no effect on subordinate effort or satisfaction.

Achievement-oriented leadership will cause subordinates to have more confidence in their ability to achieve challenging goals. Leaders who set challenging goals and show confidence in subordinates attaining the goals will increase subordinates' effort–performance expectancy in situations where they undertake ambiguous and non-repetitive tasks. In situations where subordinates

275

have repetitive, highly structured tasks, achievement-oriented leadership will have little or no effect on subordinate expectancies or effort.

Participative leadership will increase subordinate effort in a situation where subordinates have an unstructured task. When participating in decision-making, subordinates learn more about the tasks and their expected roles. Role clarity will be increased and subordinates will have a higher effort–performance expectancy. In a situation where subordinates have a highly structured task and clear understanding of the job, participative leadership will have little or no effect on subordinates' effort–performance expectancy.

Hersey and Blanchard's situational leadership theory

Hersey and Blanchard's situational leadership theory considers the two broad categories of leadership behaviour and the maturity of the followers. The two categories of leadership behaviour correspond to the initiating structure and consideration behaviours of the Ohio state Leadership Studies. They have been defined by Hersey and Blanchard (1977: 104) as task behaviour and relationship behaviour:

Task behaviour:
the extent to which leaders are likely to organise and define the roles of members of their group (followers); to explain what activities each is to do and when, where and how tasks are to be accomplished; characterised by endeavouring to establish well-defined patterns of organisation, channels of communication, and ways of getting jobs accomplished.

Relationship behaviour:
the extent to which leaders are likely to maintain personal relationships between themselves and members of their group (followers) by opening up channels of communication, providing socio-emotional support, 'psychological strokes' and facilitating behaviour.

The maturity of the subordinate is measured only in relation to a

276

particular task that the subordinate is to perform. Maturity is defined by Hersey and Blanchard (1977: 161) as:

> The capacity to set high but attainable goals (achievement motivation), willingness to take responsibility, and education and/or experience.

An individual may be quite mature in relation to one task, but very immature in relation to another aspect. For example, an assistant librarian may be very responsible in helping a library user find information, but may be very casual in overseeing and controlling serials and journals.

According to the situational leadership theory, as the level of subordinate maturity increases, the leader should use more relationship-oriented behaviour and less task-oriented behaviour, up to the point where subordinates have a moderate level of maturity. As subordinate maturity increases beyond that level, the leader should then decrease the amount of relationship-oriented behaviour, while continuing to decrease the amount of task-oriented behaviour (Figure 19.1).

THE INFLUENCE OF LEADERSHIP UPON THE ORGANIZATION

Effective leadership behaviours lead to a highly motivated staff. Where leadership, organization structure, technology and corporate climate are appropriate, motivation is higher. The contingency approach to leadership views effectiveness as also being contingent upon the task and subordinate attributes. Inappropriate leadership style leads to subordinate dissatisfaction and lowered morale.

Subordinates rely upon the leadership skills of their superiors to allow them to achieve their needs of motivation, rewards and ability to perform their allocated tasks. House's Path–Goal theory recognizes this as the leader's role in reducing the roadblocks and increasing the opportunities for personal satisfaction during their work-goal attainment.

Leadership actions count for far more than motivation. Executive (leaders') actions involve them in being the creator of symbols,

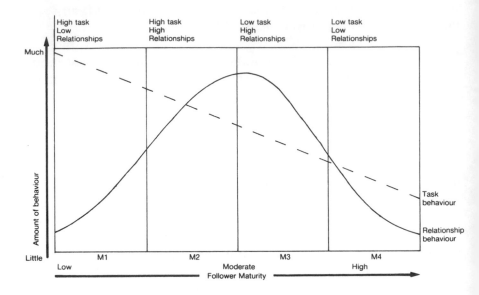

Situation M1:
Subordinates are immature in relation to the task. Leader should concentrate on task-orientated behaviour, being directive and autocratic in defining subordinate roles and establishing objectives, standards and procedures.

Situations M2, M3:
Subordinates have moderate amount of maturity. Leader should engage in considerable relationship-orientated behaviour, acting supportively and consulting with subordinates in making decisions. At the same time a moderate degree of directing subordinates and organizing the work is desirable, especially in M3 quadrant.

Situation M4:
Subordinates are very mature. Leaders should delegate responsibility to subordinates for deciding how the work is to be done and allow them to have considerable autonomy. Since subordinates are mature, they will be self-motivated by their achievement needs and will have the ability to do the work without much direction, needing little supportive behaviour.

Figure 19.1   Behaviour prescriptions in Hersey and Blanchard's situational leadership theory

ideologies, visions and other corporate cultural phenomena. Their attendance and participation at meetings where decisions are made and their involvement in the planning of agendas places them in

278

positions where symbols and language are created, where they shape ideologies and beliefs as part of their work.

True leaders see it as their responsibility to inspire subordinates to accept that which they have created, and to provide for shared meaning in terms of the organization's goals. Peters and Waterman (1982: 282) point out:

> The art of creative leadership is the art of institutional building, the reworking of human and technological materials to fashion an organism that embodies new and enduring values.

Leaders create a structure, having regard for the tasks, technologies and external environment, which harnesses the energies of others to achieve the desired result. Leaders are therefore responsible for the institutionalization of values, motivation, appropriate structure and behaviours within organizations.

REFERENCES

Fiedler, F.E. (1967), *A Theory of Leadership Effectiveness* (New York: McGraw Hill).

Hersey, P. and Blanchard, K.H. (1977), *Management of Organizational Behaviour* (3rd edn.), (Englewood Cliffs, NJ: Prentice-Hall).

House, R. (1971), 'Path–Goal Theory of Leadership Effectiveness' *Administrative Science Quarterly*, **16**, pp.321–39.

Peters, T. and Waterman, R.H. (1982), *In Search of Excellence* (Sydney: Harper and Row).

Yukl, G.A. (1981), *Leadership in Organizations* (Englewood Cliffs, NJ: Prentice-Hall).

20 Motivation issues

INTRODUCTION

Understanding the nature of human motivation is the key to successful and effective management. Motivation is one measure of a manager's performance as a leader, as the extent to which leaders motivate others determines the leader's effectiveness.

Motivation rests upon the employees perceiving that the outcomes of their behaviours will be beneficial and having an expectancy that their behaviours will actually result in a realization of the outcome. Library and information centre managers can increase the expectancy levels of their staff by providing appropriate rewards, giving praise and showing confidence in their employees, and by providing training and experience to allow employees to achieve the desired performance levels.

Individuals have different motivation needs. Abraham Maslow has arranged these needs in a hierarchy of importance. Important lower-order needs are those relating to physiological, safety and social factors. Higher-order needs relate to esteem and self-actualization.

Herzberg's two-factor theory is related to Maslow's need hierarchy. Motivation factors relate to work content and are satisfiers. Hygiene factors relate to the work environment and are causes of dissatisfaction.

Douglas McGregor lists assumptions which people hold in regard to others. These are Theory X and Theory Y. These assumptions are gained through experience, attitudes and predispositions and affect the way individuals view others in the workplace.

EXPECTATIONS AND NEEDS

Library and information centre managers can begin to explore motivation issues by understanding why employees are motivated. Victor Vroom (1964) considers that any attempted managerial influence to motivate an employee will be assessed by the employee according to the anticipated valence or value of the perceived outcome of the prescribed behaviour, and the strength of the expectancy that the behaviour will actually result in a realization of the outcome.

Influence by management will lead to motivation only where the individual perceives that his or her effort, combined with their personal ability and environmental factors, will lead to a performance which will result in a positive outcome and valence. At each step the employee takes into consideration factors which might enhance or hinder the outcomes. Thus, an individual will increase his or her efforts if he or she feels that this will lead to high performance. To increase the performance level, the individual must have the required mental or physical skills, knowledge or expertise to perform the task, and the organizational environment must also be conducive to the increased performance. If either of these factors are missing or inhibiting it will affect the individual's level of effort.

Expectations of outcomes will only have an impact if the employee perceives that he or she has the personal capacity to achieve the resultant performance, and if he or she makes the connection between the desired behaviour and the valued pay-off. If he or she does not associate the rewards as being the outcomes of certain increased efforts or performances there will be no motivation for further increased effort.

The individual will weight the outcomes to determine whether any changes in performance will lead to valued outcomes. To ascertain what employee values are, library and information centre managers should survey current employee wants and consider their basic human needs. Outcomes have two values for employees: the immediate or primary outcomes and secondary outcomes.

Immediate outcomes are represented by money, promotion, feelings of achievement, recognition by peers or, negatively, by being shunned by fellow employees. Secondary outcomes arise out of the immediate outcomes. They include the new car which is purchased from the payrise, the self-esteem which arises out of promotion, or the feeling of loneliness when an employee is shunned by fellow employees.

Library and information centre managers can increase their employees' expectancy levels by increasing their employees' confidence in their capacities to achieve the required level of performance. Well trained and experienced staff will have a higher estimation of their abilities than untrained staff or staff who have not been allowed to experiment or increase their level and range of experience in a variety of tasks.

Managers should be quick to praise their staff, pointing out that desired outcomes arise out of certain efforts or performance levels. If these connections are not made, employees may view the associated events as outcomes of luck or fate.

Most library or information centre managers are in positions to give rewards. Rewards which lead to improved performance through increased motivation and effort do not always have to be monetary. Praise, either public or private, the leader's personal interest, status symbols such as employee of the month awards, peer acceptance and approval, consultation and subordinate participation in managerial decision-making and promotion to positions with higher responsibility are all rewards over which the manager has some influence. However, not all of these rewards will have the same influence upon the motivation of the staff, since needs differ widely among individuals. Whilst one member of staff may be motivated by the expectation of a payrise, another may be motivated primarily by recognition.

Individuals translate their needs into behaviour in different ways. Some may express their wants and desires, whilst others' needs may be latent. Likewise, individuals' actions may not always be consistent, nor the needs that motivate them. At various stages of their careers, librarians and library staff will be motivated by different needs. Finally, individuals may react in different ways when they fail to fulfil their needs. Some may become withdrawn whilst others may become aggressive. Some may even increase their performance levels.

Motivating staff is therefore a complex issue. The library or information centre manager must get to know their staff and their staff's values well, treating each one as an individual and applying the most appropriate reward structure to each.

MASLOW'S HIERARCHY OF NEEDS

Abraham H. Maslow (1943) proposed that people have a complex set of needs which are arranged in a hierarchy of importance (Figure 20.1).

There are four basic assumptions in the hierarchy:

1. A satisfied need is not a motivator. When a need is satisfied, another need emerges to take its place, so people are always striving to satisfy some need.
2. The need network for most people is very complex, with a

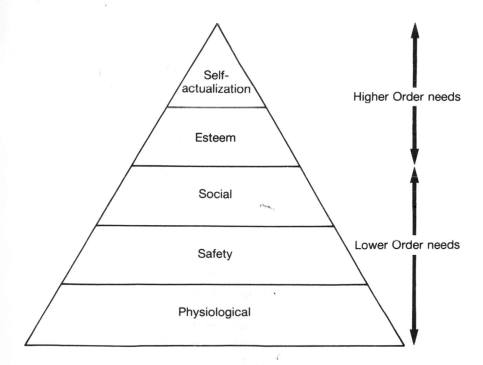

Figure 20.1   Maslow's hierarchy of needs

283

number of needs affecting the behaviour of each person at any one time.

3. In general, lower-level needs must be satisfied before higher-level needs are activated sufficiently to drive behaviour.

4. There are many more ways to satisfy higher-order needs than there are for lower-order needs.

The basic need in all humans is the physiological need. This is the need which relates to the biological maintenance of oneself – for example, the need for food and water. In a working situation basic needs relate to heating or air-conditioning, basic salaries and working conditions.

The second lower-order need is that of safety. Safety incorporates the need for security and protection, and, stability in the physical and interpersonal events of day-to-day life. In libraries and information centres safety refers to safe working conditions, job security and stable work relationships.

The third lower-order need is a social need. Individuals need love and affection and a sense of 'belongingness' in their relationship with their peers. In libraries and information centres social needs are found in compatible work groups, friendships at work and an approachable and relationship-oriented boss.

Esteem is a higher-order need. Individuals who have the lower-order needs satisfied will have a need for the esteem of others demonstrated by respect, prestige and recognition. They will also have a need for self-esteem and a personal sense of competency. Library and information centre managers will recognize esteem needs as having responsibility, or having an important job or high-status job title.

The highest order need is that of self-actualization. This is a need to fulfil oneself and to grow and use personal abilities to the fullest and most creative extent. Self-actualization is demonstrated in libraries or information centres by challenging jobs, creative task demands, advancement opportunities and achievement in the profession or the parent organization. Self-actualization will only be desired in the areas where the individual is capable of achievement. It has a low priority on the needs scale and is not a motivator of priority unless the needs of love, self-esteem, social approval and self-assertion are fairly well satisfied.

284

Work satisfies the lower-order needs in that it provides the means to purchase food and shelter. As individuals proceed up the management hierarchy, their hierarchy of needs are generally met. Whilst different individuals give priority to some needs more than others, managers will, in general, attribute more importance to the intrinsic rewards of work or higher-order needs than their subordinates. Library and information centre managers should be aware that the factors which satisfy their own motivation needs will most probably be different to those of their staff. They should not assume that those factors which motivate them will also motivate others.

HERZBERG'S TWO-FACTOR THEORY

Herzberg and his associates examined the relationships between job satisfaction and productivity among a group of accountants and engineers. They noted that the aspects of jobs that produced satisfaction were different from those that produced dissatisfaction. The satisfied worker was not a person in whom dissatisfaction was always minimal, as satisfaction and dissatisfaction were evoked by different stimulus conditions.

Dissatisfaction was caused by extrinsic factors such as pay, supervision, working conditions and company policies and so-called hygiene factors. However, the removal of these unsatisfactory extrinsic factors was not in itself satisfying, or indeed motivating. It merely eliminated dissatisfaction. For instance, whilst low pay or bad supervision could both lead to dissatisfaction, good pay or good supervision may not necessarily lead to satisfaction. This was because satisfaction and motivation came from a different set of factors called 'motivators'. Motivators include recognition, achievement, responsibility, and personal growth.

The two sets of factors identified by Herzberg are called motivation factors and hygiene factors. Motivation factors relate specifically to work content and are the satisfiers. Hygiene factors relate to the work environment and are the causes of dissatisfaction.

The hygiene and motivation factors can be equated with Maslow's need hierarchy. They can be used as motivators in two stages. First, the library or information centre manager must ensure that the hygiene factors are adequate. Salaries should be appropriate, the work environment should be safe, supervisors should have adequate knowledge of the technology and be experienced in imparting their knowledge and in supervising staff, and interpersonal relations should be good. By providing for these needs, the library or information centre manager will not provide any motivational stimulus, but will ensure that employees are not dissatisfied.

The second stage incorporates the motivators. By providing recognition and opportunities for achievement or advancement, library or information centre managers will create high levels of satisfaction and motivation (see Table 20.1).

MCGREGOR'S THEORY X

Douglas McGregor (1960) has listed some key assumptions which people hold in regard to others. There are two sets of assumptions, which McGregor termed Theory X and Theory Y.

Theory X assumptions are mainly held by traditional managers and hold that work is inherently distasteful to most people; that

Table 20.1
Integration of Maslow's hierarchy of needs with Herzberg's two-factory theory

Maslow's Need Hierarchy		Herzberg's Two-Factor Theory
Needs	Hygiene Factors	Motivation Factors
Self-actualization		Satisfiers:
		Achievement:
Esteem		Recognition
		Work itself
Social		Advancement
	Dissatisfiers:	
Security	Interpersonal relations	
Physiological	Supervision	
	Salary	
	Working conditions	

most people are not ambitious, have little desire for responsibility, and prefer to be directed; that most people have little capacity for creativity in solving organizational problems; that motivation occurs only at what Maslow called the 'physiological' and 'safety' levels; and that most people must be closely controlled and often coerced to achieve organizational objectives.

Theory Y assumptions rely upon self-control and self-direction and hold that work is as natural as play, if the conditions are favourable; that individual self-control is often indispensable in achieving organizational goals; that the capacity for creativity in solving an organization's problems is widely distributed throughout the organization; that motivation occurs at the social, esteem, and self-actualization levels, as well as at the physiological and security levels; and that people can be self-directed and creative at work if properly motivated.

The point of McGregor's work is that an individual's assumption about others affects the way that they treat them. A manager who holds Theory X assumptions takes a rather pessimistic view of his or her subordinates and will treat them accordingly. A Theory Y manager will hold the converse view. Individuals develop Theory X and Theory Y assumptions based on their experiences, attitudes and predispositions toward people.

JOB ENRICHMENT AND JOB ENLARGEMENT

Variety and challenge in a job can increase job satisfaction at the higher-order levels of motivational theories. Job enrichment and job enlargement are two different methods of providing variety and challenge in library work. Job enlargement occurs when additional responsibilities of a horizontal nature are given to employees. If the additional responsibilities are of a vertical nature, encompassing self-control, the process is called job enrichment.

Variety can be produced by adding functions or job enlargement, thus possibly reducing monotony. An additional psychological value may also be derived if the job enlargement allows the individual to see the completed process within which he or she works. The identification and performance of the initial and end tasks and/or processes, together with all of the tasks in between, will succeed in making the library job more meaningful to the employee and provide a sense of achievement and purpose. However, the type of work assigned to provide for job enlargement should be carefully screened. There is little usefulness in enlarging a job merely by adding to a worker's list of disagreeable tasks further onerous duties at the same level. If anything, this will have a negative effect on motivation.

Job enrichment is not the allocation of more tasks, but the allocation of autonomy and responsibility to the employee. As the job becomes more meaningful by seeing the operation as a whole and through the provision of feedback, the level of motivation increases. By providing a level of responsibility for certain tasks and a knowledge of the operating results, motivation, performance and satisfaction increases.

Responsibility and autonomy can be increased in libraries and information centres by allowing individuals to set their own work schedules; by varying the workplace; by changing the duties of subordinates on a regular basis; by allowing experienced personnel to train less experienced workers, by library personnel establishing direct relationships with the library users; and by encouraging staff to make their own quality checks.

Job enrichment will only work when the motivating potential of the job is high. The psychological needs are very important in determining who can, and who cannot, be internally motivated at work. Library workers with high growth needs will eagerly accept the added responsibility. Library workers whose growth needs are not so strong may respond less eagerly, or at first react negatively at being 'stretched' or 'pushed' too far.

As with job enlargement, the process has to be instituted selectively and with an acute knowledge of the motivational forces of the workers. In the worst case, job enrichment may have a negative effect on employee morale if they perceive the organization as increasing duties and responsibilities without the proportionate increases in pay. The motivational issues will then be lost in a jungle of pay disputes in which the organization will be viewed only as a 'money-saving' entity with no regard for its employees.

HACKMAN AND OLDHAM'S THEORY OF JOB ENRICHMENT

A fairly specific theory of job enrichment has been developed by

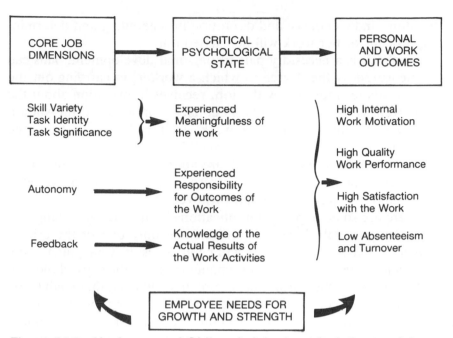

Figure 20.2   Hackman and Oldham's job characteristics model
Source: Hackman and Oldham (1980) © 1980, Addison-Wesley Publishing Co. Inc., Reading, Mass. Reprinted with permission.

psychologists J.R. Hackman and G.R. Oldham (1976). They suggest that certain core job dimensions have an impact on a number of psychological states, which in turn relate to attitudes and behaviour on the job (Figure 20.2).

The core job dimensions are found in skill variety, task identity and task significance. Each of these three job dimensions represents an important route to experience meaningfulness in the work.

Skill variety is the facility which enables the workers to perform activities that challenge their skills and abilities. The involvement of several skills in performing a job will avoid the monotony of performing the same task repeatedly. Task identity is achieved when the job requires the completion of a 'whole' or identifiable piece of work. Task significance is found in the job which has a substantial and perceivable impact on the lives of other people, whether in the immediate organization or the world at large.

Increased responsibility for work outcomes is achieved through autonomy – that is, the degree to which the job gives the worker freedom, independence and discretion in scheduling and determining how his or her work will be carried out.

Feedback is a necessary part of personal development. This can be measured by the degree to which a worker, in carrying out the work activities required by the job, receives information about the effectiveness of his/her efforts. Feedback is most powerful when it is received directly from the work itself rather than from the supervisor.

Personal and work outcomes are found in high internal work motivation, high-quality work performance, high satisfaction with work, and low absenteeism and turnover.

There are some important implications in this theory. Changes in only one core job dimension will change only one of the critical psychological states, and there will be little result. Changing the job will change behaviour only by changing the critical psychological states. If the psychological states remain unchanged there will be no behaviour change. The theory will only work for those who value the higher-order needs of autonomy, growth and responsibility. Library and information centre managers should therefore be selective in their use of this theory.

REFERENCES

Hackman, J.R. and Oldham, G.R. (1976), 'Motivation through the design of work: test of a theory', *Organizational Behaviour and Human Performance* August, pp.250–79.

Hackman, J.R. and Oldham, G.R. (1980), *Work Redesign* (Reading, Mass.: Addison Wesley).

Herzberg, F. (1968), 'One more time: how do you motivate employees?', *Harvard Business Review* January–February, pp.53–62.

Herzberg, F., Mausner, B. and Snyderman, B. (1959), *The Motivation to Work* (New York: Wiley).

McGregor, D. (1960), *The Human Side of Enterprise* (New York: McGraw-Hill).

Maslow, A.H. (1943), 'A Theory of Human Motivation', *Psychological Review*, **50**(4), July, pp.370–96.

Vroom, V. (1964), *Work and Motivation* (New York: Wiley).

21 Strategies for managing conflict

INTRODUCTION

Conflict occurs as the result of a disagreement, threat or opposition between individuals or groups, or within an individual or group. Whilst it may be destructive if it is not handled correctly, conflict is usually a sign of organizational growth and competition.

Both individuals and groups have two drives. These are to maintain psychological equilibrium and harmony, and to actualize their potential. Conflict arises when an individual or group perceives either a threat or opposition to one or both of these drives; when two antagonistic drives or needs have to be satisfied simultaneously; or where there is a tendency to simultaneously accept and reject a course of action.

Conflict has traditionally been viewed as destructive – a state of affairs which should be suppressed or eliminated. Managers are now beginning to realize that there are some positive actions in conflict and that, in many instances, conflict can be a sign of a healthy organization. In fact, if conflict within an organization ceased, stagnation would set in.

Conflict can serve as a unifying factor and a source of feedback. It acts as a safety valve and brings issues to the surface which may otherwise never arise. Competition generally leads to improved organization performance.

Individuals who are faced with personal conflict may react in either of two ways – flight or fight. Whilst the source of the conflict may not be in the organization, its effects will still be felt there through the individual's actions. When such actions begin to affect the output of other staff members, the library or information centre manager must become involved.

There are various methods and styles for resolving conflict, some more effective than others. In most instances, it depends upon the conflict situation.

SOURCES OF CONFLICT

Conflict is inevitable. It serves as a catalyst for change, which in turn leads to the adaptation necessary for the survival of any living species, be it an organization or an individual. Within libraries and information centres there are many sources of conflict. These include the structure of the organization, technology, role expectations, communication channels, interpersonal relations and behaviours, personal interests of individuals or groups, physical separations and the dependency of one party on another.

Organization differentiation

People in libraries perform different kinds of work. As a result, departments have different time horizons, values, goals and management styles. The greater the differentiation between departments, the greater the likelihood of conflict and the greater the need for mechanisms that will integrate these departments. It is the integration which is a source of conflict. Complex library institutions often expect very different departments to integrate their efforts towards accomplishing organizational objectives without having an understanding of their differences.

External environment

There is a likelihood that internal conflict will increase as uncertainty and complexity increases in the external environment. In order to accommodate these complexities the library or information centre will require their human resources to acquire different skills and attitudes. A different internal structure may be needed and corporate goals may need to be modified. This will inevitably lead to conflict between individuals or groups.

Uncertainty also leads to conflict. Where the future is certain, activities are routine and predictable. Rules and regulations are relied upon. In a rapidly changing environment, the basic rules and regulations may no longer be relevant: conflicting opinions arise, new problems have to be solved and conflict is inevitably the result.

Expansion in size of organization

As libraries or information centres increase in size, regulations evolve to control behaviour. These are not always effective and so conflict occurs.

Expansion of the library, or the organization to which it belongs, usually creates additional levels in the hierarchy. Conflict will arise as individuals and departments vie for the higher positions in the hierarchy. Takeover bids are likely to occur whereby individuals and departments inevitably win and lose. Libraries will be involved in such takeover bids from time to time.

Material technology

Material technology, which determines the interdependence and independence of departments, is another source of conflict. Departments and groups who have to share material resources may require them at conflicting times. To overcome this, departments may strive for their independence, thereby creating further tensions and conflict as departments demand their own technology systems. Where departments 'own' their own systems, they may not share their technology or information with others. As a result, conflict over ownership often arises. Integrated library automation systems overcome this to some extent, but conflicts will always arise over levels of authority to access relevant information and procedures.

Professional terminology

Due to the complexity of modern organizations and their high degree of differentiation, communications between departments and within departments can easily become distorted and lead to conflict. Library and information centre managers and professionals in general speak the language of their training or profession, which is not always recognized or interpreted by others in the same way. In other words, technical terminology used to describe events or objects with which professionals are familiar does not always extend to other departments either within the library or within the organization as a whole.

293

Policies

Conflict can arise between individuals and groups over policies, practices and plans where these are not in the main interests of one of the parties.

Role expectancies

Differences between subordinates and managers in terms of role expectancies, goals or even personal characteristics are often sources of interpersonal conflict. Managers are used to directing, yet subordinates receive orders; managers usually work for a salary and negotiate for payrises, subordinates often work for wages and work to keep their jobs. Managers have higher-order, promotion-seeking goals and usually perform interesting tasks, whilst subordinates often have lesser-order goals and perform routine, often boring, tasks. Often the dividing line between the responsibilities and tasks of managers and subordinates is not clearly defined and overlaps. Jurisdiction becomes ambiguous and consequently there is a high potential for conflict.

Competition

Conflict of interest exists where there is competition between parties for scarce resources or where one group gains at the expense of another. This is a common occurrence in organizations comprising highly dependent and interdependent departments, and where the economic climate makes financial resources scarce.

Conflict of interests

Individuals may also experience personal conflicts of interests. Librarians can experience a conflict of interests between professional values and organizational demands. Library and information centre managers may have to compete vigorously for funds for their libraries, yet cooperate at all other times with their peers.

Many library personnel experience a conflict of interests in having to work long, hard hours in order to obtain promotion in the library

294

or information centre, whilst at the same time balancing their home life, furthering their professional education, and pursuing their personal interests – all of which are deemed to be important.

Separation

When groups of people are physically separated by location or shiftwork, the possibilities for misunderstanding and the opportunities for conflict are increased. Libraries are particularly vulnerable to this type of conflict as librarians often work in a number of physically separated locations (branch libraries), or have to work rostered hours (shiftwork) in order to maintain the library's traditional long opening hours.

Dependency

The possibility that conflict will arise is greater when one party is dependent upon another for performance of tasks or for the provision of resources, materials or information. Conflict will sometimes occur between management and subordinates as management is dependent upon subordinates to perform tasks to achieve corporate goals. Likewise, subordinates depend upon their managers to provide the resources, materials and information which they need to carry out their tasks. Conflict between departments can also occur because of their dependencies upon other departments to provide resources, information or services which may or may not be forthcoming.

FUNCTIONS OF CONFLICT

Conflict has a place within libraries and information centres. It can serve as a unifying function within a group and as a source of feedback. Groups which are in some kind of conflict situation will find that internal differences are overcome. Similarly, any external source of conflict which is aimed at the library or information centre, such as the threat of closure, will result in departments working more closely together to achieve a more productive output, which in turn may prevent the threatened closure.

Conflict provides feedback to management in that it tends to bring issues to the surface, making it easier to identify the real issues of concern. Under stress, individuals are more likely to express their real feelings or problems. As a result, issues can be addressed which otherwise may never have surfaced. It can also act as a safety valve. Minor conflict can prevent pressure from building up to the point where it is destructive. Petty complaints are often examples of tension release.

Conflict is a test of power. Conflict situations often test the power of management and their subordinates, or their unions if they are acting on their behalf. Conflict will also test the willpower of individuals and the staying power of employees.

The main outcome of conflict is change. Changes will occur as an outcome of the resolution of conflict and these will sometimes be creative or innovative. For instance, budgetary pressures will often lead to imaginative combinations of needs and resources.

Competition is healthy as it will often result in the improved performance of each party as they strive to win the battle. Conflict can also lead to a better understanding of each party's problems. The discussions which take place may find issues which can be resolved to the advantage of both parties, or, basic common goals which were previously unknown or overlooked.

PERSONAL CONFLICT

When faced with conflict, the individual's natural instinct (which is common to all living things) is to react through either 'fight' or 'flight'. Either method of conduct is an attempt to adjust to the conflict situation.

Library and information centre managers may find that one of their most reliable staff members suddenly begins to act unpredictably. Their actions may be symptoms of conflict. The source of conflict may not be within the library or information centre, but its effect will most certainly be felt there. In such a situation, it is the manager's duty to try to help resolve the conflict either by providing advice or by referring the individual to an appropriate source of advice. If the source of the conflict lies within the library or information centre's internal or external environment, the manager

296

must help resolve the issue. If the source is beyond the manager's control, he or she can choose whether or not to be involved, but involvement becomes essential when other staff begin to be affected.

Fight or aggression can be identified by negativism, dominance, displaced anger or hostility. A member of staff may be contentious for no apparent reason or rebellious without cause. Some individuals may become domineering towards their peers or subordinates; or instances of anger will be levelled at subordinates rather than management. Others may become sarcastic, or make cutting comments or criticize. All of these are symptoms of an underlying conflict which must be resolved.

Flight can be identified by absenteeism, apathy or hypochondria. A staff member who suddenly begins arriving late for work or absences themselves from work without due cause; or isolates themselves from others by being aloof or refusing to become involved is using flight as an escape mechanism from a source of conflict. Other examples of flight are daydreaming and absentmindedness, an overindulgence in food, drink, drugs, or continual tiredness.

Occasionally other adjustments to conflict are made. The individual may establish defence mechanisms or perform attention-getting activities in an effort towards self-deception. Compensation tactics may be used, the individual substituting satisfaction for one kind of achievement for the lack of it in another area, in order to reduce the sense of uselessness.

A less well adjusted form of compensation is used when an individual will bask in the reflected glory of another. Individuals may push the blame on to someone or something else, such as the boss or library computer; or attribute to others the faults which really reside in themselves.

To help individuals to adjust to conflict, there needs to be an understanding of what lies behind the conduct, in order to help the individual substitute acceptable and efficient attitudes and responses.

MANAGING AND RESOLVING CONFLICT

The process of managing conflict is important if the conflict is to be turned into a positive force for organizational change. Management needs to recognize the existence and usefulness of conflict; to consider the management of conflict as one of their major responsibilities; and to encourage opposition. In so doing, they should define conflict management in such terms as to stimulate as well as resolve conflict. For conflict to be effectively managed, the organization's goals should be identified to all concerned.

In resolving work conflicts between management and staff three techniques can be used. These are win–lose, lose–lose, or win–win.

Win–lose methods

In win–lose methods the manager or supervisor inevitably wins and the employee inevitably loses. Win–lose methods constitute an authoritarian approach to conflict resolution as legitimate or coercive power is often used to bring about the employee's compliance. Managers will pursue their own outcomes at the expense of others, and employees will be forced into submission, often by the use of threats. Majority rule and the failure of the manager to respond to requests for change are also considered to be win–lose methods. Whilst win–lose methods may prove satisfactory to the manager they result in employee resentment and can have negative effects on performance.

Where the employees win in a win–lose situation the manager or supervisor will lose his or her position power. They may, as a consequence, build a resentment towards their subordinates which sometimes leads to grudges or retaliatory action, such as assigning awkward tasks to subordinates. This may cause a further breakdown in the relationship and the associated loss of control will affect work output. In any event, respect for management will be diminished, who will in turn lose their self-esteem.

Whilst the examples here are described as dealing with conflict between management and staff, the techniques can also be used between other groups or individuals.

Lose–lose methods

Lose–lose methods leave no one entirely happy. One such method is the compromise which is based on the assumption that half a solution is better than none. Another lose–lose strategy involves side payments. One party agrees to a solution in exchange for a favour from the other party later. A third strategy is to submit the issue to a neutral third party. The results of this action may be disappointing as arbitrators frequently resolve issues at some middle ground between the positions held by the disputants. Although each gains something, the outcome is rarely satisfying to either side.

Win–win methods

Win–win methods provide a solution which is acceptable to all. Win–win conflict resolution strategies focus upon ends and goals, identifying the sources of conflict and then presenting these as problems to be solved. Superordinate goals – goals which are greater than the individual departmental goals and objectives – are established. They reflect the corporate goals which all parties must work towards.

The identification of the superordinate goals reminds conflicting individuals or departments that, even though their particular goals are vitally important, they share a goal which cannot be achieved without cooperation. The win–win approach uses participative management techniques in order to gain consensus and commitment to objectives. The desired solution is one which achieves both individual or departmental goals and the organization's goals, and which is acceptable to all parties.

INTERPERSONAL STYLES FOR MANAGING CONFLICT

Whilst it would be nice to think that all conflict was handled by managers in a positive and successful way, this is not always the case. Managers use different styles in managing conflict.

Avoidance style

Sometimes a manager attempts to dispose of the problem by denying that it exists or avoiding the issue. They may try to remain neutral or withdraw from it. Examples of this can be found where managers are unavailable in their office, defer answering a memo, fail to return a telephone call, or refuse to get involved in the conflict. In most instances the conflict will not go away – in fact, it often grows to a point where it becomes unmanageable.

The avoidance style is suitable in three instances: where the issue is of minor or passing importance that it is not worth the time or energy to confront it; where the person's power is so low in relation to the other party that there will be little or no positive outcome by being involved; and where others, for example the subordinates, can more effectively resolve the conflict between themselves.

Smoothing style

The smoothing style refers to the tendency to minimize or suppress the open recognition of real or perceived differences in conflict situations, while emphasizing common interests. This style of management fails to recognize the positive aspects of handling the conflict openly. The manager acts as if the conflict will pass with time and appeals to the need for cooperation. He or she will try to reduce tensions by reassuring and providing support to the parties.

The smoothing style encourages individuals to cover up and avoid expressions of their feelings. It is effective on a short-term basis in three situations: when there is a potentially explosive emotional situation which needs to be defused; where harmonious relationships need to be preserved or where the avoidance of disruption is important; and where the conflicts are of a personal nature between individuals and cannot be dealt with within the organizational context.

Forcing style

The forcing style refers to the tendency of the manager to use coercive or reward power to dominate the other party. Differences are suppressed and the other party is forced into adopting the manager's position. This style results in winners and losers. The losers do not usually support the final decision in the way that the winners do and this can create more conflict.

The win–lose forcing style is appropriate when there is an extreme urgency and quick action is needed. It can also be used when an unpopular course of action is necessary for the long-term survival of the library or information centre. It is sometimes used as self-protection when a person is being taken advantage of by another party.

Compromise style

The compromise style is used when negotiating. There is often a tendency to sacrifice positions when seeking a middle ground for the resolution of conflict. Early use of compromise results in less diagnosis and exploration of the real nature of the conflict. The real issues often surface much later in the negotiating or conflict resolution process.

The compromise style is desirable when both parties recognize that there is a possibility of reaching an agreement which is more advantageous than if no agreement was reached. It is also useful if there is a likelihood that more than one agreement could be reached, or where there are conflicting goals.

Collaborative style

The collaborative style requires the willingness of the manager to identify underlying causes of conflict, openly share information, and search out alternatives considered to be mutually beneficial. Conflicts are recognized openly and evaluated by all those concerned. Sharing, examining, and assessing the reasons for the conflict leads to a more thorough development of alternatives. Collaborative style is inappropriate when time limits are imposed to the extent that they inhibit direct confrontation of feelings and issues involved in the conflict and when there are no shared meanings (norms, values, feelings) between management and subordinates.

The collaborative style uses win–win methods to resolve conflict. It is used more by managers who are relationship-oriented than task-oriented. It is found more frequently in open or organic organizations than in mechanistic ones. The collaborative style is recommended when individuals have common goals, when consensus should lead to the best overall solution to the conflict, and where there is a need to make high-quality decisions on the basis of expertise and information.

Each style has its purpose and, if used appropriately, will be successful. If a style is used to avoid or suppress an issue it will have a negative effect on individuals and the organization.

SOME METHODS FOR THE DETECTION OF CONFLICT IN LIBRARIES AND INFORMATION CENTRES

Grievance procedures

Conflicts can be detected through grievance procedures whereby dissatisfaction is communicated to management through official channels. Such procedures assume that the individual has the courage to submit their complaint for discussion and that the manager is approachable.

Observation

Direct observation may often identify interpersonal or intergroup conflicts. Conflicting motives are usually apparent when clashes between individuals or groups occur or work output deteriorates.

Suggestion boxes

Suggestion boxes may be used for library staff as gripe boxes. Employees can make suggestions to overcome conflicts whilst preserving their anonymity. Alternatively, the open-door policy is often used to create open communication and reduce conflict.

Exit interview

The exit interview can be one of the most reliable indications of subversive conflicts within libraries or information centres. Employees may be willing to discuss such matters when they have no further affiliation with the organization. Sometimes conflict may lead to the resignation of an employee and, in such cases, the employee may not be willing to discuss their dissatisfaction for fear that this may affect some future job reference. The interviewer should be impartial and stress the positive outcomes of the exit interview for resolving future conflicting situations.

22 Strategies for managing stress

INTRODUCTION

Stress can be defined as an environmental force, either real or imagined, that interacts with an individual's tolerance and which has a motivational or stimulatory effect. If the stressor's force exceeds the individual's stress tolerance level it will have a derogatory effect upon the individual.

Stress is the response that the human system makes in adjusting to demands or activating life events. It is not the event itself. The life event is known as the stressor. All individuals are victims of stress; being constantly exposed to life events which are threatening. However, stress tolerances differ between individuals, some being more able to control or manage their responses to stress than others.

Stress is not necessarily unhealthy. Everyone needs a certain amount of stress in order to function well. It is constant or excess stress which produces unpleasant or harmful side-effects. The conditioned responses to aid the body, characterized by arousal to meet the situational demands and relaxing when the task is accomplished, are natural characteristics of survival in transitory stress-producing situations. If these responses are allowed to accumulate beyond the adaptive capacity of the body they can result in physiological or psychological illnesses. This is because the build-up of physical energy inside the body is inappropriate to the modern life situation. Man is no longer a primitive animal requiring sudden bursts of physical energy for survival.

Stress implies a vulnerability to a stressor. Individual vulnerability to specific stressors varies widely. Vulnerability alters with age and is related to phases involving change and failures in the life cycle. Vulnerability also changes according to day-to-day events, moods and individual experiences, roles of individuals in particular settings, perceptions of expectations held of the individual by others, and the ability to control or alter the situation. Stressors produce symptoms only when the context and vulnerability are ripe. The individual must be particularly vulnerable or be in a generally threatening environment to experience the effect of the stressor. Personality has a particular relationship to stress. Certain characteristics predispose individuals to experience more or less stress than their peers.

Occupational or status level bears no relationship to the incidence of stress-related disease: stress is only related to vulnerability. However, each stage of life has its particular vulnerability, and it is important that these stages are recognized by the library or information centre managers so that they may be in a position to assist themselves and their staff to manage their stress levels.

The young adult is at the stage of transforming him or herself from child to adult. This is characterized by growing, maturing and learning. The twenties is generally spent establishing a home and career. The thirties provide minor crises of uncertainty concerning career choice. Thirty-five to fifty-five is the so-called mid-life crisis. This is a potentially stressful age when most people reach their status in life. It is a time associated with reflection, significant changes in occupation, interpersonal values and commitments, and role conflicts between family and career. The more ambitious a person is, the more he or she is likely to suffer. The latter work years may be associated with apprehension of retirement or feelings of competition from younger members of staff.

Stress may be controlled or reduced by management techniques which can be employed at individual or organizational level.

STRESS IN THE WORKPLACE

Library and information centre managers and their staff experience potential stressors in their everyday work situation. Role conflict, role ambiguity, role overload and role underload all have the potential to be stressors depending upon the vulnerability of the individual.

In their boundary-spanning roles managers will be involved in investigating complaints, troubleshooting and interacting with the environment, all of which may cause stressful situations. Planning,

304

decision-making, interacting with others, motivating, controlling and having responsibilities are other managerial tasks which have stress potential.

The organization's structure and climate, government legislation, external group activities, economic or time pressures, technological change, obsolescence, health and safety practices, the physical setting (lighting, air-conditioning), and organization, union and work group values are factors in the organizational environment which can produce stress.

Potential stressors for any individual in the work-place can be found in job insecurity, lack of work autonomy, bad work relationships, group conflict, constant work interruptions, lack of a defined career path, organization demands, promotions, demotions or transfers, or management's attitude to employees. Some employees are guilty of perfectionism and place excessive demands upon themselves. These types of people are their own stressors.

Employees often feel that change imposed from above is intended to meet the goals of management, or to increase productivity and reduce costs. Often it occurs to improve working conditions, reduce stress or increase opportunity, pay or security. This presents motivational problems for management who have often tried very hard to obtain the improved conditions.

Dual career-families, where both parties have major responsibilities, have enormous implications for work. This is particularly found in problems of relocation and in conflict between responsibilities for career and family.

Despite all of this, work is a vital part of coping with life stress. Without work, the potential for boredom and meaninglessness is increased immeasurably. Work is the primary means through which people feel useful in society and life, and so develop a sense of identity. Work may be a form of coping and a refuge for personal distress.

STRESS AND PERSONALITY

Stress that relates from pressure is highly related to the individual personality of each employee. Certain personality characteristics predispose individuals to experience more or less stress than their peers. Managers of libraries and information centres will find that some of their contemporaries and staff will handle pressure better than others.

Introverted people, for example, are not very sociable and cannot easily cope with interpersonal tensions from others. A promotion may trigger a strong stress reaction if it results in a job which involves working with other people. Additional responsibility is not the problem – just the act of being placed in unknown company.

Extroverts are people who need other people for various reasons. They work well in jobs requiring the establishment of interpersonal relationships but this need makes them vulnerable as they are dependent upon something outside of themselves. If they are confined to a lonely job they can become stressed.

The rigidly structured individual is security-oriented and afraid to take risks. They are stressed by anything which upsets their routine. They are uneasy in implementing new ideas or solutions which have not been tested. The hard-driving, work-oriented individual is stress-prone. They compulsively push activities to capacity and are extremely performance-conscious and goal-oriented. They seek honour and recognition but rarely achieve self-confidence as they are always looking at acquiring ever-increasing skills. This stress-prone individual's outlook causes continuous work overload.

The stress-reducer may be as serious as the stress-prone about getting the job done, but will seldom become impatient. They are less competitive and less likely to be driven by the clock. They work without agitation and find time for fun and leisure. Aware of capabilities and confident about themselves, they lead a fuller, less stressful, richer life than their stress-prone counterpart.

Risk-avoiders are overly careful. They are afraid of making decisions as this threatens their security. They experience constant inner tensions through feelings of inadequacy and dependency. Restrictive in innovative thinking, they avoid exploring new ideas. They will also avoid transfers or promotions, clinging to positions which have given them security and success in the past.

Flexible people usually have healthy, mature egos and can adapt to changing situations, whilst tolerating a high degree of stress. Challenges may be seen as stressors, but this will not impede their ability to cope.

Individuals who have a high self-esteem can deal with stress and frustration more easily. Faced with a pressure situation, performance is likely to improve. There is a strong sense of confidence in their ability to conform and an optimism in their approach to performance. Individuals with low self-esteem will be overwhelmed and show a sharp decrease in performance if stress is applied. This is particularly true if stress is associated with a new job.

TYPE A AND TYPE B BEHAVIOURS

Type A individuals

Type A individuals have behaviours which are typical of many managers. These behaviours are highly linked to stress-induced illnesses. Type A personalities are extremely competitive, constantly struggling with the environment at work, in sport and at social functions. They focus upon gaining power, recognition, money and possessions in a short period of time, and portray excessive strivings for achievement accompanied by underlying feelings of hostility towards other people, caused by their perception of people in the environment as being roadblocks. The hostility may be subtle or undetected until people stand in their way.

Whilst Type A personalities are outwardly confident and self-assured, they have an underlying insecurity. They often overreact and are generally hypercritical both of themselves (to themselves) and of others.

Type A individuals are fast-talking, having a sense of urgency concerning time. They thrive on deadlines, create them if they are not set and become impatient if goals and objectives are not achieved. Their work habits and their interpersonal relationships are critical in contributing to the fact that Type A personalities are three times more likely to develop heart disease or hypertension than Type B personalities.

Type B individuals

In contrast, Type B personalities have an easy-going relaxed approach to life. They hold a rational approach to achievement and recognition. They experience positive interpersonal relations and maintain a balance between work and work events. They rarely have desires to become materialistic.

As history shows that the more successful managers display Type A behaviours, it is best that managers do not reduce these behaviours. Rather, they should learn to manage, or seek assistance to manage their stress and so reduce the risk of cardiac disease.

STRESS MANAGEMENT STRATEGIES

Professional and personal relationships are among the most useful weapons against the distress of work and people demands. A library or information centre manager who is willing to delegate to competent line and staff personnel will get instrumental support for his or her projects and will be able to accomplish much more.

Communication is also important. Effective listening skills and the seeking of further information, advice and/or feedback will make decision-making less reactive and crisis-oriented. Managers should always be truthful and honest in their working relationships.

In building up supportive working relationships, work stress will be reduced. The social support offered by the relationships has a buffering effect upon the job demands, providing psychological and emotional support for the individual's well-being.

Personal planning processes can provide successful coping mechanisms for achievement-oriented individuals. The analysis of an individual's strengths and weaknesses and the periodic reassessment of their vocational, societal and personal goals and aspirations may allow more realistic goal horizons to be set.

Meditation, appropriate exercise and rest, progressive relaxation techniques and moderation in diet and drinking alcohol will also help alleviate stress.

Preventative stress management strategies can also be employed by libraries and information centres. Stress is often the result of an interaction of an individual with a demand. By altering, modifying or eliminating unnecessary or unreasonable organizational demands, managers can reduce stress in the workplace. Second, necessary coping skills can be provided. These should be aimed at

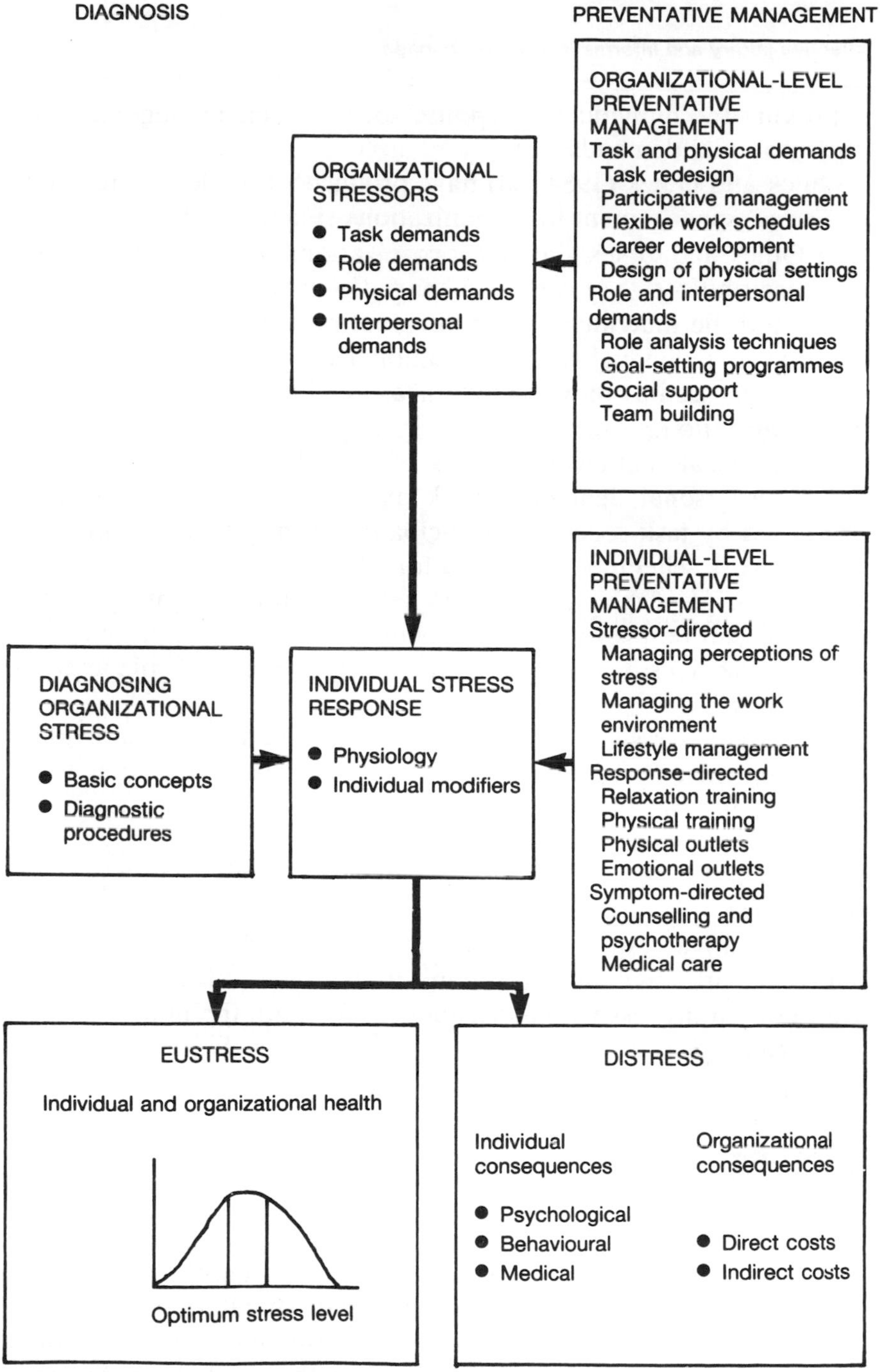

DIAGNOSIS   PREVENTATIVE MANAGEMENT

ORGANIZATIONAL-LEVEL PREVENTATIVE MANAGEMENT
Task and physical demands
  Task redesign
  Participative management
  Flexible work schedules
  Career development
  Design of physical settings
Role and interpersonal demands
  Role analysis techniques
  Goal-setting programmes
  Social support
  Team building

ORGANIZATIONAL STRESSORS

● Task demands
● Role demands
● Physical demands
● Interpersonal demands

DIAGNOSING ORGANIZATIONAL STRESS

● Basic concepts
● Diagnostic procedures

INDIVIDUAL STRESS RESPONSE

● Physiology
● Individual modifiers

INDIVIDUAL-LEVEL PREVENTATIVE MANAGEMENT
Stressor-directed
  Managing perceptions of stress
  Managing the work environment
  Lifestyle management
Response-directed
  Relaxation training
  Physical training
  Physical outlets
  Emotional outlets
Symptom-directed
  Counselling and psychotherapy
  Medical care

EUSTRESS

Individual and organizational health

Optimum stress level

DISTRESS

Individual consequences

● Psychological
● Behavioural
● Medical

Organizational consequences

● Direct costs
● Indirect costs

Figure 22.1 A model of preventative stress management for organizations

Source: Quick and Quick (1984: 28) Reprinted, by permission of the publishers, American Management Association, New York. All rights reserved.

improving the individual's response to, and their management of, organizational demands.

Quick and Quick (1984: 28) have produced a model of preventative stress management for organizations (Figure 22.1).

In Quick and Quick's model, organizational stressors have to be diagnosed before they can be managed. On the basis of the diagnosis, and the individual's own personal response to the stressors, appropriate individual and organizational actions are taken. Actions can also be used as preventative measures by both individuals and the organization.

At organizational level stressors are found in task, role, physical and interpersonal demands. Task and physical demands can be prevented by task redesign, participative management techniques, flexible work schedules, provision for adequate career development and the design of the physical work settings. Role and interpersonal demands can be prevented from being stressors by team-building, providing social support, goal-setting programmes and role analysis techniques.

Individual stressor demands can be controlled by the individual managing their perceptions of stress, and by managing their work environment and lifestyle. Individuals should also have access to physical and emotional outlets such as sporting activities, exercise routines and interpersonal relationships. Counselling and psychotherapy may also be needed.

The positive results are found in what Quick and Quick term 'eustress', or individual and organizational health. Negative results are found in distress with consequences for both the individual and the organization.

REFERENCES

Quick, J.C. and Quick, J.D. (1984), *Preventative Stress Management at the Organizational Level, Personnel*, September–October, pp.24–34.

PART VII
STRATEGIES FOR MANAGING THE GOALS AND VALUES SUBSYSTEM

Introduction

Part VII considers the goals and values subsystem of libraries and information centres, the chief component of which is the corporate culture. This subsystem is influential in the extent to which libraries can successfully cope with changing environments. However, its importance is often overlooked. More attention is now being paid in the literature to the topics of corporate culture and entrepreneurship as being critical to the success and survival of organizations.

The development of a strong corporate culture which creates and supports an innovative environment is a challenging task for a library or information centre manager. Chapters 23 and 24 provide some advice as to how this could be achieved.

Chapter 24 introduces the reader to the concept of corporate cultures in libraries. Successful libraries are those which have a corporate culture that matches their own characteristics. Several cultures are identified to assist the library manager to determine the most appropriate culture and organizational characteristics.

The concepts of values, beliefs, norms and shared meanings are considered in a library context so that the reader can gain an appreciation of their role in moulding the corporate culture. Many activities in libraries are expressions of corporate rituals. Descriptions of some of these rituals have been included in this chapter to illustrate the corporate culture at work in organizations.

Finally, some advice is offered on how to develop a corporate culture.

Chapter 24 discusses the need for innovation in libraries and information centres. Some methods for creating an innovative environment within a library or information centre are discussed. Also included is a list of critical success factors for innovative libraries.

23 Corporate culture in libraries and information centres

INTRODUCTION

All organizations have a corporate culture – some more noticeable or stronger than others. A corporate culture is the system of values, beliefs, norms and behaviours which create a certain organizational climate. Tangible factors such as task and job design, technologies, organization size and structure, leadership and decision-making styles, market certainty and external environmental influence also create the corporate culture.

Corporate culture is the product or outcome of behaviour patterns and standards which have been built up by individuals and groups over a number of years. Successful libraries have strong corporate cultures which serve to identify the guiding beliefs and values upon which all policies and actions take place. Effective corporate cultures translate cultural values at the organizational level into behaviours at the individual level.

Libraries and information centres can have many different corporate culture types. In small libraries there will only be one culture, but in larger libraries they may be many subcultures in addition to the overall culture. Handy (1976), and Deal and Kennedy (1982), have identified several different culture types which exist and which affect the goals and values, psychosocial, managerial, technical and structural systems in organizations.

Organizational subcultures arise out of the functional differences between departments. They are natural, healthy phenomena in libraries and information centres unless they interfere with or detract from the overall corporate culture.

Effective corporate cultures are developed by managers in their

314

activities and behaviours. They can be reinforced by the selection interview, induction process, training and development processes, performance appraisal interview and reward systems. To be successful, there needs to be an appropriate match between the manager's style and behaviour and the corporate culture of the library or information centre.

CORPORATE CULTURES IN LIBRARIES AND INFORMATION CENTRES

The founding librarian creates the initial, and usually the strongest, corporate culture. This is achieved through both conscious and unconscious acts. For example, their values and beliefs will be translated into policies and procedures. They will recruit staff who share the same ideas and values to further their means. These values will then be unconsciously manifested into norms and behaviours over a period of time. If the culture is strong and effective, it will remain long after the founding librarian has left the service.

In libraries and information centres where traditions and values are deeply rooted, certain behaviours and customs become deeply ingrained. New employees quickly have to learn how the library operates in order to 'fit in'. Many of these behaviours are tangible issues, such as whether appointments have to be made with secretaries to see the chief librarian, the executive officer or other heads of department, or whether employees are encouraged to make suggestions. Others are more intangible, such as an acceptable topic of conversation in the lunchroom (there may be taboos on certain subjects), who goes to tea first or whether superiors are addressed formally by title, or informally by first name.

Corporate cultures in libraries are shaped by factors such as organizational clarity, management philosophies, and management's orientation towards their staff and users of the library. Strong corporate cultures have clear-cut goals and objectives accepted by all, linked to strategic values and expressed as certain ethics of behaviour. The philosophies of management and managerial orientations will determine whether the culture of the library is

315

progressive and service-oriented, traditional, or oriented towards the good of the organization rather than the user.

Corporate cultures are expressed as languages, symbols, myths, stories and rituals. Library terminology, corporate logos, myths and stories of heroes and their successes, receptions for important visitors, and ceremonies to launch new services are examples of these. They are symbolic devices which serve to identify and reinforce the guiding beliefs and values upon which all policies and actions take place. In fact, the library's culture may be more influential on employee behaviour than the organization structure because of its subtlety and pervasiveness. As Peters and Waterman (1982: 280) point out:

> . . . the basic philosophy, spirit and drive of an organisation have far more to do with its relative achievements than do technological or economic resources, organisational structure, innovation and timing.

Corporate culture translates organizational values such as accuracy or efficiency into behaviours at the individual level. This is achieved when employees share a common management philosophy and set of values, and demonstrate this in their work practices.

CORPORATE CULTURE TYPES

Libraries and information centres can have many different corporate culture types. In small libraries and information centres there will be only one culture, which should reflect the corporate culture of the parent organization. In larger libraries, where extensive differentiation occurs, there may be more than one culture in existence.

Handy (1976) and Deal and Kennedy (1982) have identified several different culture types within organizations. These are based upon different organizational influences such as organization structure, the amount of risk associated with decision-making and feedback received from the environment. Whilst none of these culture types have been specifically identified for libraries, they are useful to consider as all organizations will display the characteristics of a certain corporate culture. In order to create a 'culture–

316

organization characteristic match', it is useful to identify the description which best fits the library or information centre or its parent organization.

The characteristics of the culture type are found in the various systems which operate in organizations – namely the goals and values, technical, structural, managerial and psychosocial systems. Having identified the characteristics, the type of corporate culture is known. Alternatively, having identified the corporate culture of the parent organization, the library or information centre manager can begin to design their library service's systems to fit the overall culture. There is no universally right culture. The culture of the organization should be appropriate for the circumstances and the people involved.

Handy

Handy (1976: 178–85) identifies four cultures relating to organization structure. These are power culture, role culture, task culture and person culture:

1. *The power culture.* Frequently found in small entrepreneurial organizations, traditionally in the robber-baron companies of nineteenth-century America, occasionally in today's trade unions, and in some property and finance companies.
2. *The role culture.* Often stereotyped as bureaucracy.
3. *The task culture.* Job- or project-oriented.
4. *The person culture.* Not found in many organizations. It exists only for the people in it without any superordinate objective, examples being barristers' chambers, architects' partnerships, hippy communes, social groups, families and some small consultancy firms.

Each of these four cultures display unique characteristics within the particular organizational systems (Table 23.1).

Deal and Kennedy

Deal and Kennedy (1982: 108–23) linked the amount of risk associated with decision-making and the feedback received from the

317

Table 23.1

Descriptors of organizational culture types according to Handy

	Power Culture	Role Culture	Task Culture	Personal Culture
Environmental Suprasystem	Possible political influence.	Must be stable, organization needs to be able to control environment. Monopoly or oligopoly.	Appropriate to flexible and sensitive environments. Most suited to coping with changes to market or product.	
Goals and Values System	Strong and proud. Faith in individuals. Judgement by results and tolerant of means. Tough and abrasive.	Role or job description is more important than the person who fills it. Slow to perceive need for change and slow to change. Offers security and predictability to the individual.	Team work obliterates individual objectives and most status and style differences. Culture most in tune with current ideologies of change and adaptation, individual freedom and low status differentials.	Provides a base upon which individuals' careers and interests can be furthered. Allegiance to professional group(s) rather than the organization. Organization is subordinate to the individual.
Technical System	Non-continuous, discrete operations, one-off job, unit production. Rapidly changing technology.	Undiversified. Product life is long. High degree of interdependence, systemized coordination, standardization. Market stable, predictable, controlled.	Product is important. Rapidly changing technology. Non-continuous, discrete operations, one-off productions. High degree of control over work. Market is competitive, product life is short, speed of reaction is important.	Professions, specialists.

Structural System	Web connected by functional/specialist strings. Small. Growth achieved by spawning new webs. Few rules and regulations. Little bureaucracy.	Bureaucracy coordinated by narrow band of top management. Controlled by procedures, rules and regulations, authority and job descriptions.	Job/project teams formed, reformed, continued. Matrix structure.	Structure exists only to serve individuals within organization. No formal control measures or management hierarchies.
Psychosocial System	Individuals will prosper and be satisfied to the extent that they are power-oriented, politically minded, risk-taking.	Individuals selected for satisfactory performance of role. Role could be filled by a range of individuals. Performance over and above role not required. Could even be disruptive.	Individuals have high degree of control over their work, judgement by results.	Individuals do what they are good at. Specialists.
Managerial System	Central figures determine whether organization moves in the right direction. Requires resource and personal power at centre in order to survive. Power and influence spreads out from central figure.	Use of position power. Expert power tolerated. No influence, organization relies upon rules and procedures.	No presiding deity, right people at the right level and get on with the task. Expert rather than position or personal power. Team-oriented, team leaders will compete for resources if scarce.	Influence is shared. Power base, if necessary, is expert.

Source: Adapted from Handy (1976).

Table 23.2
Descriptors of organizational culture types according to Deal and Kennedy

	Tough-guy/Macho Culture	Work-hard/Play-hard Culture	Bet-your-company Culture	Process Culture
Environmental Suprasystem	Encourages values of risk-taking. High-risk, quick feedback.	Small-risk, intensive feedback.	High-risk, slow feedback.	Low-risk, slow feedback. Financial stakes are low.
Goals and Values System	Young culture. Focus on speed not endurance. Tough. Intense pressure, frenetic pace. War games. Individualistic. Outlaw heroes are the norm. Chance plays a major part. Superstitions prevent learning from mistakes.	Activity is everything. Primary values centre upon customers and their needs. 'Find a need and fill it'. Heroes are the supersales people. Worth of their activities measured in volume. Energetic games contests, meetings, promotions, conventions. Short-term perspective, many quick fixes. Language is important in culture.	Primary ritual is the business meeting; people from all levels attend, but seating strictly by rank. Values focus on future and importance of investing in it. Careers, products and profits last a lifetime.	Workers get no feedback. Start to develop artificial ties, small events become important. Values centred on technical perfection. Rituals centred upon work patterns and procedures. Attention paid to titles and formalities.
Technical System	High financial stakes.	System full of checks and balances to keep job from being high risk. Volume is important, can displace quality.	High investment – capital goods. High-quality inventions, major scientific breakthroughs, not mass-scale.	Heavy regulated industries. Government agencies.

Structural System	Bonding – exclusive and exclusionary. Cabals.	Teams and/or groups produce results.	Large systems	Formalized work patterns and procedures. Tightly structured hierarchy.
Psychosocial System	Immature, point scoring. Temperamental, short-sighted. High turnover.	Active people who thrive on quick, tangible feedback. Young people with stamina.	Self-directed and tough. Need stamina to endure long-term ambiguity with little or no feedback. Cautious and deliberate. Spend long periods evaluating. Share hard-won knowledge. Look to mentors.	No feedback, therefore focus upon how they do something rather than what they do. Protective and cautious. System's integrity is protected rather than the individual. Orderly, punctual, attend to detail. Carry out written procedures without querying why.
Managerial System	Quick decision-maker. Aggressive. Tolerate all or nothing risks because of instant feedback.	Friendly, carousing. Team–group effort. No one individual is more important.	Decision-making is top-down, once all inputs are obtained. Self-directed, tough. Authority and expertise is important. Confident in approach.	Bureaucratic. Emphasis upon procedure.

Source: Adapted from Deal and Kennedy (1982).

environment to different types of corporate culture. They have identified four cultures based on these factors:

1. *The tough-guy, macho culture.* A world of individualists who regularly take risks and get quick feedback on whether their actions were right or wrong – for example, movies, television, advertising.
2. *The work-hard/play-hard culture.* Fun and action are the rule here, and employees take few risks, all with quick feedback. To succeed, the culture encourages them to maintain a high level of relatively low-risk activity. It is found in sales-dominated industries.
3. *The bet-your-company culture.* Cultures with big stakes decisions, where years pass before employees know whether decisions have paid off. A high-risk, slow feedback environment. Aviation companies like Boeing are examples of this type of company culture.
4. *The process culture.* A world of little or no feedback where employees find it hard to measure what they do; instead they concentrate on how it is done. This bureaucratic culture is typical of banks, government agencies and trade associations.

These cultures also have an influence upon the systems within organizations (Table 23.2).

VALUES, BELIEFS, NORMS AND SHARED MEANINGS

Values

A library or information centre's culture can be identified by the value system it ascribes to and the climate it creates. Values comprise those matters most important to an individual, group or organization. They have a moral dimension and influence the beliefs and attitudes of individuals and groups. Examples of such values are honesty, loyalty and performance. Values reflect desired behaviours or states of affairs and can influence a person's or group's perceptions of situations and problems. They are the basis

322

of human activities. Values also influence choices, preferences and decisions.

Values are the core of organizational culture. They are important for the understanding of similarities and differences between libraries and information centres, and groups and individuals. Libraries and information centres, and their parent organizations, may not necessarily share common values. Different departments may place different emphases on work processes, behaviours and priorities. As a result, different values emerge.

The organization may view different departments as having different priorities or levels of importance. Management will reflect these priorities and allocate resources, power and prestige to these departments according to priority or importance.

Because corporate values reflect much more than meaning and they stand for clear, explicit philosophies about the library's or organization's goals and objectives, successful libraries and parent organizations are those in which its own corporate values are shared between management and subordinates. Library managers have a duty to shape and fine-tune values to conform to the external and internal environments and communicate these to subordinates.

Beliefs

Beliefs are the acceptance of values or convictions about values. They are to a great extent shaped by the consistencies or inconsistencies between value statements and actions or behaviours of superiors or powerful individuals within the library or information centre or parent organization. If there is consistency then their actions will influence the beliefs that would be expected to evolve from the stated values. Inconsistencies between value statements and actions will result in different beliefs in accord with the actions of superiors and weaken the organizational culture.

To be successful, corporate beliefs should be visible, known and acted upon by all members of the organization. This can only be the case if they are communicated throughout the organization and reinforced through human resource management processes, recognition and rewards. They then become permanently infused and accepted as norms by which the organization exists.

Norms

Norms are standards of behaviour. Everyday behaviours based upon rules and systems become norms when they are transmitted unconsciously within organizations.

Shared meanings

Shared meanings are different to social norms as they focus upon message exchange, interpretation and interaction sequencing. Shared meaning assumes that people have similar attitudes, values, views of the world and feelings about situations.

Most positive actions take place on the basis of shared meaning or on an assumption that people in the same situations share common experiences and viewpoints. Shared meaning is consequently the system which allows actions, events, behaviours and emotions to take place.

CORPORATE RITUALS

Many activities in libraries are expressions of corporate rituals, the consequences of which go beyond the technical details. Examples include induction, training, organizational development activities, sackings, collective bargaining and Christmas parties. Trice and Beyer (1984: 653–69) have identified some organizational rites or activities which have social consequences in organizations and these are described below.

Rites of passage

Rites of passage begin with the induction and basic training processes. These allow employees to part with their past identities and statuses and take on new roles. They minimize the changes which occur in the transition from old to new and re-establish the equilibrium in ongoing social relations. The induction interview with the chief librarian, or the assigning of a new office, form part of the incorporation rite. Retirement ceremonies and farewell parties are part of the rites of passage when employees retire or resign.

Rites of degradation

Rites of degradation take place when the chief executive or person of high authority is fired and replaced, thereby dissolving his or her social identity and power. Such an action may be interpreted as the organization's public acknowledgement that problems exist. As a consequence, group boundaries may be redefined to take into account previous close supporters of the executive. These supporters may or may not be incorporated into the newly formed groups. The replacement of the executive is an act which re-affirms the social importance and value of the role. If the position is not filled, it is accepted that it had no importance in the organization.

Rites of enhancement

Enhanced personal status and the social identification of individuals who have been successful within the corporate or professional environment are provided for by 'rites of enhancement'. Examples of such are the granting of membership to an élite group, or the granting of a fellowship or life membership to a member of a professional organization such as a library association. Such a membership is usually jealously guarded by those who have attained such status.

Rites of enhancement spread good news about the organization or association. They also emphasize the social value of performance. As Trice and Beyer (ibid: 660) point out:

They provide public recognition of individual accomplishments from which all derive benefits and seem to enable the organisation to take some share of the credit for these accomplishments. Another obvious, not-so-latent consequence is to motivate other members to greater efforts.

Rites of renewal

Rites of renewal are provided in organizational development

activities such as corporate plans, management by objectives programmes, job redesign, team-building and leadership effectiveness training programmes. These are rites which are intended to refurbish or strengthen existing social structures and thus improve their functioning.

The latent consequences of rites of renewal are that members are reassured that something is being done to correct organizational problems. However, they can be used to focus attention away from one problem to another. Many of the activities give rise to certain rituals which legitimize and reinforce the existing systems of power and authority.

Conflict reduction rites

Conflict reduction rites involve collective bargaining or feigned fights of negotiation where parties may become hostile, threaten to boycott or walk out of the negotiating process whilst the other parties speak of compromise, point to areas of cooperation and attempt to overcome the anger in a ritualistic way. These actions may deflect attention away from solving problems.

Other forms of conflict reduction rites in libraries or information centres are the formation of committees, advisory groups, task forces, affirmative action committees or quality circles. Most of these groups serve to re-establish equilibrium in disturbed social relations. Confidence is often renewed when it is known that a committee or advisory group has been formed to investigate or advise on a problem.

Rites of integration

Rites of integration encourage and revive common feelings that bind members together and commit them to a social system. Such rites are found in the library's Christmas party. They permit emotions to be vented and allow the temporary loosening of various norms.

ORGANIZATIONAL SUBCULTURES

Organizational subcultures arise out of the functional differences between departments in libraries or information centres. These include the use of different technologies; the identification of different values and interests; the use of different terminologies or languages; the employment of different approaches to problem-solving techniques; and the different aspects of the interactive external environment.

Subcultures can also be based on gender, occupation, status, task, tenure, or race of the work group. Socioeconomic and educational backgrounds can also lead to subcultures being formed. Although they are sometimes blamed for poor organizational performance, in libraries, where strong cultures exist, subcultures do not cause problems as the overall values and beliefs are strong. However, in weak cultural environments they can be very destructive as they can obscure overriding values and result in cultural drifts.

STRONG AND WEAK CORPORATE CULTURES

Successful libraries or information centres have strong corporate cultures. Strong cultures provide meaning and direction to members' efforts. Everyone knows the library's goals; people feel better about what they do and, as a consequence, are likely to work harder. The organization's networks carry the beliefs and values.

Strong cultures come from within and are built by the founders and by individual leaders, not consultants. These people care about their employees. No matter how distant departments are from the head office, all sites are treated appropriately. This is important in libraries, where sites may be geographically dispersed over wide areas.

Strong cultures are created, sustained, transmitted and changed through social interaction – through modelling and imitation, instruction, correction, negotiation, storytelling, gossip and observation. They are communicated and reinforced by organization-wide action. High-performing libraries or information centres will have well conceived human resource programmes which will reinforce the culture.

Strong cultural values are important to libraries and information centres as they provide employees with a sense of what they ought to be doing, and a knowledge of how they should behave to be

327

consistent with organizational goals. Strong cultures represent an emotional feeling of being a part of the library or parent organization, and lead to greater employee commitment and motivation.

Strong cultures can still be found in poor performing libraries or information centres. Conversely, a strong culture may not necessarily be an effective or healthy one. In these cases it is usual for the pervading culture to be dysfunctional; usually focusing upon internal politics rather than external commitments such as user requirements.

DEVELOPING THE LIBRARY'S OR INFORMATION CENTRE'S CORPORATE CULTURE

As a service organization, a library's or information centre's culture should be the set of norms and values that affect employee behaviour in areas of user service, management style and concern for quality and innovation. These should be manifested in cultural values such as good customer service, a commitment to quality and productivity improvement, increased employee pride and loyalty, effective problem-solving and conflict resolution.

Cultural values such as these can be achieved in part by the various human resource management processes which operate in libraries and information centres. The selection interview, induction process, training and development practices, performance appraisal, career development and reward systems all provide opportunities for the cultural values to be reinforced.

Prospective employees can be questioned about their attitudes to certain key library values, such as quality of service, during the selection interview. All other things being equal, those who hold similar values and beliefs to the desired culture should be given priority over those who do not.

The induction process provides the ideal situation to communicate the desired cultural values. These should be later reinforced by consistent actions in order to instil beliefs. The library's or information centre's philosophies and values and the associated management practices should be discussed with the new employee. This will provide them with reasons why certain norms and behaviours are acceptable and others are not. All training and development programmes should reinforce these foundation values and philosophies.

The performance appraisal interview provides the opportunity for feedback and reinforcement of the required values and philosophies. It may also be used to detect underlying subcultures which may need correction if they contradict the overall culture. Employees should be given the opportunity to discuss their own values and beliefs and how these fit into those of the library or information centre.

The reward system should be structured so as to reward those values which are held in high regard. Incentives should be linked to key library values. This serves to reinforce the important values in employees' beliefs and enables them to initiate behaviours leading to good organizational performance.

Appropriate leadership and management styles are needed to match and develop the corporate culture. Employees look to managers to shape shared meanings, define and create values and demonstrate corporate beliefs. They act as agents for change and minimize the conflict between inner and outer directed beliefs – that is, the conflicts which often exist in libraries and information centres between organizational and professional beliefs. Library managers are responsible for the convergence of these values and beliefs.

For their activities to be effective, the managers' styles and behaviours must be congruent with the organization's values and behaviours. An authoritarian style in a democratic culture would be nothing short of disastrous.

REFERENCES

Deal, T.E. and Kennedy, A.A. (1982), *Corporate Cultures: the rites and rituals of corporate life* (Reading, Mass.: Addison-Wesley).

Handy, C.B. (1976), *Understanding Organisations* (Harmondsworth: Penguin).

Peters, T. and Waterman, R.H. (1982), *In Search of Excellence* (Sydney: Harper and Row).

Trice, H.M. and Beyer, J.M. (1984) 'Studying organizational cultures through rites and ceremonials', *Academy of Management Review*, **9**, October, pp.653–9.

24 Strategies for survival: fostering innovation and intrapreneurship in libraries and information centres

INTRODUCTION

In order to survive major changes in the environment, libraries have to become more innovative. Innovation exploits change and provides libraries with the means to deal with the unstructured problems arising out of changing environments. Innovation is championed by intrapreneurs.

The internal environment of the library or information centre is the most important factor which leads to successful innovative practices. Staff must be receptive to innovation and willing to perceive change as an opportunity rather than a threat. Although conflict inevitably occurs during change and innovative processes, such conflict needs to be managed to ensure that creativity is not stifled.

Innovation also involves risk. Management should be willing to take risks and allow their staff to make mistakes as part of the learning process.

An innovative climate is created through policies and management practices. Open communication channels are necessary; encouragement and support for creative ideas must be forthcoming; unnecessary bureaucratic procedures should be discontinued. Managers should communicate and reinforce their values and beliefs to all staff when wandering around work activity areas. Innovative teams can be built from within the library or information centre. The key functions should be matched with the individuals who have strengths in these areas.

330

Successful innovation requires a balanced mix of idea generation, intrapreneurship, project-leading, management, gatekeeping, coaching and operating. These key functions require people with specific skills and personal attributes. This in turn requires a variety of compensation, staffing and management practices.

THE NEED FOR LIBRARIES TO BE INNOVATIVE

Libraries and information centres are generally seen as conservative organizations with traditional values and time-honoured practices which have served them well in the past. Whilst there have been some innovative libraries, as a group libraries have never been seen by administrators, politicians or the public as particularly entrepreneurial. In most cases they are attached to public service or not-for-profit organizations which are themselves resistant to change and which foster a traditional approach to management.

Until recently, this has had a cushioning effect upon the management of libraries. Activities have been based upon budgets rather than directly aligned to results and performance. The library or information centre has been funded as a service institution whose tangible benefits have been difficult to measure in real terms. In response, the library has sought to maximize its potential rather than optimize it. Arguments for funds have been based on the percentage of users in the service population. If it could be shown by the membership figures that a high proportion of people made use of the library, the budget allocation was expected to match this.

There are two major environmental factors which are bringing pressure on libraries to change their outlook. These are the nature and provision of income or funds, and the changing perception of information and its use. Both will affect the long-term survival of traditional library and information services.

The current source of funding for most libraries and information centres is the public purse. Pressures for less direct taxes will decrease the amount of funds available from traditional sources, such as direct government grants or subsidies, and increase the need for the library or information centre to become more entrepreneurial in its quest for funds. Aging Western populations are also causing shifts in the tax base from wages, or earnings to indirect taxes such as consumption taxes and pay-as-you-use systems for public sector services.

The traditional function of the library as a repository for the printed word no longer justifies its costs. The library should, and can, do much more. Information is now an important commodity, not just for day-to-day living but for industry and commerce. A whole new sector has been created called the information industry. As people who are trained to correctly store, organize, manage and disseminate information, librarians and information professionals can play a key role in this sector.

Libraries and information centres have access to information technologies and other facilities (material and human). They can be brought to the front of the information sector if they are prepared to pay the cost of change. These costs should not just be measured in financial terms. There are also costs associated with risk, with changes in professional attitudes and work practices. Organizational disruptions may accompany some strategies used to withstand outside threats for the long-term benefit of the library and its users. Even more importantly, the costs to libraries in terms of their long-term survival are much greater if nothing is done to enhance the role which libraries play in storing, organizing and providing information.

Innovation and intrapreneurship are the keystones to change and the future success of libraries and information centres. They are necessary facilitators for ideas and change. Innovation exploits change and provides the means to deal with the instructured problems facing libraries. Intrapreneurs are the intracorporate entrepreneurs who champion change.

The internal environment of the library or information centre is the most important factor in the process of innovation. For innovation to take place, it is not just a matter of having creative or entrepreneurial people who have the necessary creative-thinking skills. These people have to be able to champion their cause in an open environment which is motivating, risk-taking and ready to accept change.

332

CREATING AN INNOVATIVE ENVIRONMENT

To be an innovative library is not easy. The cross-specialized talents of the entrepreneurs, risk-takers, idea-generators, gate-keepers, and so on lead to natural love–hate relationships, confrontation and conflict. Interdepartmental rivalries and conflicts need to be resolved with care to ensure that creativity is not stifled, that ineffective compromises are not made and that interdepartmental communication and cooperation is not adversely affected.

The conversion of a library holding traditional management styles and values into one which is entrepreneurial and risk-taking takes considerable skills and foresight. A culture needs to be created which not only values better performance, leadership and entrepreneurship, but also sustains that commitment year after year. This means a major shift in the values for some staff, not just a slight increase in awareness of entrepreneurship or the establishment of one or two new programmes or activities for the year.

Staff must be able to accept change, and alter their work tasks and behaviours accordingly. They should be willing to perceive it as an opportunity rather than a threat. Most people are creatures of habit and resist change, seeing it as threatening their existence. It takes management skills to create an environment in which change is accepted as the norm.

There must be a willingness by management to take risks and allow staff to make mistakes. If failure means the loss of a job or not being given the opportunity to try something new again either on a group or individual basis, innovation will be discouraged. The corporate culture of the library will hold the belief that if you value your job, do not try anything difficult or challenging. Risk-taking does not, however, mean short-term orientations, giving the impression that only winners get promoted, or proceeding with an action prior to considering all its possible consequences.

It should be noted that innovation is achieved through long-term outlooks and strategies. It is not achieved through management control systems or short-term efficiency: the pay-off to innovative practices occurs at least five years hence. This is not to say that short-term efficiencies should not exist. These are still important but are not linked to innovation.

Innovation relies upon open communication channels with the external environment. The library or information centre manager must develop reliable networks in the external environment in order to disseminate and obtain information. Timeliness in sensing environmental changes and responding to them is a prime requisite for effective marketing strategies in innovative libraries or information centres.

Timeliness refers to making contacts with politicians to get questions asked in Parliament about the development of new libraries or national information policies. It refers to contacts with key figures in the community suggesting that they write to their elected members about proposed cut-backs in library services in an effort to prevent them. Timeliness is also important in obtaining up-to-date information, an example being the knowledge of proposals to build a shopping centre in a new subdivision of land and the ability to incorporate a library into the scheme before the plans are finalized.

Open internal communication of information and advice is important. Unnecessary bureaucratic procedures should be discontinued as these tend to stifle innovation. Staff should be allowed to exchange ideas and experiences with people of different levels throughout the organization. They should be encouraged to make suggestions, and all ideas should be evaluated.

Some staff will be more creative than others. Whilst all staff should be encouraged to be creative, divergent thinkers should be particularly motivated. Individuals with talent should be recognized and encouraged to champion their ideas. All staff should be aware that even the most unusual idea will be considered by management.

Innovation can be stifled if there is lack of support from top management, lack of necessary time for thought and discussion, and a lack of funds. Thus, library and information centre managers should allow time in their busy schedules to communicate to their employees the values and beliefs which encourage innovation. These should not just be communicated at formal meetings, but also by talking to staff when touring the work rooms, reference or issue desks. It is necessary that communication is a two-way process, allowing staff the opportunity to provide feedback, as it is this informal, two-way communication of values and beliefs which is most effective in creating an innovative corporate culture.

334

An innovative climate is also created through innovative opportunities being built into policies and practices. Staff should be given the freedom to try new ways of performing tasks, and work pressures should be moderate to provide time for thinking. All staff should be given challenging, yet realistic, goals. Immediate and timely feedback on performance should be given.

Participative decision-making and problem-solving should be encouraged. Responsibility should be delegated to allow staff to be self-guiding in their work.

Innovative libraries or information centres create a culture in which there is a broad acceptance of responsibility and a commitment to the organization which goes beyond the individual's functional role. Such a culture is unique as libraries and information centres usually comprise staff who are cosmopolitan in outlook. It occurs because the staff see their library as an example for the profession. This in turn reinforces their commitment and dedication to the organization in their determination to keep it so.

CRITICAL SUCCESS FACTORS FOR INNOVATION

Successful innovation relies upon a balanced mix of seven different functions: idea generation; entrepreneurship or championing; project-leading; management; gatekeeping; coaching; and operating (see Table 24.1). It is also dependent upon routine technical problem-solving, problem definition, idea-nurturing, information transfer, information integration and programme-pushing.

These functions can only be successfully performed by people who have a diversity of skills or by different types of people who need to be recruited and managed differently. Associated with this is the need to measure and reward performance by different means as each individual will be motivated by different incentives. They will also require different types of goals, measures and controls.

Routine management units should not be mixed with entrepreneurial ones. Those people who are responsible for organizing, exploiting and optimizing what already exists should not be responsible for championing new ideas, although this should not prevent them from becoming involved with them. The library should be structured to permit innovative ideas to rise above the daily

Table 24.1

Critical functions in the innovation process

Critical function	Personal Characteristics	Organizational Activities
Idea-generating	Expert in one or two fields. Enjoys conceptualization; comfortable with abstractions. Enjoys doing innovative work. Usually is an individual contributor. Often will work alone.	Generates new ideas and tests their feasibility. Good at problem-solving. Sees new and different ways of doing things. Searches for the breakthroughs.
Entrepreneuring or Championing	Strong application interests. Possesses a wide range of interests. Less propensity to contribute to the basic knowledge of a field. Energetic and determined; puts self on the line.	Sells new ideas to others in the organization. Gets resources. Aggressive in championing his or her 'cause'. Takes risks.
Project-leading	Focus on decision-making, information, and questions. Sensitive to the needs of others. Recognizes how to use the organizational structure to get things done. Interested in a broad range of disciplines and in how they fit together (e.g. marketing, finance).	Provides the team leadership and motivation. Plans and organizes the project. Ensures that administrative requirements are met. Provides necessary coordination among team members. Sees the project moves forward effectively. Balances the project goals with organizational needs.

Gatekeeping	Possesses a high level of technical competence. Is approachable and personable. Enjoys the face-to-face contact of helping others.	Keeps informed of related developments that occur outside the organization through journals, conferences, colleagues, other companies. Passes information on to others; finds it easy to talk to colleagues. Serves as an information resource for others in the organization (i.e., authority on who to see or on what has been done). Provides informal coordination among personnel.
Sponsoring or Coaching	Possesses experience in developing new ideas. Is a good listener and helper. Can be relatively objective. Often is a more senior person who knows the organizational ropes.	Helps develop people's talents. Provides encouragement, guidance, and acts as a sounding board for the project leader and others. Provides access to a power base within the organization – a senior person. Buffers the project team from unnecessary organizational constraints. Helps the project team to get what it needs from the other parts of the organization. Provides legitimacy and organizational confidence in the project.

Source: Roberts and Fusfeld (1981: 25).

demands. Routine processes and procedures should not be allowed to cut off the generation of good ideas and block their movement through the library system.

Innovation and intrapreneurship requires people who:

1. know what they are supposed to do;
2. want to do it;
3. are motivated towards doing it; and,
4. are supplied with the tools and continuous affirmation which enables them to do it.

A mix of champions, sponsors, innovative leaders and creative, flexible staff achieves this.

Champions are people who believe that a new idea is really critical. They will push ahead with their idea, no matter what the roadblocks. Champions are necessary for innovative libraries and information centres as they get things done, often at considerable personal costs to themselves.

Innovative ideas also need sponsors – people sufficiently high up in the organization to marshall the required resources to support the proposed intrapreneurial activity. Once convinced of the activity's value, sponsors provide the resources: people, money and time.

Innovative libraries also require managers who are innovative leaders – that is, managers who set challenging goals for themselves and for others. The library's or information centre's goals should not be vague or easily reached but ones which force the library to be innovative in order to achieve them. The library or information centre manager need not necessarily be creative, ideas-driven people themselves. However, they should recognize the necessity of innovation for success and survival. They should welcome change, accepting that this is part of the innovative process.

Finally, innovation cannot be achieved without a mix of bright, creative minds and an experienced, flexible staff who convert the ideas into outcomes through their performance in carrying out the required tasks.

In acknowledging the need for challenging goals, it should also be understood that there needs to be a clear definition of the library's or information centre's mission in order that the intrapre-

338

neurs know what the library is trying to do. Innovation does not equal diversification. Indeed, most innovative libraries are tightly focused and do not try to be all things to all users.

Above all, innovation and creative ideas must be congruent with the mission statement and have clear set directions. The intrapreneurs and other creative people need to focus upon the real needs of the marketplace and create a distinctive level of performance which matches those needs. Level of performance may not necessarily mean more services. Outcomes such as lower costs for existing services, better performing services, or better features for existing services all require successful innovative strategies.

REFERENCES

Roberts, E.B. and Fusfeld, A.R. (1981), 'Staffing the innovative technology-based organization', *Sloan Management Review*, Spring, pp.19–32.

PART VIII
CONTROL STRATEGIES
FOR LIBRARIES AND
INFORMATION CENTRES

Introduction

This section introduces the reader to the topics of budgeting and economic analysis, programme reviews and performance measures and managing change.

Chapter 25 deals with strategies which provide the means for control of the library's financial resources. This is important as finance is a significant resource within any organization and must be managed effectively and efficiently.

The chief librarian will be personally accountable for all expenditure and income received by the library or information centre. Chapter 25 describes how budgets are framed and expenditure is controlled. The preparation of the budget necessitates the calculation of expenditure and some advice is offered on how this can be done. Some insight is also given to various budgeting methods, such as zero-based budgeting. Finally, a basic introduction to microeconomics provides the reader with some methods of determining the optimum use of staff and other cost analysis techniques which can aid efficiency.

Performance measures do not themselves aid performance. They provide the controls by assessing how the library or information centre is performing, and can be used as accountability measures to the stakeholders of the library. Chapter 26 discusses the issues which arise out of trying to measure the quality and quantity of a library's or information centre's performance. The function of a library manager in either the private or public sector is to ensure that the services meet the particular needs of their marketplace at an acceptable cost. Performance is therefore assessed according to efficiency and effectiveness.

Library managers operate in an environment in which demands for service continue to rise while the availability of resources is increasingly constrained. The ability to measure and demonstrate the value and benefits of the library or information centre will provide some means of ensuring support from the stakeholders.

Finally, the aspect of change is considered in Chapter 27. Change is a necessary part of organization life. It can occur through external or internal environmental influences, or may be instigated to correct poor performance. Change will create apprehension for a number of reasons. A knowledge of why this is likely to occur will assist the library manager in introducing change. Techniques for overcoming resistance to change are also presented in this chapter.

25 Budgeting and economic analysis

INTRODUCTION

Library and information centre budgets are framed by library managers to account for the proposed revenues and expenditures for a specific time period. Whilst the initial preparation of the budget and its ongoing control is often delegated to mid-level managers, final accountability for the budget rests with top management.

The budget is related to the corporate planning process as it is the means by which resources and activities are funded to achieve the library's or information centre's goals. Zero-based budgets and planning–programming budgeting systems are two more recent budgeting techniques which attempt to relate the budgeting process to the planning process.

Budgets are broken down into either functions, cost centres (branch libraries or departments), or cost units (services or programmes). All budgets must be fully supported with documentation and should be prepared for by a series of reports on library activities and proposed developments to executives beforehand. Proposals for new activities should never be presented in a budget report without having been previously discussed at executive meetings.

Since budgets are prepared in advance, some forecasting of costs are necessary when calculating levels of expenditure and revenue. Expenditure should be divided into capital and operating costs, and can be further divided into fixed and variable costs.

Annual budgets should be checked regularly to see that income and expenditure is controlled throughout the year.

Finally, microeconomic analysis can be used in libraries and information centres to determine the optimum use of staff and to budget effectively.

BUDGETING

The term 'budgeting' refers to the act of planning for expenditure and revenue over a specific time period. All library and information centre activities are subject to expenditures and revenues which must be accounted for in a budget. The budget is the financial statement which is prepared and approved for a specific period of time and which provides details of the proposed expenditure and revenues. Usually it is prepared to cover a financial year, but can cover a longer period of time – for example, a triennium. Occasionally, a half-yearly budget is planned.

A budget is prepared prior to expenditure taking place and constitutes both the means of control as to how monies are spent and a check on what monies should have been received.

Preparation of the budget

The preparation of the budget is the responsibility of the library or information centre manager, who is also entrusted with administering the allocated funds within the library's overall programmes and activities. Whilst this responsibility is often delegated to mid-level management or activity centre managers, such as branch librarians or department heads, overall coordination and accountability rests with the manager in charge of the total library service.

In the larger library systems, departmental heads or branch librarians will prepare their own budgets and submit these to the library director or chief librarian. Discussions should take place about the items on the budget and the justifications for them. The library director or manager should be kept fully informed on all aspects of each cost centre's budget.

The library manager is rarely the final arbitrator on the amount of funds to be allocated to the library. This decision is usually made at the executive or ownership level of the parent organization. It is most important that managers of both large and small libraries keep the executives and stakeholders of the parent organization fully informed of the library's progress throughout the year.

Whilst it is important that the proposed budget is fully supported with documentation justifying the proposals and linking these with approved plans, it is not enough. Justification for funds is an ongoing, year-round exercise. The executives of the parent organization and representatives at the ownership level should have their views sought on policy directions and matters for the forthcoming budget well before the presentation of the library's budget. Executives and budget committees do not usually view too kindly strange budget proposals for items which have not previously been discussed. Proposals for new services should be introduced in regular or special reports, not in the budget documentation.

Library and information centre managers should take the time and effort to understand the politics of the budget process within the parent organization. They should also learn how to win budget arguments. If not already invited, they should ask to sit in on the budget deliberations so that they may learn why, sometimes, their bids are rejected. Networks should be formed with key people in the treasury or finance department in order to put the library's point of view forward and gain support for certain proposals.

The lack of opportunity personally to participate in the final budget deliberations should not prevent the library manager from obtaining their required budget allocation. Credibility of the budget details and a recognized value of the library service is what matters most. Justification for the library's budget will already have been made if the arguments for services have been well presented in detailed and timely reports throughout the year. If the librarian's personal network has been effective, key members of the budget committee will be supportive of the library and its budget.

RELATIONSHIP WITH THE CORPORATE PLANNING PROCESS

The budget should be related to the corporate planning process in that it is the means by which resources and activities are funded to achieve the library's or information centre's goals and objectives. It is necessary for library or information centre managers to forecast the monies required to finance the library's planned programmes and activities. The budget then earmarks the amounts of expenditure and anticipated income for certain items or services used in these. For example, it will identify the amount of money which has

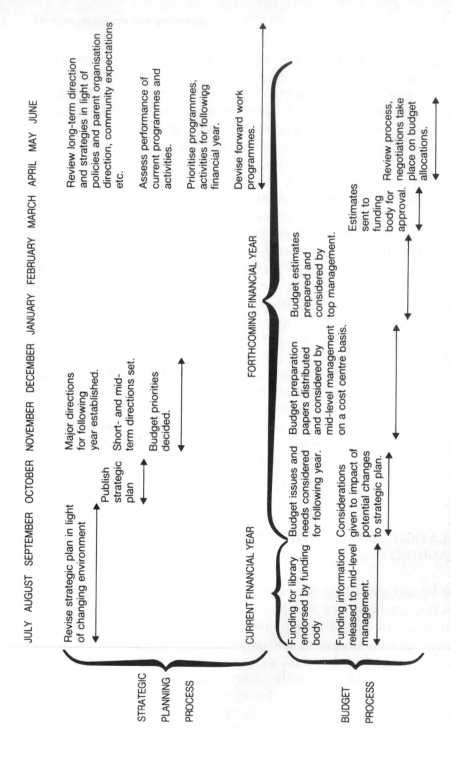

Figure 25.1 Relationship between the corporate planning process and budget process

been approved for expenditure on books, serials, online information searchers or CD-ROMS.

Budgets are often broken down by either programmes or activities (cost units) or location (cost or activity centres). Small libraries and information centres will probably break down their budgets according to the programmes or activities (services) which they provide – that is, on a cost unit basis. Larger library services which consist of departments, branch libraries or both generally use a mix of the cost centre and cost unit methods to break down their budgets.

Figure 25.1 illustrates how the budget process fits the ongoing corporate planning process as part of the annual planning cycle.

CALCULATION OF EXPENDITURE

The preparation of a budget necessitates the calculation of expenditure, which consists of capital expenditures and operating expenditures. Capital expenditures are one-off items of expenditure such as a photocopying machine or new blinds for the windows. Capital expenditures can re-occur, but they are not ongoing costs. They represent long-term investments.

Operating expenditures are current, ongoing costs associated with the day-to-day operations of the library or information centre. These may be divided further into fixed and variable costs:

- Fixed costs relate to annual overhead charges such as rent, general insurance and energy costs.
- Variable costs vary according to usage and relate to salaries, workers' compensation premiums and postage costs.

A further explanation of fixed and variable costs is given later in this chapter.

Within the library's budget, each cost unit's or cost centre's budget will be broken down into capital and operating costs. A further breakdown according to items is often necessary. This allows for various revenues and expenditures to be categorized. For example, an item on the budget just labelled 'staff' provides very little management information, but if this item is broken down into salaries, superannuation on salaries, workers' compensation insurance, training and staff development, conference fees, advertising staff appointments, it is much more meaningful.

Some operating expenditure costs will be harder to calculate than others. Some fixed costs will be known at the time of framing the budget. Public utilities such as energy commissions, post offices, may have already announced their rates or increases in charges for the year and so expenditure in these areas can be calculated quite easily. Cleaning contract costs or maintenance agreements for certain equipment may already be known. Sometimes overheads for library buildings are conveniently reduced to a rate per square metre per annum for budget calculations.

Salaries are usually one of the hardest items to calculate in the library's budget. In most libraries or information centres few staff are paid on the same salary scale. Some staff receive annual increments in their salaries, whilst others do not. The annual increments may be adjusted according to age or years of experience. As a result, some staff have their salary adjusted on their birthdate, whilst others have their salary adjusted according to the date they commenced employment in a particular position. Each position needs to be assessed individually and the appropriate salary figure calculated for the following year.

Inflation rates, international currency exchange rates, salary increases, insurance rates, public utility charges, and so on, are all subject to variances from year to year and within years. Some, such as exchange rates, will fluctuate, whilst others will increase at different rates. These all have to be taken into account when preparing the budget. Usually the library or information centre manager obtains the most recent rates and then discusses the matter with knowledgeable people in the external environment and with members of the finance or treasury department.

Budgetary provision for library materials is often easier to calculate. Published materials price indices can be used. Subscription agencies often advise on likely increases in serial subscriptions. Previous invoices can be scanned to detect increases in prices.

It is important to anticipate the library's income correctly. Any income in excess of expenditure at any given time is often invested by the parent organization on the short-term money market to provide additional cash flow for the organization. Variances in income will disrupt the parent organization's ability to plan its investments wisely. Although some changes in income levels will be unavoidable, any anticipated changes in policies which may affect the library's income should be accounted for in the budget. Examples would be the anticipated increased income in photocopying fees as the result of an additional photocopying machine being installed in the library, or, the increased income obtained as the result of higher fines being introduced.

In planning for the annual budget there is a time-delay process. Planning often commences up to six months prior to the budget being ratified and the necessary funds being available to purchase items. This is particularly the case with such capital expenditure items as furniture and computer terminals which are costed in preparation for the budget several months before they can be purchased. There is even a longer lead-time for major undertakings such as when budgeting for the building of a new library. Allowances to cover price increases may need to be built-in to the budget.

BUDGET CONTROLS

Whilst the preparation of the budget is an annual event, often being a long drawn-out affair, with deliberations lasting several weeks, the budget control process is a day-by-day, month-by-month, year-round process. All expenditures must be made within the framework of the amount stated in each item approved by the reviewing authority.

Expenditure is usually divided into three categories on the weekly or monthly budget report. These are the total expenditure amounts budgeted at the beginning of the financial year, the actual expenditure to date and the committed expenditure to date.

Actual expenditure refers to expenditure amounts for goods or services received and for which invoices and/or statements have also been received and paid for. Committed expenditure refers to the outstanding expenditures for goods or services which have been ordered but not yet paid for. The goods or services may or may not have been received by the library. In calculating total expenditure costs to date, both the actual and committed expenditure amounts should be added together.

Statements of committed and expended funds should be regularly checked and continually kept under review in order to control the budget. Any anticipated increase in expenditure above that provided by the budget must be offset by a decrease in expenditure activity in that area. Unexpected expenditures such as costly emergency repairs to buildings, bookmobiles, and the like should incur a reallocation of funds from elsewhere. Such a readjustment of funds will usually occur twice or three times per year, and may need to be referred to, or authorized by, top management or the ownership level.

It is important that appropriations for the various items of the budget are expended solely for the purposes specified in the budget. However appropriate techniques for making changes and revisions to the budget should be provided to allow for unexpected events which could not possibly be foreseen when the budget was framed.

BUDGETING TECHNIQUES

Line-item budgets

This is the most traditional approach to budgeting. It divides expenditures into broad categories such as salaries, other operating expenses, equipment maintenance, materials, capital expenditures, and sundries. There are further subdivisions within these categories. Most line budgets are prepared by projecting current expenditures to next year, taking likely cost increases into account.

Whilst they are easy to prepare, very few organizations use line-item budgets today as they have many disadvantages when compared with the more modern approaches. They do not relate to the organization's goals and objectives, and the benefits or outcomes of the allocated monies cannot be assessed.

Line-item budgets foster a temptation to disguise needs and ask for more monies than are actually needed. There is often no attempt made to ascertain whether items are really necessary. It is also possible for the line-item budget to lock the library or information centre manager into a particular piece of equipment itemized on the budget, when an alternative solution may be appropriate.

352

Zero-based budgeting

Zero-based budgeting or ZBB combines corporate planning and decision-making with budgeting. At the operational level in a library there exists a number of activities which can be grouped together to achieve a common purpose and which make up programmes. The grouping of these activities or programmes is the lowest level entity for which a budget may be prepared. Each programme should be large enough to be identifiable as having functional responsibilities to which costs can be allocated, but small enough to be manageable.

Prior to the budget, the objectives and activities of the programme are examined. Alternative methods of providing the programme are evaluated. The advantages of retaining the programme's current activities, the consequences of not having the programme, and its overall efficiency are considered. The required resources and associated costs for the programme are calculated.

The programmes are then grouped into a series of decision packages. Each package responds to a statement of purpose, and is in accordance with the library's goals and objectives. They are ranked according to their cost–benefit by management.

At some point in the ranking of the decision packages there is a cut-off point. This is the point which allows some programmes to be funded and others not. The cut-off point corresponds to the library's total budget allocation. Those programmes which are ranked in priority above the funding line are funded; those below it are left unfunded. If further funds become available, those ranked at or immediately above the original funding line are funded.

Zero-based budgeting does not allow for incremental growth in budgets. It considers efficiency and the relevancy of programmes in achieving organizational goals. It exposes all library activities to the same scrutiny, preventing programmes from being approved solely on the basis of tradition. More efficient ways of achieving the corporate goals and objectives are sought by examining different methods of service delivery or activities.

The decision package statement provides a statement of purpose for the programmes activity descriptions, the anticipated benefits from the desired results, alternatives, consequences and costs. It is both an operating plan and a budget. The budget is thus the product of the operating decisions.

As Chen (1980: 66) points out, zero-based budgeting requires a thorough knowledge of the organization. Library and information centre managers need to be aware of the library's characteristics and objectives, and the types of people who use its services. Activities and programmes must be well conceived. The library's or information centre's strengths and weaknesses should be known. Managers and staff should know why they want to spend money, where and what to spend it on and the outcomes of spending the money.

Zero-based budgeting identifies the trade-offs among the programmes and goals so that top management can decide what funding level they can afford versus the programmes and goals they must afford to do without.

There are some disadvantages to zero-based budgeting. It requires great commitment of time and effort; it involves a great deal of preparation, planning and organization; and it relies upon all participants being aware of formalized policies and planning priorities. To be effective, it requires extensive training in its techniques and should not be introduced without due consideration of the time and effort involved.

Programme budgeting

Programme budgeting is based upon the provision of library services rather than individual items or expenditures. It allocates monies to services or programmes; having previously explored different means to providing services which have been identified as needed by the library's clientele. In a public library major programmes may be provided to serve the housebound, young adults, children, business and commerce, and adults. Each programme has certain funds allocated for staff, operating expenses, materials, publicity, and so on. There are no overall budget allocations to the library, only to the individual programmes.

Performance budgeting

Performance budgeting bases its expenditure on the performance of

354

activities and services. It is similar to programme budgeting in format but is concerned with efficiency. It uses cost–benefit analysis techniques to measure performance and requires large amounts of data. Performance budgeting has been criticized as it emphasizes economics rather than quality of service.

Planning–programming budgeting systems (PPBS)

PPBS combines the best of programme budgeting and performance budgeting. It combines the functions of planning, programming and budgeting into one.

The library's goals and objectives are established and short-term objectives are stated in a quantifiable manner. Alternative means of achieving the objectives are considered and selected on the basis of cost–benefit. These activities are then grouped into programmes and funded.

Once the programmes are established they are controlled by comparing them with the stated objectives to see if the goals are being achieved. The results are evaluated so that corrective actions can be taken. PPBS allows costs to be assigned to programmes so that the benefits can be measured in relation to cost.

PPBS is a time-consuming budgetary procedure. Whilst the approach appears to be simple, it is complex in practice. It is based upon planning steps which may not, in reality, be evaluated during the actual budget preparation. It does not provide an operating tool for line managers or provide the mechanism to evaluate the impact of various funding levels on each programme. Finally, it does not force the continued evaluation of existing programmes and activities.

LIBRARY COST ACCOUNTING

Cost accounting can be used in libraries to determine the anticipated value of certain activities or for comparative purposes to measure efficiency. Cost accounting is the simple process of breaking down resources to the activity being carried out and then collating the monetary cost to show the cost of the activity. Cost accounting is not an end in itself. It is used to determine if the resources have been used effectively.

Library cost accounting falls into two categories: routine costing which is used to provide regular financial and management information; and special exercise costing which deals with specific questions.

Routine cost–output or cost–activity ratios are used on a comparative basis to measure the efficiencies of certain library functions, cost centres or services. By themselves these ratios serve no real purpose. When used to compare branch libraries within a system or to make external comparisons between similar types of organizations they provide valuable management information. Efficient and inefficient services, functions or centres can be highlighted using routine costing procedures.

Special costing exercises are concerned with particular activities or groups of activities. They are used to answer specific questions such as the comparison of costs of current operations with the estimated costs of alternative methods. In preparing special costing exercises, it is important to remember that the costs of proposed systems need to be related not only to the existing systems but also to the other benefits which will result. It may well be that a new system is approved not so much on the grounds of costs savings but on the benefits and improvements of the new service to the user.

ECONOMIC ANALYSIS

Although most libraries and information centres operate in the public sector, this should not prevent library managers from looking at costs of services from an economic point of view. This section is intended to provide a basic introduction to microeconomics which can be used to determine the optimum use of staff and to budget effectively.

Fixed and variable costs

Fixed costs are those which do not vary with output. Costs which vary with output are called variable costs. Knowledge of both fixed and variable costs is necessary in order to budget effectively. As an example, the total costs of a library's operations will rise if more

356

Expenditure

Salaries – research	6,000
data entry	2,000
Insurance – workers' compensation	200
Superannuation on salary	100
Stationery	2,000
Printing	2,000
Art fees	500
Word processing use	300
TOTAL	**$13,100**

Print run 5,000

Unit cost of production $\dfrac{13,100}{5,000} = \$2.62$

Income

Proposed income from sales 4,990 @ $4	19,600
Profit	$6,500

Figure 25.2   An example of unit costing to determine the price of a library publication

books are purchased. This rise will not apply to all items in the budget or be in proportion because some library costs will not be affected by the increase in the number of books bought. Electricity costs, for example, will remain the same if 3,000 or 6,000 books are purchased. Electricity costs will only increase if more processing time is involved, increasing the amount of time in which the lights are left on. Expenditure on safety equipment or telephones will remain unchanged unless the number of staff is increased considerably. Electricity, safety equipment and telephone costs will be fixed costs in this example. If an additional staff member is appointed to process the items the salary component in the budget will be increased. Salaries are therefore a variable cost.

Unit costs

Unit costs are used to measure output. As it is not always easy to compare the rising curve of total costs, library managers and

357

economists convert the total cost figures into unit costs. They do this by dividing the total cost of the activity by the number of units – for example, the number of interlibrary loans or number of books processed. This results in a figure for the average cost per unit of output. Unit costs can also be used in time terms. They are used in libraries to measure performance by comparing inputs to outputs.

Unit costs concepts can be used to allocate a cost to a library product or service; they can also be used to develop a standard for a job in either time or cost terms.

Fixed costs per unit

Fixed costs per unit can be used to determine budget allocations and efficiency in libraries and information centres.

Fixed costs per unit of output fall as output rises. If a library has fixed costs (electricity, conference fees, telephone) of $10,000 a year and it issues 5,000 books per year, each book issued will have a fixed cost of $2. If output rises to 10,000 issues, the unit share of fixed costs of an issue will shrink to $1. At 100,000 issues it would be 10¢ (See Figure 25.3).

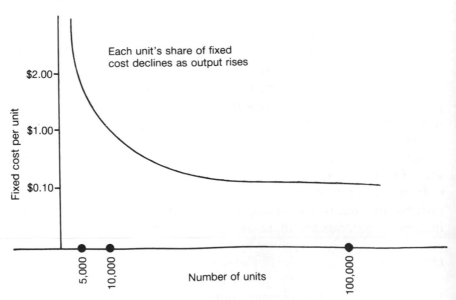

Figure 25.3   Profile of fixed costs per unit

With regard to variable costs per unit, the situation is more complex. It depends upon marginal productivity and the productivity curve (law of variable proportions).

Productivity curves: law of increasing returns

Productivity curves can be used to determine the optimum levels of efficiency in libraries and information centres.

Physical productivity changes when different amounts of one factor are combined with fixed amounts of others. In a new library or information centre with a stock of 2,000 books, a certain amount of equipment may be needed. Apart from the librarian, there is no need for additional labour. If another person is hired, the library has the capacity to process and catalogue more books. The capacity increases again when a third person is hired and so on.

The appointment of the second librarian will have value as the two can begin to specialize and divide the work. Each will perform the jobs they are better at and save time formerly wasted by moving from one job to the next. As a consequence this division of labour may allow the library to catalogue and process a further 5,000 books per year. Since the difference in output is 3,000 books, the marginal productivity of labour when the two librarians are working is 3,000 books.

The marginal productivity of labour should not be spoken of in terms of the second librarian as, by themselves, their efforts would be no more productive than those of the first librarian. If the first librarian left, the second librarian would still catalogue and process only 2,000 books. What makes the difference is the jump in the combined production of the two librarians once specialization can be introduced. Hence we speak of the changing marginal productivity of labour, not the individual.

Increased specialization takes place with the third, fourth, fifth librarian so that the addition of another unit of labour as an input in each case brings about an output larger than was realized by the average of all the previous librarians. This does not necessarily mean that each successive librarian is more efficient and productive. It means that, as units of one factor [librarians] are added, the total mix of these units plus the fixed amounts of other factors forms an increasingly efficient technical combination. The range of factor inputs, over which average productivity rises, is called a range of increasing average returns.

Every time a factor is added, efficiency rises. The rate of increased efficiency will not be the same, for the initial large marginal leaps in productivity will give way to smaller ones. However, the overall trend whether measured by looking at total output or at average output per librarian will still be increased. This continues until a point of maximum technical efficiency is reached.

Law of diminishing returns

The law of diminishing returns is used to detect the point of maximum technical efficiency in libraries and information centres.

At a certain point, the point of maximum technical efficiency, the marginal output no longer rises when another librarian is added to the staff. Total output will still be increasing, but the last librarian to be employed will have added less output than their predecessor. Labour is now beginning to 'crowd' equipment or the premises. Opportunities for further specialization have become non-existent.

This condition of falling marginal performance is called a condition of decreasing or diminishing returns. The library is getting back less and less not only from the 'marginal' librarian but from the combined labour of all the other librarians.

Table 25.1
Law of diminishing returns

Number of Librarians	Total Output (Books Catalogue)	Marginal Productivity (Change in Output)		Average Productivity (Total Ouput – Number of Librarians)	
1	2,000	2,000	Increasing marginal productivity	2,000	Increasing average productivity
2	5,000	3,000		2,500	
3	8,500	3,500		2,853	
4	11,800	3,300	Decreasing marginal productivity	2,950	
5	14,800	3,000		2,960	
6	17,300	2,500		2,883	Decreasing average productivity
7	19,500	2,200		2,785	

If labour goes on being added, a point will be reached at which the contribution of the 'marginal' librarian will be so small that the average output per librarian will also fall. Eventually, if even more librarians were added, the factor mix would be so disrupted that the total output would actually fall resulting in a condition of negative gains (Table 25.1).

The marginal productivity begins to diminish with the fourth librarian who catalogues only 3,300 books not 3,500 as did the predecessor. Average productivity continues to rise until the addition of the sixth librarian, because the fifth librarian, although producing less than the fourth, is still more productive than the average output of all four cataloguers. Therefore marginal productivity can be falling while average productivity is still rising.

In summary, as successive units of one factor are added to fixed amounts of others, the marginal output of the units of the variable factor will at first rise and then decline. This is called the law of variable proportions or the law of diminishing returns or, the physical productivity curve (Figure 25.4).

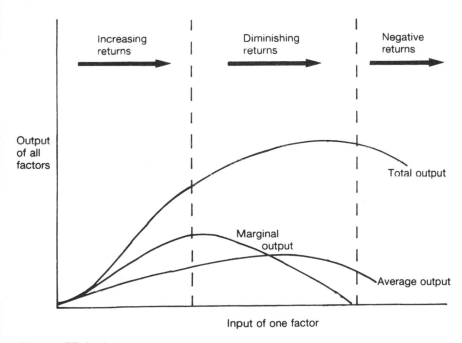

Figure 25.4   Law of variable proportions

Variable costs per unit

Variable costs per unit can be used to cost increased efficiency in libraries.

Table 25.2
Schedule of physical productivity

Number of Librarians	Total Outputs (units)	Marginal Product
1	2,000	2,000
2	5,000	3,000
3	8,500	3,500
4	11,800	3,300
5	14,800	3,000
6	17,300	2,500
7	19,500	2,200

As in the case of the librarians processing and cataloguing the books, the total number of books catalogued (units produced) will rise at first rapidly, then more slowly with the addition of more librarians (Table 25.2). To convert the schedule of physical productivity into a unit cost figure, the total variable cost for each level of output should be calculated. This should then be divided by the number of units to obtain an average variable cost per unit of output (Table 25.3).

Table 25.3
Calculating the average variable cost per unit output

Number of Librarians	Total Variable Costs at $20,000 per Librarian	Total Output (units)	Average Variable Cost per Unit of Output (cost–output)
1	$ 20,000	2,000	$10.00
2	40,000	5,000	8.00
3	60,000	8,500	7.05
4	80,000	11,800	6.78
5	100,000	14,800	6.75
6	120,000	17,300	6.93
7	140,000	19,500	7.18

The average variable costs per unit (book catalogued) declines at first and then rises. This is because the variable cost increases by a set amount ($20,000 per librarian). Output, however obeys the law of variable proportions, increasing rapidly at first and then displaying diminishing returns. The variable cost per unit of output will therefore fall as long as output is growing faster than costs. It will begin to rise as soon as additions to output start to get smaller.

Total cost per unit

A complete costing schedule can now be established for the combined fixed and variable costs of processing and cataloguing the books in the library or information centre. This is useful for calculating a processing charge if a book is lost and an account has to be sent for the true value of the book – that is, the cost of the book and the cost of cataloguing and processing it.

Fixed costs (overheads such as electricity, telephones) are added to the variable costs of the salaries of the librarians to give the total cost. The total cost is divided by the output to give the average cost per unit of output. The changing marginal cost per unit is calculated by dividing the increase in total costs by the increase in output, each time an extra librarian is appointed (Table 25.4).

Table 25.4
Calculating the average cost per unit of output

Number of Librarians	Total Costs ($10,000 fixed costs + $20,000 per librarian)	Output (units)	Cost per unit of output			
			Average (total cost – output)		Marginal (changes in cost – changes in output)	
1	30,000	2,000	$15.00			
2	50,000	5,000	10.00	Falling	$6.61	Falling
3	70,000	8,500	8.23	average	5.71	marginal
4	90,000	11,800	7.63	cost	6.06	Rising
5	110,000	14,800	7.43		6.66	marginal
6	130,000	17,300	7.51	Rising	8.00	cost
7	150,000	19,500	7.69	average	9.09	

REFERENCES

Chen, Ching-chih (1980), *Zero-Based Budgeting in Library Management: a manual for librarians* (Phoenix, Az.: Oryx).

26 Programme review and performance measures

INTRODUCTION

An important process of management is that of reviewing the library's or information centre's programmes and measuring its performance in attaining the corporate goals. This has two purposes: as an assessment of how the service is performing, and as an accountability factor to the stakeholders.

The most common means of measuring a library's or information centre's performance and value has been through its outputs. Some people have also attempted to measure outcomes or the library's impact on its target markets and the environment.

Outputs provide a neat, measurable focal point. They can be compared with inputs to measure efficiency, and with the corporate goals to measure effectiveness. Outputs also become outcomes when an attempt is made to measure the impact of the outputs on the environment. Outputs therefore allow management to measure the effectiveness and efficiency of the library's or information centre's systems, policies, procedures, leadership, resources, and so on, in meeting the needs of the defined target markets.

The user's ability to utilize the library's services to create further output is a measure of the library's performance in the form of an outcome. If the library's services are such that they cannot be put to use as part of a continuing system cycle, the programmes need to be reviewed.

In order to measure performance, information needs to be collected and analysed about the library's or information centre's programmes. The library or information centre manager must determine what pieces of information are needed to evaluate or measure the library's performance. These are called performance indicators. They provide the formula through which measurement can be made. Information for performance indicators has to be obtained through a data collection process.

Performance measures and programme reviews serve to prove and improve. If the planning process has served its purpose, the library or information centre will be able to prove its worth by meeting or exceeding the set goals and objectives. If challenging goals have been set, it follows that the library and its services must also have improved.

MEASURING PERFORMANCE IN DIFFERENT TYPES OF LIBRARIES

As the missions and goals of various types of libraries and information centres are different, it follows that their outputs and outcomes will also differ. Special libraries and most information centres provide information which assists in the internal functioning of an organization. Their measures of performance will be linked to how successful the organization is in achieving its objectives. Such libraries add value to the quality of knowledge within the organization by acquiring, organizing and disseminating accurate and timely information. Their outcomes are found in the added values to knowledge and information within the organization which help to make it successful against its competitors.

Whilst some public libraries provide special library and information services to their local authority, they principally exist to serve an external agency, the public. Public libraries add value to the quality of life of individuals, and occasionally commerce, through the provision of educational, informational, recreational and cultural services. Their measures of performance are linked to the societal marketing concept of customer satisfaction, long-run public welfare and the creation of an informed society by the most cost-effective methods.

There are three measures of performance common to all libraries and information centres. These are efficiency and two other aspects, 'How good is the service?' and 'How much good does it do?'. The latter can be expressed as quality and value or effectiveness and benefit. Orr (1973: 318) states:

The ultimate criterion for assessing the quality of a service is its capability for meeting the user needs it is intending to serve, and the value of a service must ultimately be judged in terms of the beneficial effects accruing from its use as viewed by those who sustain the costs.

If the special library or information centre is supplying pertinent and timely information in an efficient manner which enables the organization to take advantage of its competitors, it will be perceived as being a valuable asset by management and funded accordingly. If it fails to do so, it may be endured as a luxury or status symbol until such times as an economic recession forces its closure through lack of support.

A similar situation exists in public libraries. Good public libraries, whose services are efficient and reflect the needs of the community, are usually well supported. Ratepayers convey positive feedback on the library service to the elected members and executives of the local authority. Tangible effects are felt upon the quality of life in the community. Community spirit and support for the library grows. A poor, inefficient library service results in disillusionment for both staff and users. Negative feedback from the ratepayers often results in negativism on the part of those who hold the purse-strings and unless performance is enhanced, declining funding follows.

Orr's framework

Orr's loop and propositions are useful to consider here (see Figure 26.1). Orr's (1973: 318) basic propositions are:

i) that, other things being equal, the capability of the service will tend to increase as the resources devoted to it increase, but not necessarily proportionately.
ii) that, other things being equal, the total uses made of a service (utilization) will tend to increase as its capability increases, but not necessarily proportionately.
iii) that, other things being equal, the beneficial effects realized from a service will increase as its utilization increases, but not necessarily proportionately.

iv) that, other things being equal, the resources devoted to a service will increase as its beneficial effects increase, but not necessarily proportionately.

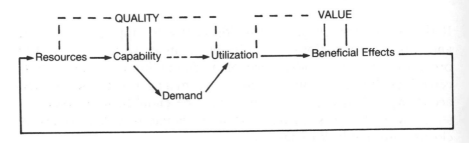

Figure 26.1   Orr's Relations among criterion variables
Source: Orr (1973: 318). Reprinted by permission of Aslib.

The cause and effect sequence is useful in that it points out that funds invested in programmes or libraries may not necessarily have the same impact. There are always other important interactions which will have just the same, if not more, effect on the library and its programmes.

In the past it was considered that a library's performance was directly related to the size of its budget. Librarians, somewhat naively, measured their library's budget against others in terms of what was 'biggest' must be 'best'. They measured quantity of input rather than quality or output. Today, it is recognized that output, quantity and quality play an important part. In fact, in times of economic restraint, it is quality not quantity which distinguishes a library service. The knowledge and resourcefulness of library staff can have more impact on the quality and value of the service than the funding level.

The level of funding obviously still has some bearing upon the output and performance of the library or information centre. Without finance to provide the necessary inputs in the forms of human, technical and material resources, the library's services will gradually decline in use. If the library is not viewed as being of value it will suffer when resources are being allocated. However, funds alone do not constitute a good service.

A good library or information service depends upon the effectiveness of its policies and practices, on its staff competence and morale and on the leadership skills of management. In reviewing the programmes and assessing their performances, the systems operating in the library or information centre will be the first to be scrutinized. If the marketing strategies are correct, and the policies, operations, technical and material resources are adequate and effective, attention should then be turned to the staff. Their competence, skills and experience and productivity levels should be assessed. The staff are responsible for putting into action the policies and operations. If they lack the skills or competence, both will be ineffective.

Finally the leadership skills of management should be evaluated. Their mix of technical, human relations and conceptual skills should be appropriate to their level of management. Without effective leadership skills the goals of the organization, management and employees will not be reconciled. As a consequence, the performance of the library or information centre will suffer. Management information systems can play a vital role in providing information upon which performance-based decisions can be made.

MEASURING PERFORMANCE

One of the problems that library and information managers have is in proving their worth or value in quantitative terms. So many of the benefits are intangible. The quality of the service may be recognized by the users and stakeholders or executives, but it is still hard to apply any comparative measures between libraries in order to try to improve it still further.

In returning to Orr's loop, Orr (ibid, 319), states:

Of the four variables in the loop, resources lend themselves most readily to quantification in that they seem, at least superficially, to have 'natural' units, which should be countable.

369

Resources are inputs to the service. They do not measure quality of service for the reasons mentioned above.

Utilization, according to Orr (ibid.) is somewhat more difficult to quantify. This is mainly because of expense and the fact that most services are heterogeneous. Utilization is quantified in simple output measures such as number of reference questions handled, number of issue transactions and so on.

Sometimes an attempt is made to assume some sort of qualitative measures by applying a time-scale to the quantitative measures – for example, the number of reference enquiries taking 15 minutes or more – the assumption in this case being that the longer the period of time taken, the more in-depth and valuable the service given. It should be noted that there is not necessarily a correlation between time and quality.

The problem with using performance measures of this type is that we do not know what the user is going to do with the information that is provided. There have been cases where users have walked out of libraries completely dissatisfied but, out of politeness and consideration for the staff, have made them feel helpful and successful. The questions of quality and value or capability and benefit arise.

Capability and benefit are much more difficult to measure directly. Indirect measures have been used, but as Orr points out (ibid.: 320), the relationship between capability and utilization is mediated through demand, which is itself a highly complex variable.

Quality and value are linked to the usefulness of the outputs – that is, the effect the particular output has on the performance of the recipient or on an organization. As an output, libraries and information centres provide information both in the form of a product and a service. Taylor (1986: 181–4) has defined several qualities or attributes which should be used as a basis for auditing information as an output.

The audit should be at a definable point in the process such as the number of abstracts completed or requests for information processed. The activities should be easy to count and defined. For example, reference transactions can be classified as taking under 1 minute, 1–3 minutes, 5–10 minutes, and so on.

A defined output should also be consistent with existing information systems and, if possible, covered by historical data. Like should be compared with like. The historical context is important as it allows for comparisons over a period of time.

The output should have a terminal quality. It should be isolated and counted at the point where it changes function and status. The issue of a book changes the status of the book from a library resource or input to a source of information, education, culture or recreation for the library user. By counting issue transaction statistics, public libraries are counting one of the sources of added value to the quality of life in their communities. The outputs should be the result of a process in which value is added. Libraries add value to information by organizing it.

The output should be in a form useful in the future as input to other processes. Either as a product or service, information is acquired, organized, stored, retrieved, analysed, packaged and transmitted for some purpose. It has an outcome in a future act, decision or knowledge change. This is the area that librarians and information centre managers need to know more about in assessing their library's performance and in demonstrating accountability to the stakeholders.

PERFORMANCE INDICATORS

A performance indicator is the formula which management uses to measure the progress of a programme towards achieving the organization's goals and objectives. It is the means of knowing whether a library's or information centre's specific objectives are being achieved (Table 26.1). However, even success in producing outputs and achieving outcomes does not necessarily mean that there are not better ways of achieving the same results at least cost. The results should always be analysed.

Performance indicators must combine the elements of inputs, outputs and outcomes. Generally three types of indicators are used. These are:

1. *Workload indicators*: output oriented and measure amount of work done
2. *Efficiency indicators*: compare resource inputs against resulting outputs

Table 26.1
**Examples of performance indicators which may be found
in information centres**

Category	Objective	Performance Indicator
Workload	To bibliographically organize 600 books per year.	Actual books processed per year (reported monthly)
Efficiency	Provide a SDI service at a maximum cost of $100.00 per person per month.	The actual cost of providing an SDI service (based at unit cost)
Effectiveness	To provide an information service which satisfies 90% of client demands for information within 3 days.	Analysis of information service against client demand/requests for information and time taken to provide information, summarized monthly.

3. *Effectiveness indicators*: measure the extent to which programmes achieve objectives.

Performance indicators must be relevant to the cause and should
clearly relate to the specific objectives of the programme. Above
all, they should be measurable. The information used must be
reliable and valid. Data collection should be accurate, unbiased and
collected in time for proper use to be made of it. It is most important
that the indicators can be translated into meaningful information for
use by all who require them.

Each indicator should be unique. It should reveal some important
aspect of performance that no other indicator does. Finally, the
value of the information should be weighed against the costs of the
collector's and analyst's time, efforts and resources. This is the most
important criterion of all. It is necessary to consider the degree to
which routine operations will be impeded in collecting the data, and
the acceptable levels of staff time and operating expenses for the
value of the information provided.

REFERENCES

Orr, R.H. (1973), Measuring the goodness of library services: A general framework for considering quantitative measures', *Journal of Documentation*, **29**(3), September, pp.315–32.

Taylor, R.S. (1986), *Value Added Processes in Information Systems* (New Jersey: Ablex).

27 Managing change

INTRODUCTION

Change can be defined as an alteration in the relationships or environment of one or a group of people.

Change has always been part of the human condition. What is different now is the pace of change, and the prospect that it will accelerate, affecting every part of life, including personal values, morality and religion, which seem almost remote from technology and libraries. Change is a necessary part of organizational life. It occurs through the impact of both external and internal sources. It is also associated with the various stages of development in the organizational life cycle. Changes can either be pro-active or reactive. Pro-active or planned changes are superior as they provide time for thought.

There will often be some resistance to change. This is usually caused by feelings of loss and uncertainty which in turn leads to insecurity. The most effective way of overcoming resistance to change is through encouraging those involved to become part of the planning and decision-making process. Education and training, open communication and evidence of clear, tangible benefits as an outcome of change will also facilitate the change process.

ORGANIZATION CHANGE

When one or more elements in a library change it is called organizational change. Organizational change will occur either as a result of changes in the external environment which impact upon the library or through internal forces. Some internal forces may be an indirect reflection of the external forces acting upon the library or information centre.

External forces most likely to affect libraries or information centres are those relating to technologies, economic and financial conditions, supplies of information materials, cultural and social conditions. Internal forces are most likely to come from a revision of organizational goals, shifts in employee's sociocultural values, changes in work attitudes, hours or working conditions. Many of these changes will be rooted in the external environment such as equal opportunity legislation, award changes or affirmative action.

Some organizational change is planned well in advance, such as the changes to a library's organization structure as the result of computerization. Other changes come about as a reaction to unexpected events – for example, cutbacks in services as a result of unanticipated budget cuts.

Planned change is change that is designed and implemented in an orderly and timely fashion in anticipation of future events. Reactive change is a piecemeal response to problems as they develop. As such changes are always executed quickly with little time for thought the results are not as preferable as those of planned change.

Organizational change affects the library's technology, products or services, employees and managerial systems. A change in any one of these will affect the others.

Technical changes are usually designed to make the technical processes more efficient or to produce greater throughput with the same number of staff. Such changes involve automating the library's functions or changing the techniques of information retrieval by introducing CD-ROMS. The introduction of any new technology will result in the need for staff retraining and changed work practices. The need for library user education in using the new technology should not be overlooked, as they will be using some of the tools of the new technology – for example, OPACs or CD-ROMS.

Changes in a library's or information centre's services or products are generally introduced as a result of technological change, in response to consumer demand or through the identification of a market niche not previously served. These changes will often require staff time and expertise in promoting the new services and in educating the users about them.

People changes refer to changes in attitudes, skills, expectations and behaviour of employees. Increasing the technical skills of librarians or information professionals, discouraging smoking in

375

work areas, improving interpersonal relationships are all people-changing activities.

Managerial changes involve the supervision and management of the library. They include changes in the organization structure, goals, policies, reward and compensation systems, labour relations, management information systems, and budgeting and accounting systems. As the organization grows, changes will automatically take place. An explanation for this can be found in the analysis of an organization's life cycle, which follows later in this chapter.

INTRODUCING CHANGE

When introducing change into a library or information centre several issues should be considered, the first being the implications of the proposed change. By determining the implications of the change some of the answers as to how people will react to change may be provided.

The magnitude of the change alters the way in which the change processes should be managed. Radical or major changes which have the potential to affect the whole organization are managed quite differently to minor changes or those which affect one or two people. Changes at policy level also need to be managed differently from those at procedural level.

The timing and frequency of the change needs to be considered. Wherever possible, changes should be implemented at a time when the organization is least pressured. However, this is not always possible, particularly in the case of reactive change. The frequency of change and the duration of the change affects the way in which the change is managed. Permanent change needs to be managed differently to short-lived change.

ORGANIZATION LIFE CYCLES AND CHANGE

Organizations are subject to a life cycle which leads them towards a bureaucratic or mechanistic style of management and thence onwards to an integrating or matrix structure and management style. These styles and structures are discussed in Chapters 4 and 9.

376

As the library or information centre and its parent organization progresses through the organization life cycle, changes in managerial structure and style will occur. The fundamental reason for this is found in systems theory. As systems grow they move in the direction of differentiation and elaboration with greater specialization of function. As differentiation proceeds, it is countered by processes that bring the system together for unified functioning.

When a library or information centre is first established, the emphasis is on creativity. Services and products are created in order to prove its worth. The founding librarian devotes his or her energies to establishing and marketing the services. As there are generally few staff, the organization and management style is informal and non-bureaucratic. Control is based on the librarian's personal supervision. Long hours are often experienced. There is often not enough time for proper procedures to be documented; most decisions are based upon professional knowledge.

As the library grows, more staff are added. People are promoted from within. It is an exciting place to work but, unless the policies and goals have been formally documented, it begins to lose direction. The founding librarian may not be interested in management, more in his or her professional work. Strong management is needed to guide the library or information centre through this stage.

If the leadership is strong, clear goals and direction are provided. Differentiation occurs, specialization takes place, departments are established, and a hierarchy of authority is formed. This marks the beginning of the division of labour. Management systems are introduced for accounting budgets, inventory and acquiring items. Communication becomes more formal, and elements of bureaucracy are apparent.

As growth continues, restrictive practices begin to impede the service. First-line and mid-level managers need to be able to exercise discretion. Top managers begin to delegate responsibility to mid-level managers, concentrating more on long-term planning and coordination. The internal control systems have by now formalized communication to the extent that it becomes less frequent. New specialists and services are added. Consultants are often hired to review policies and procedures as the organization appears to be ineffective. As a result, task forces, project and matrix groups are formed to improve coordination, but the proliferation of systems and bureaucracy strangles innovation. The solution to this crisis is in collaboration and cooperation. Managers develop skills for confronting problems and resolving interpersonal differences. Formal systems are simplified. Attempts are made to create a more open, reactive organizational environment.

The developments in the organization life cycle produce significant changes from one stage to the next. Library and information centre managers need to know the stage at which their library is in the organization life cycle in order to prepare for the future and avoid some of the pitfalls.

RESISTANCE TO CHANGE

In planning for change, library managers and information professionals should take it into account that they will experience resistance to change. There are a variety of reasons why people resist change. Often the uncertainty of impending change leads to anxiety, particularly in relation to people's ability to cope with new technology or methods. This has been demonstrated by some library staff in their use of computer terminals and library automated systems. They may have quite happily used typewriters, but become anxious at the thought of using a 'typewriter with a screen'. They fear the thought of having to master something new and the possibility that they may not be able to do this immediately.

Change is also resisted because there are often different perceptions of the employee's and management's assessment of the situation. Changes in organizational structure or workplace may cause the severance of old relationships with feelings of loss and disruption to existing social networks. The promotion of an internal candidate to the level of top management may sever the close relationships which existed beforehand between the candidate and mid-level management.

Resistance can also occur because of previous life experiences. If the change is coloured by a previous negative encounter with a similar life experience, there will often be resistance.

Familiarity with existing procedures and lack of psychological energy to acquire new skills or change direction also causes resist-

378

ance to change. Staff may argue that they are too old to learn new systems. Change may also produce a threat to an individual's or group's self-interest or status. Their position of authority or power source may be threatened if they are placed in a situation of being dependent upon others whilst they are in a learning situation. An organization's culture may also present resistance to change.

TECHNIQUES FOR OVERCOMING RESISTANCE TO CHANGE

The most effective technique for overcoming resistance to change is by encouraging participation in the decision-making and planning processes. Employees who participate in planning and implementing change are better able to understand the reasons for it. Uncertainty is reduced and self-interest neutralized through the opportunity to express their own ideas.

Education, training and communication about expected work practices and results should reduce resistance. If open channels of communication are established and maintained, uncertainty can be minimized. It is also helpful to introduce change gradually to minimize resistance and facilitate the unfreezing process.

In order to minimize resistance it is important that changes result in a positive and relative advantage, the benefits of which should be clearly apparent to the individuals being asked to change. The earlier these benefits can be identified by those involved, the more likely they are to accept and continue their change-related practices. The changes being advocated must be compatible with the existing values and experiences of the individuals otherwise they will be discarded as threatening or inappropriate.

If resistance to change continues it may be the symptom of one of two causes: either that the correct 'fit' between the change situation, change agent and people has not been found, or that the proposed change is a poor strategy and is not in the organization's best interest.

Change for change's sake has no inherent organizational value; only change which contributes to the library's or information centre's goals is organizationally rational.

SYMPTOMS OF UNSUCCESSFUL CHANGE

A successful change will barely be visible. Unsuccessful change can be recognized by the absence of feedback, even though a feedback mechanism is available; or, by strong feedback in the form of protests or complaints. A drop in productivity below that anticipated by the learning curve will also indicate a problem.

Withdrawal symptoms characterized by lack of cooperation, absenteeism, resignations or transfers also indicate that something is wrong.

When any one of these symptoms appear, it should be immediately investigated in order to isolate and correct the problem.

EPILOGUE

28 The final strategy: effective management

Library and information centre managers have a responsibility to provide effective and efficient services relevant to their markets' needs. Effective libraries satisfy the demands and expectations of their stakeholders. They achieve their goals smoothly and efficiently, without strain. Effective managers achieve this through a mix of management strategies.

Organizational processes are planned, controlled, coordinated and organized to meet corporate goals. These are managerial tasks which provide for synergy within the library. Planning allows the library to adjust to changing conditions. Coordination integrates the diverse activities of the library, whilst control maintains the organizational activities within limits. Together, they maintain the library in a position where it can adequately achieve its mission.

Effective coordination can be achieved by ensuring that the type of organizational structure fits with the environment's needs and that levels of management reflect the duties, requirements and responsibilities of those in certain positions. There is a growing trend towards the school of thought that matches organizational structure, leadership style and subordinate attributes to the technologies used in the organization and its internal and external environments. This requires managerial competence and foresight in order to determine both the activities of the environment and the organization.

Effective managers strategically place the library or information centre in its environment which ensures its continued success and security. This requires top management to continually monitor the external environment in order to detect changes before they have a significant adverse impact upon the library or information centre. It also prevents unrealistic decisions from being made, and allows the library to take advantage of opportunities as they are presented.

A library or information service can only be effective when it responds to its users' needs, and where there is a good working relationship between the management and the stakeholders. A total understanding of each other's needs and how these are representative of the library user's needs is very necessary. For example, the funding body may wish to save the taxpayer money by reducing funding to libraries, whilst the library may seek to provide the services the taxpayers (users) indicate they need by requesting an increase. This dilemma can only be overcome through the establishment of policies and action programmes, the setting of goals and objectives, and by applying modern budgeting techniques.

Effective managers are able to acquire and manage the necessary human, technical, financial and information resources. Open systems theory relies upon continued input. The effective manager or information professional has to ensure that this is the case. This requires skills in acquiring staff, technical and material resources, financial resources and new ideas.

A systematic human resource selection programme involving manpower planning to accurately forecast personnel needs according to both type and numbers, job analyses to accurately define job descriptions and job specifications, and an objective recruitment process, should ensure that only the most appropriate and professionally competent staff are engaged.

Effective personnel management does not stop at this point; worker productivity must be maintained on an ongoing basis through motivation, training and self-development techniques. The concept of 'the boss is always right' is vanishing along with the traditional protestant work ethic. In its place is a recognition of the necessity to accommodate the needs of individuals in fitting together the task, the person and the situation or, where this is impossible for the organization, modifying the behaviour or outlook of the individual to accommodate its needs.

There will be times when the goals of the library, the parent organization and the employees will not be compatible. Effective managers use successful negotiation practices which preserve good working relationships and the sensitivities of others, and which result in creative outcomes.

Library and information centre managers are in the business

of communicating. They are responsible for the management of organizations involved in the storage and dissemination of ideas, beliefs and information. In order to do this they have to communicate their requirements upwards to their funding and administrative bodies, downwards to subordinates and laterally to colleagues and library users. They are also reliant upon others communicating effectively with them to gain information. Many different communication techniques can be used, the most effective of which is dependent upon the situation concerned. Effective managers are aware of the most appropriate communication channel to use for a specific purpose – for example, when sending an overdue notice to an errant reader, or in applying corrective measures to an over-zealous or delinquent staff member.

Effective managers are aware that different technologies create different time horizons, values, job design and skills. They compensate for this by providing appropriate structures and management styles which fit the technology and its culture. They are also aware of the differences in social roles, motivation, senses of identity and communication processes between staff having different work orientations and expertise. Effective managers ensure that the reward and compensation systems, work environment and management techniques allow for these variations without harming the overall strategies of the library or information centre.

Successful managers have a good understanding of the various power sources and follow a contingent approach to their use. They delegate authority and responsibility as they see this as a necessary source of staff development and motivation. However, they still hold the final responsibility for the outcomes. They are also politically astute. They will be involved in organizational politics only to the extent where it enhances the library's position. They will form valuable networks with key people both within and outside the parent organization. This provides support for the library and the means for obtaining valuable information.

Libraries, like other service institutions, are being held accountable for their performance. Measures of effectiveness have been developed for interlibrary comparison and should be used by librarians to justify additional funding and to measure their performance.

The effective library manager or information professional can no longer afford to be the stereotype of a shy, retiring person who acts as a custodian of the books. They are often responsible for large budgets and large staffs, as libraries are still labour-intensive. They operate in a dramatically changing environment of information technology, requiring personal drive continually to update individual qualifications and expertise, and sound management techniques with which to introduce and manage change.

The organization to which the library or information service is attached may well be dynamic, requiring the library manager or information professional to play a high-profile role. In so doing, he or she must be adept at convincing the funding bodies of the library's importance in an economically strained environment, be outward-looking to take advantage of opportunities as they are presented, build upon the strengths, overcome weaknesses and be willing to work resourcefully within their constraints.

Effective managers ensure that the corporate culture is strong and that the goals and values of the organization are known to all. They reinforce this in their recruitment and staff development processes. Their technologies, structure, leadership and decision-making styles also complement the corporate culture. Effective corporate cultures are developed by managers in their activities and behaviours. Effective managers take the time to see that their values are communicated directly to their staff.

Whilst there must be effective control measures, the outlook for success must be towards the future. Long-term, innovative strategies are important for the success of the library. There needs to be a clear definition of the library's mission in order to plan for the future.

In conclusion, the effective library manager needs to be aware of many management techniques and principles, and be adept at using the right one at the right time.

Selected further reading

PART I: INTRODUCTION TO LIBRARY AND INFORMATION CENTRE MANAGEMENT

Chapter 1 An introduction to management

Bailey, Martha J. (1986), *The Special Librarian as a Supervisor or Middle Manager* (2nd edn.), (Washington DC.: Special Libraries Association).

Drucker, Peter F. (1974), *Management: Tasks, Responsibilities, Practices* (New York: Harper and Row).

Handy, Charles (1976), *Understanding Organizations* (Harmondsworth: Penguin).

Issues in Library Management: a reader for the professional librarian (1984) (White Plains, NY.: Knowledge Industry Publications).

Lynch, B.P. (1976), 'Role of middle managers in libraries', *Advances in Librarianship* **6**, (New York: Academic Press).

Mintzberg, H. (1973), *The Nature of Managerial Work* (New York: Harper and Row).

Sinclair, D. (1979), *Administration of the Small Public Library* (2nd edn.), (Chicago: American Library Association).

Townsend, R. (1970), *Up the Organization* (New York: Knopf).

Chapter 2 Strategic influences on modern library and information centre management

Brown, E.F. (1979), *Cutting Library Costs: increasing productivity, and raising revenues* (Metuchen, NJ: Scarecrow Press).

Evans, Edward G. (1983), *Management Techniques for Librarians* (2nd edn.), (New York: Academic Press).

Flowerdew, A.D.J. (1985), *The Pricing and Provision of*

Information: some recent official reports Library and information research report no.20 (London: British Library).

Lindsey, J.A. and Prentice, A.E. (1984), *Professional Ethics and Librarians* (Phoenix, Az.: Oryx Press).

Strassman, Paul A. (1985), *The Information Payoff – the transformation of work in the electronic age* (New York: Free Press).

Thompson, J. (1982), *The End of Libraries* (London: Clive Bingley).

Wilson, H.D. (1986), 'Library venturing', *The Electronic Library*, **4**(2), April pp.96–102.

PART II: STRATEGIES FOR UNDERSTANDING THE LIBRARY'S OR INFORMATION CENTRE'S ENVIRONMENT

Chapter 3   Situation audit

Burns, T. and Stalker, G.M. (1961), *Management of Innovation* (London: Tavistock Press).

Kast, F.E. and Rosenzweig, J.E. (1984), *The Nature of Management (Modules in Management)* (Chicago, Ill.: Science Research Associates).

Lawrence, P.R. and Lorsch, J.W. (1969), *Organization and Environment* (Homewood, Ill.: Irwin).

Lynch, B. 'The academic library and its environment' *College and Research Libraries*, **35**, March, pp.126–32.

Rowe, Alan *et al.* (1986), *Strategic Management and Business Policy: a methodological approach* (2nd edn.), (Reading, Mass.: Addison-Wesley).

Wheelen, T.L. and Hunger, J.D. (1986), *Strategic Management and Business Policy* (2nd edn.), (Reading, Mass.: Addison Wesley).

PART III STRATEGIES FOR MANAGERIAL PROCESSES

Chapter 4   The corporate planning process

Bryson, J. (1988), 'A strategic planning process for public and non-profit organisations' *Long Range Planning*, **21**, February, pp.73–81.

Detweiler, M.J. (1983), 'Planning more than a process', *Library Journal*, January. pp.23–36.

King, W.R. (1982), 'Strategic planning for public service institutions: what can be learnt from business?', in C.R. McClure (ed.) *Planning for Library Services: a guide to utilizing planning methods for library management* (New York: Harworth Press) pp.43–65.

McClure, C.R. (1978), 'The planning process: strategies for action', *College and Research Libraries*, November, pp.456–66.

McClure C.R. *et al.* (1987), *Planning and Role Setting for Public Libraries: a manual of options and procedures*, prepared for the Public Library Development Project (Chicago: American Library Association).

Palmour, V.E., Bellassai, M.C. and De Wath, N.V. (1980), *A Planning Process for Public Libraries* (Chicago: American Library Association).

Ramsey, I.L. and Ramsey, J.E. (1986), *Library Planning and Budgeting* (New York: Franklin Watts).

Riggs, D.E. (1984), *Strategic Planning for Library Managers* (Phoenix, Az.: Oryx Press).

TenDam, Hans (1986), 'Strategic management in a government agency', *Long Range Planning*, **19**(4), August, pp.78–86.

Chapter 5   Human resource planning

Ash, R.A. and Levine, E.L. (1980), 'A framework for evaluating job analysis methods', *Personnel*, **57**(6), November–December, pp.53–9.

Broome, E.M. (1973), 'Library manpower planning', *Aslib Proceedings*, **25**(11), pp.400–14.

Cowley, J. (1982), *Personnel Management in Libraries* (London: Clive Bingley).

Durey, P. (1976), *Staff Management in University and College Libraries* (Oxford: Pergamon).

Jones, N. and Jordon, P. (1987), *Staff Management in Library and Information Work* (2nd edn.), (Aldershot: Gower).

Moore, N. (1987), *The Emerging Markets for Librarians and Information Workers*, Library and Information Research Report no.56 (Boston Spa: British Library Research and Development Department).

Nkomo, S.M. (1988), 'Strategic planning for human resources – let's get started', *Long Range Planning*, **21**, February, pp.66–72.

White, Herbert S. (c. 1985), *Library Personnel Management* (White Plains, NY: Knowledge Industry Publication).

Chapter 6 Strategies for human resource development

Berkner, D.S. (1979), 'Library staff development through performance appraisal', *College and Research Libraries*, **40**(4), July, pp.335–44.

Breiting, A., Dorey, M. and Sockbeson, D. (1976), 'Staff development in college and university libraries', *Special Libraries*, **67**, July, pp.305–10.

Conroy, B. (1978), *Library Staff Development and Continuing Education: principles and practices* (Littleton, Colo.: Libraries Unlimited).

Conroy, B. (1979), 'Inservice training and staff development' *Library Management Without Bias*, Foundations in library and information science, **13**, (Connecticut: JAI Press) pp.145–53.

Creth, S.D. (1986), *Effective On-the-job Training: developing library human resources* (Chicago: American Library Association).

Ferriero, D.S. (1982), 'ARL directors as proteges and mentors' *Journal of Academic Librarianship*, **7**(6), January, pp.358–65.

Redfern, M. (1980), 'Managing the people part: the changing climate of personnel administration' *Studies in Library Management*, **6** (London: Clive Bingley) pp.177–94.

Weber, D.C. (1974), 'The dynamics of the library environment for professional staff growth' *College and Research Libraries*, **35**(4), July, pp.259–67.

Chapter 7 Strategies for decision-making

Bommer, M.R.W. and Chorba, R.W. (1982), *Decision Making for Library Management* (White Plains, NY: Knowledge Industry Publications).

Burckel, N.C. (1984), 'Participatory management in academic libraries: a review', *College and Research Libraries*, **45**(1), January, pp.25–34.

Dickinson, D.W. (1978), 'Some reflections on participative management in libraries', *College and Research Libraries*, **39**(4), July, pp.253–62.

Elbing, A. (1978), *Behavioural Designs in Organizations* (2nd edn.), (Dallas, Texas: Scott Foresman).

Likert, R. (1961), *New Patterns of Management* (New York: McGraw-Hill).

Lynch, B. (1972), 'Participative management', *College and Research Libraries*, **33**, pp.382–90.

Vroom, V.H. and Yetton, P.W. (1973), *Leadership and Decision Making* (Pittsburgh: University of Pittsburgh Press).

Chapter 8 Competitive strategies: strategic marketing for libraries and information centres

Drucker, P.F. (1976), 'Managing the public service institution', *College and Research Libraries*, **37**(1), January. pp.4–14.

Kies, Cosette (1987), *Marketing and Public Relations for Libraries* (Metuchen, NJ: Scarecrow Press).

Kotler, P. (c. 1982), *Marketing for Non-Profit Organizations* (2nd edn.), (Englewood Cliffs, NJ: Prentice Hall).

MacMillan, I.C. (1983), 'Competitive strategies for not-for-profit agencies', *Advances in Strategic Management*, **1**, pp.61–82.

PART IV STRATEGIES FOR STRUCTURAL PROCESSES

Chapter 9 Organization structures

Daft, R.L. (1983), *Organization Theory and Design* (St Paul, Minn.: West).

Lawrence, P. and Lorsch, J. (1969), *Developing Organizations* (Reading, Mass.: Addison-Wesley).

Martin, L.A. (1984), *Organizational Structure of Libraries* (Metuchen, NJ: Scarecrow Press).

Chapter 10   Strategies for the structural coordination of libraries and information centres

Battin, P. (1979), 'Changing old and planning new organisational structure', *Library Management without Bias*, C. Chen. (ed.), (Connecticut: JAI Press).

Chapter 11   Strategies for Communication in libraries and information centres

Abell, M.D. (1965), 'Aspects of upward communication in a public library' M.L. Bundy and R. Aronson (eds.) *Social and Political Aspects of Librarianship: student contributions to library science* (Albany: School of Library Science, State University of NY at Albany) pp.91–9.
Berne, E. (1964), *Games People Play* (Harmondsworth: Penguin).
Conroy, B. and Jones, B. (1986), *Improving Communication in the Library* (Phoenix, Az.: Oryx Press).
Emery, R. (1975), *Staff Communication in Libraries* (London: Clive Bingley).
Fisher, Dalmar (1981), *Communications in Organizations* (St Paul, Minn.: West).
Knapp, Mark L. (1972), *Non-verbal Communication in Human Interaction* (New York: Holt, Rinehart and Winston).
Lippitt, G. (1982), *Organization Renewal* (Englewood Cliffs, NJ: Prentice-Hall).
Mathews, A. J. (1983), *Communicate: a librarian's guide to inter-personal communication* (Chicago: American Library Association).
Powell, J.W. and Le Lieuvre, R.B. (1979), *Peoplework: communications dynamics for librarians* (Chicago: American Library Association).
Roberts, S. (1979), 'Communication studies and the management and provision of library studies' in A. Vaughan (ed.) *Studies in Library Management*, **5**, (London: Clive Bingley) pp.92–116.
Sigel, E. (1982), *Books, Libraries, and Electronics: essays on the future of written communication* (White Plains, NY: Knowledge Industry Publication).
Stevens, N.D. (1983), *Communication Throughout Libraries* (New Jersey: Scarecrow Press).

PART V STRATEGIES FOR TECHNICAL EFFECTIVENESS

Chapter 12 Managing technologies in libraries and information centres

Boss, R.W. (1984), *The Library Manager's Guide to Automation* (2nd edn.), (White Plains, NY: Knowledge Industry Publication).

Burton, P.F. and Petrie, J.H. (1984), *Introducing Micro-computers. A Guide for Librarians* (Wokingham: Van Nostrand Reinhold).

Chen, C. and Bressler, S.E. (eds) (1982), *Micro-computers in Libraries* (New York: Neal-Schuman).

Clayton, M. (1987), *Managing Library Automation* (Aldershot: Gower).

Cohen, E. and Cohen, A. (1981), *Automation, Space Management and Productivity* (New York: Bowker).

Collier, M. (ed.) (1988), *Telecommunications for Information Management and Transfer*, Proceedings of the first international conference held at Leicester Polytechnic, April 1987 (Aldershot: Gower).

Dowlin, K.C. (1984), *The Electronic Library* (New York: Neal Schuman).

Falk, H. (1985), *Personal Computers for Libraries* (Medford, NJ: Learned Information).

Fraley, R. A. and Anderson, C.L. (1985), *Library Space Planning: how to assess, allocate, and reorganize collections, resources and physical facilities* (New York: Neal-Schuman).

Gellatly, P. (ed.) (1984), *Beyond 1984: the future of library technical services* (New York: Haworth Press).

Genoway, D.C. (1984), *Integrated On-Line Library Systems: principles, planning and implementation* (White Plains, NY: Knowledge Industry).

Gillman, P. and Penniston, S. (1984), *Library Automation: a current review* (London: Aslib).

Lancaster, F.W. (1982), *Libraries and Librarians in an Age of Electronics* (Arlington, Va.: Information Resources Press).

Linder, J.C. (1985), 'Computers, corporate culture and change', *Personnel Journal*, September, pp.49–55.

Lovecy, I. (1984), *Automating Library Procedures: a survivor's handbook* (London: Library Association).

Mathews, J.R. (1980), *Choosing an Automated Library System: a planning guide* (Chicago: American Library Association).

Mathews, J.R. (ed.) (1983), *A Reader on Choosing an Automated Library System* (Chicago: American Library Association).

Reynolds, D. (1985), *Library Automation: issues and applications* (New York: Bowker).

Rice, J. (1984), *Introduction to Library Automation* (Littleton: Libraries Unlimited).

Rowley, J. (1988), *The Basics of Information Technology* (London: Clive Bingley).

Stayer, R.A. and Richardson, V.E. (1983), *The Cost-effectiveness of Alternative Library Storage Programs* (Clayton, Vic.: Monash University).

Tedd, L. (1984), *An Introduction to Computer-based Library Systems* (2nd edn.), (Chichester: Wiley).

Woodward, J. (1958), *Management and Technology* (London: HMSO).

Woodward, J. (1965), *Industrial Organisation: theory and practice* (London: Oxford University Press).

Chapter 13　Managing expertise in libraries and information centres

Caputo, J.S. (1984), *The Assertive Librarian* (Phoenix, Az.: Oryx Press).

Chapter 14　Management information systems in libraries and information centres

Brophy, P. (1986), *Management Information and Decision Support Systems in Libraries* (Aldershot: Gower).

PART VI　STRATEGIES FOR MANAGING THE PSYCHOSOCIAL ENVIRONMENT

Chapter 15　Group dynamics

Berne, E. (1963), *The Structure and Dynamics of Organizations and Groups* (Philadelphia: Lippincott).

Lacoursiere, R.B. (c. 1980), *The Life Cycle of Groups: group developmental stage theory* (New York: Human Sciences Press).

Chapter 16   Power, influence, authority and delegation

Bacharach, S.B and Lawler, E.J. (1980), *Power and Politics in Organisations* (San Francisco: Jossey-Bass).

French, J.R.P. and Raven, B. (1959), 'The bases of social power' D. Cartwright (ed.) *Studies in Social Power* (Ann Arbor, Mich: Institute for Social Research).

Grimes, A.J. (1978), 'Authority, power, influence and social control: a theoretical synthesis', *Academy of Management Review*, **3**(4), October, pp.724–35.

Katz, D. and Kahn, R.L. (1978), *The Social Psychology of Organizations* (2nd edn.), (New York: Wiley).

Korda, M. (1975), *Power: how to get it, how to use it* (New York: Random House).

Wrong, D.H. (1979), *Power: its forms, bases and uses* (Oxford: Blackwell).

Chapter 17   Strategies for personal networking and organization politics

Pfeffer, J. (1981), *Power in Organizations* (Marshfield, Mass.: Pitman).

Chapter 18   Strategies for negotiation

Pruitt, D.G. (1983), 'Strategic choice in negotiation' *American Behavioural Scientist*, **27**(2), November–December, pp.167–91.

Shaffer, K.R. (1975), 'The library administrator as negotiator: exit the "Boss" ', *Library Journal*, **100**(15), September, pp.1475–80.

Chapter 19   Leadership strategies

Fiedler, F.E. (1967), *A Theory of Leadership Effectiveness* (New York: McGraw-Hill).

Hersey, P and Blanchard K.H. (1977), *Management of Organizational Behaviour* (3rd edn.), (Englewood Cliff, NJ: Prentice-Hall).

House, R.J. (1971), 'A path-goal theory of leader effectiveness', *Administrative Science Quarterly*, **16**, pp.312–39.

Riggs, D.E. (ed.) (1982), *Library Leadership: visualizing the future* (Phoenix, Ariz.: Oryx).

Sager, D.J. (1979), 'Leadership and employee motivation' in R.E. Stevens (ed.) *Supervision of Employees in Libraries* (Ill.: University of Illinois) pp.45–55.

Sayles, L.R. (1979), *Leadership: what effective managers really do . . . and how they do it* (New York: McGraw-Hill).

Stogdill, R.M. (1974), *Handbook of Leadership: a survey of theory and research* (New York: Free Press).

Tannanbaum, R. and Schmidt, W.H. (1973), 'How to choose a leadership pattern', *Harvard Business Review*, **51**, pp.162–75.

Yukl, G.A. (1981), *Leadership in Organizations* (Englewood Cliffs, NJ: Prentice-Hall).

Chapter 20 Motivation issues

Herzberg, F. (1968), 'One more time: how do you motivate employees?' *Harvard Business Review*, **46**, January–February, pp.361–76.

Maslow, A.H. (1970), *Motivation and Personality* (2nd edn.), (New York: Harper and Row).

McGregor, D. (1960), *The Human Side of Enterprise* (New York: McGraw-Hill).

Sever, S. and Westcott, F. (1983), 'Motivational basis for compensation strategies in a library environment', *College and Research Libraries*, **44**(3), May, pp.228–35.

Vroom, V.H. (1964), *Work and Motivation* (New York: John Wiley and Sons).

Chapter 21 Strategies for managing conflict

Jones, K. (1984), *Conflict and Change in Library Organizations: people, power and service* (London: Clive Bingley).

Chapter 22 Strategies for managing stress

Cooper, C and Marshall, J. (1978), *Understanding Executive Stress* (London: Macmillan).

Cox, T. (1981), *Stress* (London: Macmillan).

McLean, A.A. (1979), *Work Stress* (Reading, Mass.: Addison-Wesley).

Parker, D.F. and De Cotiis, T.A. (1983), 'Organizational determinants of job stress', *Organizational Behaviour and Human Performance*, **32**, October, pp.160–77.

Quick, J.C. and Quick, J.D. (1984), 'Preventative stress management at the organizational level', *Personnel*, September–October, pp.24–34.

PART VII STRATEGIES FOR MANAGING THE GOALS AND VALUES SUBSYSTEM

Chapter 23 Corporate culture in libraries and information centres

Deal, T.E. and Kennedy, A.A. (1982), *Corporate Cultures: the rites and rituals of corporate life* (Reading, Mass.: Addison-Wesley).

Handy, C. (1976), *Understanding Organizations* (Harmondsworth: Penguin).

Hickman, C.R. and Silva, M.A. (1984), *Creating Excellence: managing corporate culture, strategy and change in a new age* (New York: New American Library).

Kakabadse, A. (ed.) (1982), *People and Organizations: the practitioner's view* (Aldershot: Gower).

Kakabadse, A. (1983), *The Politics of Management* (Aldershot: Gower).

Peters, T. and Waterman, R.H. (1982), *In Search of Excellence* (Sydney: Harper and Row).

Samuels, A.R. (1982), 'Planning and organisational culture', C. McClure (ed.), *Planning for Library Services: a guide to utilizing planning methods for library management* (New York: Harworth Press).

Schein, E.H. (1985), *Organizational Culture and Leadership* (San Fransisco: Jassey-Bass).

Trice, H.M. and Beyer, J.M. (1984), 'Studying organizational cultures through rites and ceremonials', *Academy of Management Review*, **9**, October, pp.653–59.

Chapter 24 Strategies for survival: fostering innovation and intrapreneurship in libraries and information centres

Brown, M. and Rickards, T. (1982), 'How to create creativity', *Management Today*, August, pp.28–41.

Drucker, P.F. (1985), *Innovation and Entrepreneurship: practice and principles* (London: Heinemann).

Galbraith, J. (1982), 'Designing the innovative organisation', *Organizational Dynamics*, Winter, pp.5–10.

McIntyre, S.M. (1982), 'Obstacles to corporate innovation', *Business Horizons*, January–February, pp.23–8.

Pinchot, G. (1985), *Intrapreneuring* (New York: Harper and Row).

Roberts, E.B. and Fusfeld, A.R. (1981), 'Staffing the innovative technology-based organization', *Sloan Management Review*, Spring, pp.19–32.

Smith, N.I. (1980), 'Creativity and organisational innovation', *Human Resources Management Australia*, Winter, pp.43–8.

Smith, N.R. and Miner, J.B. (1983), 'Type of entrepreneur, types of firm and managerial motivation: implications for organizational life cycle theory', *Strategic Management Journal*, December.

Souder, W.E. (1983), 'Organizing for modern technology and innovation: a review and synthesis', *Technovation*, **2**, pp.27–44.

Steiner, G.A. (ed.) (c. 1965), *The Creative Organization* (Chicago: University of Chicago Press).

Zeldman, M.I. (1980), 'How management can develop and sustain a creative environment', *Society for Advancement of Management, Advanced Management Journal*, Winter, pp.23–7.

PART VIII CONTROL STRATEGIES FOR LIBRARIES AND INFORMATION CENTRES

Chapter 25 Budgeting and economic analysis

Brown, E.F. (1979), *Cutting Library Costs: increasing productivity, and raising revenues* (Metuchen, NJ: Scarecrow Press).

Chen, C. (1980), *Zero-based Budgeting in Library Management* (Phoenix: Oryx Press).

Mason, D. (1973), 'Programmed budgeting and cost', *Aslib Proceedings*, **25**(3).

Prentice, A.E. (1977), *Public Library Finance* (Chicago: American Library Association).

Ramsey, I.L. and Ramsey, J.E, (1986), *Library Planning and Budgeting* (New York: Franklin Watts).

Roberts, S.A. (ed.) (1984), *Costing and the Economics of Library and Information Services*, Aslib Reader series **5**, (London: Aslib).

Roberts, S.A. (1985), *Cost Management for Library and Information Services* (London: Butterworth).

Sarndal, A.G. (1979), 'Zero base budgeting'. *Special Libraries*, **70**(12), December, pp.527–32.

Smith, S. (1983), *Accounting for Librarians: and other not for profit managers* (Chicago: American Library Association).

Trumpeter, M.C. and Rounds, R.S. (1985), *Basic Budgeting Practice for Librarians* (Chicago: American Library Association).

Chapter 26 Programme review and performance measures

Buckland, M. (1975), *Book Availability and Use* (Oxford: Pergamon).

Cronin, B. (1982), 'Taking the measure of service', Paper presented to the Department of Library and Information Studies, Queens University, Belfast, March 1982, *Aslib Proceedings*, **34**(6–7), pp.273–94.

D'Elia, G. and Walsh. S. (1983), 'User satisfaction with library service – a measure of public library performance', *Library Quarterly*, **53**(2), April, pp.109–33.

Gault, R.R. (1984), 'Performance measures for evaluating public library children's services', *Public Libraries*, Winter, pp.134–7.

Gers, R. and Seward, L.J. (1985), 'Improving reference performance: results of a statewide survey', *Library Journal*, November, pp.32–5.

Houghton, T. (1985), *Bookstock Management in Public Libraries* (London: Clive Bingley).

Lancaster, F.W. (1977), *The Measurement and Evaluation of Library Services*, (Arlington, Va.: Information Resources Press).

Lindsay, J.A. (ed.) (1986), *Performance Evaluation: a management basic for librarians* (Phoenix, Az.: Oryx Press).

McClure, C.R. and Reifsnyder, B. (1984), 'Performance measures for corporate information centres', *Special Libraries*, **75**(3), July, pp.193–204.

Orr, R.H. (1973), 'Measuring the goodness of library services: a general framework for considering quantitative measures', *Journal of Documentation*, **29**(3), pp.315–22.

Schmidt, J. (1980), 'Reference performance in college libraries', *Australian Academic and Research Libraries*, **11**(2), pp.87–95.

Stecher, G. (1975), 'Library evaluation: a brief survey of studies in quantification', *Australian Academic and Research Libraries*, **6**, March.

Taylor, R.S. (1986), *Value Added Processes in Information Systems*, (New Jersey: Ablex).

Urquhart, J.A. and Schofield, J.L. (1971), 'Measuring readers' failure at the shelf', *Journal of Documentation*, **27**(4), pp.273–86.

Zweizig, D. (1982), *Output Measures for Public Libraries* (Chicago: American Library Association).

Chapter 27 Managing change

Beer, M. (1980), *Organizational Change and Development: a systems view* (Santa Monica: Goodyear).

Drucker, P.F. (1969), *The Age of Discontinuity: guidelines to our changing society* (London: Pan).

Greinar, L.E. (1978), 'Evolution and revolution as organizations grow', *Harvard Business Review*, **50**, July–August, pp.37–46.

Jones, K. (1984), *Conflict and Change in Library Organizations: people, power and service* (London: Clive Bingley).

McCaskey, M.B. (1982), *The Executive Challenge: managing change and ambiguity* (Boston: Pitman).

McNally, Arthur M. and Downs, Robert B. (1973), 'The changing role of directors of university libraries', *College and Research Libraries*, **34**, March, pp.103–25.

Chapter 28 The final strategy: effective management

Lancaster, F.W. (1978), 'Whither libraries? or, Wither libraries', *College and Research Libraries*, **39**, pp.345–57.

Library Effectiveness: a state of the art (1980) (New York: Library Administration and Management Association/American Library Association).

Index